"This book is the first to bring together academics and professionals in youth justice to examine the benefits of exchanging their knowledge and practice. The significant, and accessible, chapters are written by leading academic authors and experienced professionals in the field and offer inspirational examples of a wide range of effective partnership between academics and professionals."
                          – Professor Raymond Arthur, Northumbria University

"The arrival of this book is really heartening. For those of us who have aspired to bridge the gaps between practice, learning and research this represents a major contribution towards furthering that aim. The authors bring their own wide range of applied knowledge, research experience and critical insights to the field at a time of great change, when there are very real opportunities to harness what we know to improve what is offered to young people who experience the criminal justice system. With a variety of contributions from differing perspectives, the book will provide a rounded view of the field, combined with a wealth of ideas about how best to align knowledge and practice to the maximum effect. Throughout the book runs a spirit of exchange and innovation, which highlights the very real gains to be made on all sides from direct and committed engagement between those dealing with the 'messy realities' of practice, and those who have the opportunity to document, reflect and inform. This will be a major asset for those involved in youth justice research and education, on all sides."
                               – Professor Roger Smith, Durham University

"This interesting, edited collection is the outcome of a productive new knowledge transfer partnership between the authors and Cheshire Youth Justice Services. Contributors are drawn widely, producing policy relevant discussions that are situated in research and practice, while demonstrating the symbiotic relationship between these domains, through placements, guest lectures and other activities. Consideration of Wales, Scotland and Belarus broadens the scope of discussion in a way that will interest readers from different backgrounds. Ultimately, this valuable volume underlines the importance of meaningful connections between different parties to benefit young people's treatment and outcomes."
                     – Professor Sarah Brooks-Wilson, University of Birmingham

Knowledge and Skills Partnerships in Youth Justice

Providing in-depth insight into different types of knowledge and skills partnerships in youth justice, this book illustrates the importance of collaborative working between academics and professionals, drawing on empirical research and practice examples to present expert analysis of knowledge/evidence production and utilisation in youth justice.

Original and cutting edge, the focus of this edited collection is on different forms of knowledge exchange (transfer) between professionals and academics in the youth justice context. Authored by experts in the field, each chapter presents a series of case studies showcasing the application of theory/evidence to practice, and shedding light on the challenges professionals experience when seeking to understand complex theory and 'make sense' of the vast array of empirical data.

Knowledge and Skills Partnerships in Youth Justice will appeal to students researching youth justice and criminal justice systems. The book will also be useful for practitioners of youth justice, as well as policymakers.

Jayne Price is a Senior Lecturer and the programme leader for Undergraduate Criminology, and Deputy Head of Division Social and Political Science at the University of Chester. She is a Senior Fellow of the Higher Education Academy (Advance HE). Jayne is a trustee of YMCA Together and sits on the Executive Committee of the British Society of Criminology. For over ten years, she has volunteered within her local Youth Justice Service working with children and young people, practitioners and other volunteers.

Sean Creaney is a Criminologist and Senior Lecturer in the School of Law, Criminology and Policing at Edge Hill University. He is a Senior Fellow of the Higher Education Academy (Advance HE). Dr Creaney is an Associate of the Children and Young People's Centre for Justice (CYCJ), and a member of the Transdisciplinary Research for Youth Justice (TRYJustice) network.

Knowledge and Skills Partnerships in Youth Justice

Edited by
Jayne Price and Sean Creaney

Routledge
Taylor & Francis Group

LONDON AND NEW YORK

Designed cover image: gettyimages.com

First published 2025
by Routledge
4 Park Square, Milton Park, Abingdon, Oxon OX14 4RN

and by Routledge
605 Third Avenue, New York, NY 10158

Routledge is an imprint of the Taylor & Francis Group, an informa business

British Library Cataloguing in Publication Data
A catalogue record for this book is available from the British Library

Library of Congress Cataloging-in-Publication Data
Names: Price, Jayne, editor. | Creaney, Sean, editor.
Title: Knowledge and skills partnerships in youth justice / Jayne Price and Sean Creaney.
Description: Abingdon, Oxon ; New York, NY : Routledge, 2024. | Includes bibliographical references and index.
Identifiers: LCCN 2024015580 (print) | LCCN 2024015581 (ebook) | ISBN 9781032532684 (hardback) | ISBN 9781032532622 (paperback) | ISBN 9781003411192 (ebook)
Subjects: LCSH: Justice–Psychological aspects. | Justice in young adults | Justice–Study and teaching.
Classification: LCC BF789.J8 K66 2024 (print) | LCC BF789.J8 (ebook) | DDC 172/.2–dc23/eng/20240422
LC record available at https://lccn.loc.gov/2024015580
LC ebook record available at https://lccn.loc.gov/2024015581

ISBN: 978-1-032-53268-4 (hbk)
ISBN: 978-1-032-53262-2 (pbk)
ISBN: 978-1-003-41119-2 (ebk)

DOI: 10.4324/9781003411192

Typeset in Sabon
by Taylor & Francis Books

Contents

Figures

Contributors

Sue Bond-Taylor is a Senior Lecturer and the Programme Leader for Criminology at the University of Lincoln. Sue's research explores the connections between social care provision, crime prevention and youth justice, with an emphasis on services for children and families with complex needs. She works closely with local children's services and organisations to promote children's rights and wellbeing, and to develop holistic approaches to support children and their families. Sue delivers the Criminology programme's Youth Justice module in collaboration with local youth offending professionals, and leads the University of Lincoln's Child Friendly Research Network.

Andrea Brazier joined HM Inspectorate of Probation as Head of the Youth Inspection Programme in July 2021. Andrea leads the youth team, and her role is pivotal in overseeing the delivery of all core youth justice inspections across England and Wales. Andrea works closely with the Youth Justice Board, the Ministry of Justice Youth Justice Policy Unit, and various stakeholders in the youth justice sector, to ensure up-to-date knowledge and understanding regarding the youth justice landscape.

Sean Creaney is a Criminologist and Senior Lecturer in the School of Law, Criminology and Policing at Edge Hill University. He is a Senior Fellow of the Higher Education Academy (Advance HE). Dr Creaney is an Associate of the Children and Young People's Centre for Justice (CYCJ), and a member of the Transdisciplinary Research for Youth Justice (TRYJustice) network. His areas of knowledge and expertise include Child First Justice, typologies, theories and models of participation and co-production, and experiential peer support and mentorship. Sean is a founding Advisory Board member of the social justice charity Peer Power, an empathy-led charity focussed on healing trauma and creating individual and system change.

Fiona Dyer is the Director of the Children and Young People's Centre for Justice. She leads CYCJ in its work to improve children and young people's lives through improving policy, practice, participation and research. This involves supporting professionals from all disciplines who work with children and young people on the cusp of – or involved in – offending, by promoting best practice, based on up-to-date evidence and research. Before joining CYCJ Fiona was seconded to the Scottish Government youth justice team for three years and a professional social work advisor, and prior to this worked for ten years as a social worker and social work manager within the fields of youth and criminal justice. She is currently co-chair of the Scottish Government's independent working group on Antisocial Behaviour.

Ross Gibson is a Practice Development Advisor at the Children and Young People's Centre for Justice, where he supports developments in policy and practice for children and young people in conflict with the law. He has a particular interest in improving care for 16 and 17 year olds, expanding diversion from prosecution, advancing Scotland's Whole System Approach, raising the age of criminal responsibility and in the delivery of secure care. Ross was a member of the Independent Care Review and through his work at CYCJ seeks to ensure that its conclusions are realised. He is a qualified Social Worker and Practice Teacher, and before joining CYCJ worked for Glasgow City Council within their youth justice social work team. He also has a history of working within residential care. He is currently undertaking a part time Ph.D. at the University of Strathclyde, focusing on children within secure care and exploring their perception of their pathways into that setting.

Kathy Hampson set up the Learning Mentor system in a large secondary school, providing support for children with wide-ranging barriers to their learning, which led to co-authorship of a practice-based handbook (*The Learning Mentor's Resource Book*). After this, she worked for several years as a case manager for a large city Youth Offending Team (YOT), completing her Ph.D. whilst there, researching the emotional intelligence of children who offend (whilst also working for the University of Birmingham on their distance learning Social, Emotional and Behavioural Difficulties M.Ed. programme). After relocating to North Wales, she worked for the charity Llamau in a hybrid strategy/research project looking at YOT practice around the resettlement of children leaving custody (which also partnered with Professor Neal Hazel and fed into the development of the YJB's preferred resettlement model 'Constructive Resettlement'). She is now a Senior Lecturer in Criminology at Aberystwyth University, where she has created the first Youth Justice M.Sc. programme in the UK mainland. She continues to research into youth justice, focusing currently on youth justice systems, Child First justice, the voice of the child, and legal education for children in schools.

Helen Mercer joined HM Inspectorate of Probation as an inspector in 2015. As Head of Standards Helen is responsible for leading the development, continuous improvement and promotion of standards across all the inspectorate's programmes of inspection. Her role is to build a shared view of quality, drive improvement and maximise the impact of inspection. Helen also provides strategic leadership and sets the direction for the inspectorate's work on lived experience and participation. Helen is keen to ensure that inspections are fair, transparent, robust and reliable.

Robin Moore joined HM Inspectorate of Probation as Head of Research in 2015. He provides strategic leadership and direction to the inspectorate's research team and oversees the team's research products and the analytical support to youth, adult and thematic inspections. The primary goal of the team is to make valuable contributions to the evidence base for high-quality youth justice and probation services – thinking carefully about 'knowledge translation' and 'knowledge mobilisation' – and to help maximise the robustness and impact of inspection.

Vicky Palmer is a Senior Lecturer on the B.A. (Hons) Youth Justice course in the Department of Social Work, Care and Community at Nottingham Trent University; commencing in 2005. She currently teaches the year-one 'Evolution of the Youth Justice System' module, the year-two 'Effective Practice in Youth Justice' module and two year-three modules including 'Law Sentencing and the Role of the Courts' and

'Dissertation'. She completed her doctoral studies in 2016 with her thesis entitled: 'A Critical Approach towards the Professionalisation of the Youth Justice Workforce: A Research-Led design of a Mental Health Module'. In 2019, Vicky completed five separate visits to the Republic of Belarus where she has been instrumental in the training of judges, prosecutors, police, defence lawyers and charitable organisations in all areas of youth justice, in readiness for their own development of a separate juvenile justice system. Her research interests include comparative youth justice, children in conflict with the law, mental disorder and neurodiversity and their connection to 'youth offending', the proliferation of managerialism in youth justice practice and the re-introduction of diversion techniques for young offenders. Vicky has 20 years' experience of working as a Probation Officer, Youth Justice Social Worker, and Youth Offending Team Case Manager, both in Leicestershire and North Nottinghamshire, and she remains a Registered Social Worker.

Jayne Price is a Senior Lecturer at the University of Chester and the programme leader for Criminology Undergraduate. She is a Senior Fellow of the Higher Education Academy (Advance HE). Jayne is a trustee of YMCA Together and sits on the Executive Committee of the British Society of Criminology. For over ten years Jayne has volunteered within her local Youth Justice Service, working with children and young people, practitioners and other volunteers. Her principal research interests lie within the youth justice/young adult agenda and the experiences of this population within the criminal justice system. Jayne also has experience of collaborative participatory research methods and engaging children and young people through lyric writing.

Nina Vaswani is a Senior Research Fellow and Research Lead at the Children and Young People's Centre for Justice. Nina oversees the research programme at CYCJ, which aims to support the synthesis and production of new knowledge to inform policy and practice development for children and young people in conflict with the law. CYCJ has a particular emphasis on participatory, coproduced and peer-led research with children and young people. Nina's specific research interests are the experience and impact of loss, bereavement and trauma in young people and how these experiences interface and shape contact with the justice system. Of particular interest is the over-representation of young men in justice settings, and how their exposure to loss, bereavement and trauma might shape their developing masculinities identities, behaviours and outcomes. As a result, Nina is also interested in institutional and organisational responses to trauma, and the realities of trauma-informed approaches in practice. Nina is also the PI on the UKRI-funded Men Minds Project, aimed at coproducing new ways of researching mental health with marginalised adolescent young men.

Foreword: The golden ticket for youth justice?

'100 miles per hour in the wrong direction is slow' is a particular favourite phrase of mine and is as applicable in Youth Justice as in other areas of life. But sometimes we are so busy 'motoring along' that we forget to check if our efforts are being utilised to utmost effect – nose to the grindstone and crack on might elicit maximum effort – but does it produce the outcomes we want? If it's in the right direction and using the evidence of what is effective practice – it is more likely! Note I didn't give an unequivocal simple answer, as the field of human behaviour and the impacts of macro-economic and social policy on the individual actions of human beings is notoriously difficult to predict. But we can use evidence to predict what is likely to achieve the outcomes we want – and thereby lies another tale, as nearly everyone has an opinion about what to do about youth crime and most are convinced by 'common sense' which is usually anything but.

Early in my career a very experienced colleague said to me in her distinctive Lancashire drawl, 'Remember Gareth, everyone knows how to deal with a kicking donkey 'cept them that has one!'

And of course many intuitively held beliefs such as 'scare them straight' have been proved to be at best ineffective and at worst to exacerbate the problem. The anti-heroin ads in the 1980s were an example of this – many young people found the images attractive, and heroin chic was a fashion statement although the damage of opiate addiction is anything but attractive.

I have always been interested in the concept of What Works in attempting to reduce the amount and impact of crime since I was a probation officer in Greater Manchester in the early 1990s, and particularly in prevention of crime by children. This interest steadily grew but was brought into particular focus in 2014 when I chaired a session at the Annual Youth Justice Convention organised by the Youth Justice Board (YJB) in my capacity as chair of Association of Youth Offending Team Managers (AYM).

As someone who was responsible for effective and efficient delivery of youth justice services in the Cheshire region for nearly 20 years, and perhaps exposing my innate and Northern parsimony, I have always been keen to see what works and why – and at what cost. It is fair to say that the contributors on the session I chaired that day impressed me enormously. The links between Swansea Youth Offending Team (YOT) with its local university seemed to me to be an eminently sensible and mutually beneficial one – and essentially cost-neutral. The partnership between Newcastle YOT and its local university were equally impressive and demonstrated real change outcomes which can be demonstrated by the rise of the Skill Mill organisation which focusses on development of skills for enhanced employment opportunities as well as allowing researchers access to suitable topics of work. A real win-win in my book!

I even tried to bend the laws of geography to allow for my organisation – Cheshire Youth Justice service, to be considered as under the umbrella of the Greater Manchester Youth Justice research project in conjunction with Manchester Metropolitan University, but my attempts were thwarted by funding rules – and common sense as the Greater Manchester consortium served coterminous other criminal justice delivery agents such as probation and police. But no harm in trying. So if we couldn't join their club – how do we start our own? And this led to the idea of building even further on our already established links with Edge Hill and Chester universities.

The benefits of close and instructive relationships with academic partners is self-evident. We need to explore what works and why but of course, as many explorers will no doubt testify, you also need an idea of where you want to go, what you expect to find, how to assess whether you were successful, and of course whether there is a better, cheaper, faster way of achieving the above. Aimlessly wandering around to see what may turn up may be a romantic ideal but is not what hard earned public money should be spent on in terms of criminal justice.

So why is this collaboration so important?

Whilst crime by children is not the political hot potato it was in the 1990s and the emergence of Youth Offending Teams following the 1998 Crime and Disorder Act has contributed to impressive reductions in youth crime, first time entrants to the youth justice system and use of custody, this is only part of the picture. Children today face additional challenges in an age of 24-hour media, social and otherwise; electronic technology which can create trauma as well as education; and political and health pressures with a global impact not least of which has been the Covid 19 pandemic. So as well as reducing crime we need to address the real issues of how children can become the best versions of themselves and live long, healthy and happy lives. Developments in academic research such as the trauma informed model, child first youth justice, contextual safeguarding, as well as victim centred approaches such as restorative justice, have made the criminal justice policy and practice world look very different to the environment I encountered as a newly quailed probation officer in 1990.

These developments are driven by research, and research requires partnership and participation of those in the system, and this is where the knowledge transfer partnership approach is so valuable. Ensuring the voice of the child is heard, understood and valued in any research project allows us all to develop practice, policy and ultimately legislation to travel in the right direction and thereby achieve our collective ambition of reducing crime, impacts of crime and allowing for the development of positive citizenship. Some may say this is naive and idealistic, to which I would respond that if you aim low you will settle for less than you should! Not dissimilar to the approach we take with individual children and families.

And of course less crime means less people impacted by the negative outcomes of such activity. The majority of victims of serious youth crime are also children or young adults.

So the 'Golden Ticket' to achieve our collective ambition is to understand and evidence what interventions, approaches, and policy and procedure are effective in reducing the amount and impact of crime by children. Collaboration is the key word for me and this book looks at the links and approaches between academia, research projects and quality assurance measurement organisations; and I am sure students, academics, practitioners and policy makers will find the contributions fascinating and useful and not merely of interest.

The partnership between Cheshire Youth Justice, Edge Hill University and Chester University started primarily as a localised response to the themes I have mentioned. At

Cheshire Youth Justice we have extensive experience of promoting academic research – Ph.D. dissertations particularly – as well as practical work-based placements and input to criminology and other courses to inform and debate with students actual practice, not just the theory of youth crime. This is a two-way process as of course the research informs the practice at both local and national level, and the Association of YOT Managers has a longstanding commitment to such an approach, as does the Youth Justice Board and Home Office.

In some ways our local situation originated in the relationships between the main protagonists, as many projects do, and is growing and developing further, and I hope that many of my colleagues in Youth Justice take inspiration from the fundamental approach we adopted which was without additional funding, or indeed any funding. We have developed a mutually beneficial and collaborative approach that gives many positive outcomes but collectively aims to achieve our prime aim – reducing crime, impacts of crime and improving lives. I am confident that the culture of practical learning and research we have established will continue to develop and impact long after the original protagonists have moved on.

I thank all the contributors who have given generously of their time, their thoughts and findings, and their hours of hard work.

I trust you will find this a stimulating, informative and inspiring read.

Gareth Jones
Former Head of Cheshire Youth Justice services
January 2024

Acknowledgments

The Editors would like to take this opportunity to thank all the authors for contributing to this collection. All the contributors to this book are respected within their field and we are delighted they agreed to be involved. It has been a pleasure working with them, and their commitment to meeting deadlines and supporting this collection forming is hugely valued. Thanks to Dr Kathy Hampson for proofreading the introduction and conclusion chapters, providing important comments, observations and proofreading-type corrections on versions of the manuscripts. Thanks to Susan Gillen and Dr Nicholas Longpre for proofreading some of the chapters and for providing helpful comments.

Thank you to Lydia de Cruz (Commissioning Editor) and Medha Malaviya (Senior Editorial Assistant) who both work at Routledge, Taylor & Francis (Informa), for providing extensive support and guidance throughout the whole process.

We are very grateful to Gareth Jones who established the partnership in Cheshire and has maintained a keen and reciprocal relationship between academia and practice throughout. Tom Dooks has similarly also been open to academic involvement within the service and encouraged these links across relationships with academics and practitioners.

As readers will see from the first chapter, practitioners working within Cheshire Youth Justice Service demonstrate huge pride and commitment to their work with children and young people and we are proud to work with them. They are passionate individuals who are keen to develop themselves professionally and seek out opportunities to do so. In every instance, they have been warmly welcoming and supportive of students undertaking placements, seeking to ensure they have a rich professional experience. The professionals within the research group are hugely generous with their time within these meetings and any empirical work undertaken within the service. They are responsive to research findings and feedback, alongside shaping the conceptual thinking of academics involved in the partnership. We are also grateful to all the children and young people who have engaged with the researchers as part of the knowledge and skills partnership.

Introduction

Knowledge/evidence production and utilisation

Sean Creaney and Jayne Price

Rationale for the book

There are different types of knowledge relevant and applicable to the youth justice context that can be developed or acquired through engagement in academic study/scholarship and mastered through professional practice. Evidence-based practice, defined in different ways, is informed and guided by empirical research, theoretical insights, young people's narratives and professional knowledge/expertise (Baker et al., 2011). The focus of this edited collection is on forms of knowledge exchange (transfer) between professionals and academics in the youth justice context. The phrase 'Knowledge and Skills Partnerships' is invoked, and covers a spectrum of meanings, employed as an umbrella term that encompasses the exchange and transfer of knowledge between stakeholders and translation of theory/evidence into practice. This emphasis on the construction and dissemination of knowledge in youth justice was the theme of an event on Wednesday 8 June 2022. Dr Jayne Price, Dr Sean Creaney and Gareth Jones chaired a one-day online conference[1] about 'Knowledge Transfer Partnerships' between youth justice practice and academia. The event was hosted by Cheshire Youth Justice Services, Edge Hill University and the University of Chester, and focused on knowledge/evidence production and utilisation in youth justice practice. The catalyst for the event was HM Inspectorate of Probation's (2021:6) report on Cheshire Youth Justice Services:

> We were impressed with the [Youth Justice Service] YJS's use of evidence and academic research to inform and develop practice and services. This is some of the strongest we have seen.

The inspectorate alluded to the benefits of a well-established knowledge and skills partnership and how evidence is used to inform practice. It was heartening to see such value placed on research-informed and evidence-based practice, highlighted in the final inspection report that was then published online (HM Inspectorate of Probation, 2021). It is important to emphasise the opportunity which this conference and book presents of drawing together other expertise in this area. This includes creating a space to disseminate achievements (including proactive knowledge exchange strategies), engage academic/practice experts and heighten the importance of knowledge and skills partnerships by creating a space for professionals to reflect upon their own beliefs and values, including principles that underpin meaningful knowledge exchange activity. Understanding the environments within which practitioners operate is of paramount importance, (re)attaching value to 'knowledge *from* practice, or practice wisdom'

DOI: 10.4324/9781003411192-1

(Gibson, Vaswani and Dyer, 2024), when seeking to nurture the development of evidence-based policy and practice within organisations.

The conference was an opportunity to share insights into the multifaceted ways in which 'youth justice services are grounded in reliable and robust evidence' (Moore, Brazier and Mercer, 2024). It was also an opportunity to explore why nurturing reciprocal relationships between professionals and academics is key when building the evidence-base and maximising effective practice across the sector. The 'ivory tower' (Case, 2016) of academia may be a phrase invoked by some to level criticism at criminologists and criminal justice researchers for being detached from the realities and complexities of 'policy making' within child and youth justice services or indicating a lack of understanding of the 'real world' decision making processes within youth justice practice. Whilst academics may be, to an extent, remote from practice/coalface youth justice delivery, this could be due to a lack of insider or tacit knowledge about what is happening within organisations. Within knowledge and skills partnerships, academics have experienced the pressing concerns and ideas of frontline professionals; *working together* to identify the issues, co-producing solutions, conceptualising novel approaches to problems detected or uncovered through fieldwork and meaningful dialogue between stakeholders.

The online conference brought together stakeholders from youth justice practice, academia (including students), the Association of Youth Offending Team Managers (AYM), and the Inspectorate, to recognise and showcase how bilateral communication between interested parties (including researchers) can enhance practice and help to facilitate positive outcomes for children and young people and their parents/carers. Speakers included:

- Dr Robin Moore (HM Inspectorate of Probation)
- David Parks (The Skill Mill)
- Ross Gibson (Children and Young people's Centre for Justice)
- Dr Sue Bond-Taylor (University of Lincoln)
- Dr Sarah Brooks-Wilson (University of Birmingham)
- Emma Day (Edge Hill University)
- Dr Kathy Hampson (Aberystwyth University)
- Dr Anne-Marie Day (Manchester Metropolitan University)
- Hazel Williamson (Association of Youth Offending Team Managers)
- Tom Lang (Manchester Youth Justice Service)

We considered different expressions of knowledge transfer partnerships, how they can develop the knowledge base and are realised in practice. We promoted opportunities for further collaborations at the event, capitalising on a rich tapestry of shared insights, culminating in this book. We were interested in producing an edited collection that was accessible to practitioners working in the field, with an interest in advancing best practice. We also felt this collection would be of interest to educators and criminology (and related disciplines) students who are researching work-related learning opportunities and/ or keen to study how practice informs, and is led by, research, theories and knowledge. Our aim is to interest educators who are practice-focused and interested in developing research-informed teaching materials or undertaking consultancy and evaluative work.

Students with experience of placements and research projects within Cheshire Youth Justice Services also presented at this knowledge transfer partnership event, illustrating the power of 'Student as Producer' (Neary, 2019; Strudwick, 2017). Whilst the use of this concept in a youth justice context is underdeveloped, there are examples of it being employed as a guiding principle driving curriculum design and the development of inno-vative educational projects focused on the study of youth crime and justice (Bond-Taylor and Davies, 2019). At its core, the concept builds on 'student voice' scholarship to view students as capable knowledge creators who can educate, influence professionals and academics alike, undertake empirical work, obtain data 'to fill critical evidence gaps in practice and theory' (Butts et al., 2024: 215) by disseminating discoveries. For this to be realised in practice, tutors need to carefully monitor power dynamics within relationships and provide students with valuable opportunities to achieve maximum outcomes from their studies and extra-curricular engagements, especially research activity and skills development.

Aims of the collection

This book is the first of its kind to offer comprehensive analysis of knowledge and skills partnerships in the youth justice sector. The text is original and cutting-edge, shedding light on the challenges professionals experience when seeking to understand complex theory and 'make sense' of the vast array of empirical data. The wealth of research evidence and aca-demic ideas presented to practitioners can be perceived as 'a multitude of noisy, argu-mentative criminological perspectives' (McLaughlin and Muncie, 2006: xiii). Practitioners may also feel disempowered if their practice expertise, experience of working in the field, or professional judgement appear to be devalued by the academy, especially if they feel compelled or are instructed to comply with certain agendas that they feel are futile or bureaucratic. It is worth noting here that this collection is not a synthesis of criminological theories (Hopkins Burke, 2018), nor is it a detailed account of children first philosophy (Haines and Drakeford, 1998) or an introductory text unpacking the concepts of desistance (Wigzell, Paterson-Young and Bateman, 2024). It is, however, a text that seeks to address gaps in understanding about knowledge/evidence production and utilisation. In other words, it explores co-design (between researchers and non-academic partners) and the application of knowledge/evidence/theory into practice. This is achieved by the expert author team who skilfully navigate the complex terrain of knowledge exchange, especially in relation to translating theory and evidence into practice. The collection combines a blend of skills, knowledge (evidence), values and lived or life experience of various stakeholders who hold a shared commitment/vision to improve justice *for* and *with* children and young people. At its core, the purpose of the collection is to showcase – through illustrative examples and rich case studies – effective knowledge exchange/transfer in the youth justice context, including analyses of the mechanisms that help or hinder the theory/practice nexus, and factors that influence approaches to service delivery.

The collection

The authors present an expert analysis of knowledge/evidence production and utilisation in youth justice, drawing on empirical research and practice examples. The text presents a series of case studies to showcase the application of theory/evidence to practice. The chapters within this collection, authored by practice and academic experts, explore the benefits and challenges of knowledge production in youth justice. This book will appeal to both national and international audiences who are interested in learning about knowledge exchange initiatives and approaches to building evidence-based practice in a range of youth justice jurisdictions (Belarus, Scotland, Wales and England).

Chapter 1: 'Enablers and barriers to the development of knowledge and skills partnerships in youth justice'. Dr Jayne Price and Dr Sean Creaney

The chapter by **Dr Jayne Price and Dr Sean Creaney** explores why knowledge and skills partnerships between academics and practitioners can be a useful mechanism to apply criminological theory and research evidence in practice. Through consultancy, evaluation work and training or coaching activities, empirical evidence and criminological theories can be applied in practice and used to inform or influence policy developments across and within multi-agency child and youth justice services. As the authors assert, this vision has been achieved in practice through co-founding a research group to operationalise a commitment to research informed practice, in so doing identifying and promoting progressive and principled ways of working. As part of the Knowledge and Skills Partnership (KSP), practitioners and researchers have also co-designed a relationship-based practice framework and identified key principles necessary to help create and sustain meaningful partnerships between children and professionals. The KSP has also facilitated opportunities for academics to undertake research, which has led to changes in orthodox ways of working within the service, recognising the value of relationship-based practice and the social prescribing of more creative/participatory interventions.

Chapter 2: 'Criminology placements and work experience opportunities in youth justice'. Dr Sean Creaney and Dr Jayne Price

The chapter by **Dr Sean Creaney and Dr Jayne Price** presents insights into the types of practice and research placement opportunities available as part of the 'Building Professional Skills for Youth Justice' (BPSYJ) programme. Within this chapter, the 'in focus' case studies presented provide an in-depth illustrative account of how students have been involved directly in the learning process. Creaney and Price offer a credible and persuasive account of the power of work-based learning opportunities. As the authors assert, the chapter may help to pave the way for other youth offending team/university collaborations to enrich the experiences of students with an interest in youth justice practice. Furthermore, some of the themes presented here may be of relevance to other professions and disciplines, especially interested parties who are jostling with ideas to secure work experience or mobilise research placements for students or bolster forms of critical thinking and reflective practices.

Chapter 3: 'How the inspectorate works with external academics/researchers'. Dr Robin Moore, Andrea Brazier and Helen Mercer

The chapter by **Dr Robin Moore, Andrea Brazier and Helen Mercer** provides insight into how the Inspectorate collaborates with external academics and researchers. As the authors assert, HM Inspectorate of Probation provides authoritative and evidence-based judgements and guidance through reviewing, developing and promoting the evidence-base for high-quality services. The authors provide an insightful and engaging account of ways to maximise the knowledge, experience and skills of various stakeholders and interested parties who are invested in the generation, use or application of evidence. The authors outline different types of knowledge exchange activity undertaken by the Inspectorate, showcasing how it has been beneficial and impactful. The chapter includes a series of practice examples and detailed accounts of how the Inspectorate has worked in collaboration with commissioned partners. The authors also reflect upon some of the challenges, including ways to navigate competing/differing academic perspectives and the importance of nurturing research/evaluation cultures within services to advance evidence-informed approaches in youth justice.

Chapter 4: 'Youth Justice Still Live! The centrality of relationships to the maintenance of a youth justice community of practice in challenging times and beyond'. Dr Sue Bond-Taylor

The chapter by **Dr Sue Bond-Taylor** provides a detailed account of *Youth Justice Live!* an educational development project involving students, practitioners and academics, premised on ideas of a Community of Practice. The project is collaborative, providing a platform for differing perspectives to be shared and valued, including the knowledge and insights of students. Within this space, students nurture critical thinking skills through critiquing practices within youth justice, including assessment processes. The teaching and learning activities within *Youth Justice Live!* are interactive, student focused and related to contemporary policy and practice developments. Not only are students taught relevant theory and principles of effective practice within the co-delivery of a degree-level module, but they also explore career development opportunities within the youth justice sector and have the space to acquire and develop the necessary skills (graduate attributes) to work within multi-disciplinary child and youth justice services. Alongside an acknowledgment of the limitations of employability-focused extra-curricular activities within the discipline of criminology, the chapter also includes examples of how the university/youth justice service knowledge exchange partnership has catalysed the use of evidence and research to develop and enhance practice. The chapter ends by setting out some key principles that can be described as core components of effective practice, necessary to drive innovative practices within the realm of knowledge exchange.

Chapter 5: 'The Dyfed Powys Hwb Doeth partnership'. Dr Kathy Hampson

The chapter by **Dr Kathy Hampson** showcases effective and innovative practices through a practice-academia group formulated within the Welsh youth justice context. It begins by setting the scene for the discussions that follow. The author provides relevant and useful context by setting out the purpose and key features of the Dyfed Powys and Hwb Doeth practice/research focused initiatives. The chapter presents insights from members involved in the partnership. The knowledge transfer partnership opens up the space to reflect on and discuss current issues, share insights into the application of findings from research studies into practice, reflect on the efficacy of certain interventions, identify gaps in knowledge and understanding, and work together to decide how to overcome barriers or issues impacting on service delivery. Practitioners working within youth justice services in Wales have designed and delivered practice-focused guest lectures to undergraduate students, and have also benefited from being in receipt of training delivered by academics. Furthermore, the partnership has facilitated student research projects; worthwhile opportunities to evaluate a new pilot or intervention. The author of the chapter also reflects on some of the challenges with regard to knowledge exchange/transfer in a Welsh youth justice context.

Chapter 6: 'Supporting practice in Scotland: Lessons from the Children and Young People's Centre for Justice'. Ross Gibson, Dr Nina Vaswani and Fiona Dyer

The chapter by **Ross Gibson, Dr Nina Vaswani and Fiona Dyer** provides in-depth insight into the work of the Children and Young People's Centre for Justice (CYCJ) in Scotland, a trusted Knowledge Exchange Centre for Excellence. The chapter explains how the Centre facilitates effective knowledge exchange through adopting and implementing novel approaches. The authors define and critique key terminology, including types and uses of knowledge, and provide an overview of the interconnected workstreams. As the authors assert, through networking and relationship-building, knowledge and evidence gaps can be identified. In addition to presenting key arguments and reflections on how evidence has been used to influence responses to children in conflict with the law, it also presents case studies to illustrate the impact and influence of the Centre on policy and practice developments.

Chapter 7: 'Advancing best practice in juvenile justice in Belarus'. Dr Vicky Palmer

The chapter by **Dr Vicky Palmer** presents insight into an internationally collaborative knowledge transfer partnership between academics and criminal justice professionals in England and Belarus. The author provides an in-depth account of its origins, purpose, implementation and accomplishments, including reflections on the challenges of designing and delivering a project of this nature. A series of high-quality seminars was delivered to juvenile justice stakeholders via a range of teaching methods and learning activities, including real-life case studies and anonymised court reports. Palmer concludes the chapter by reinforcing the importance of knowledge transfer partnerships locally, nationally and internationally.

Conclusion: 'Knowledge and skills partnerships'. Dr Sean Creaney and Dr Jayne Price

This chapter by **Dr Sean Creaney and Dr Jayne Price** revisits the purpose of the collection, including justification for an edited collection about knowledge/evidence production and utilisation in youth justice practice. It then identifies key themes and summarises the arguments set out in this collection. It ends by identifying some of the key principles necessary for the development and sustainability of knowledge and skills partnerships across the youth justice sector. Such principles or prerequisite features include relationship-building, collaboration, reciprocity, constructive dialogue, and participation.

Note

1 The event was supported by the Association of Youth Offending Team Managers (AYM) and sponsored by Edge Hill's Law and Criminology Department and the Institute for Social Responsibility (ISR) (Edge Hill University).

References

Baker, K., Kelly, G. and Wilkinson, B. (2011) *Assessment in Youth Justice*. Bristol: Policy Press.

Bond-Taylor, Sue and Davies, Ceryl (2019) Youth Justice Live! Flexible pedagogies in an online/offline community of practice. In: *Flexible Pedagogies in Practice: Implementing flexibility in higher education through online learning communities*. Rotterdam: Sense Publishers.

Butts, Jeffrey A., Roman, John K. and Pugliese, Katheryne (2024) Evidence-oriented Youth Justice. In: Brandon C. Welsh, Steven N. Zane and Daniel P. Mears (eds) *Oxford Handbook of Evidence-Based Crime and Justice Policy*. New York: Oxford University Press.

Case, S. (2016) Negative Youth Justice: Creating the youth crime 'problem'. CYCJ. Available from: https://www.cycj.org.uk/negative-youth-justice-creating-the-youth-crime-problem/.

Creaney, S. and Burns, S. (2023) Freedom from Symbolic Violence? Facilitators and barriers to participatory practices in youth justice. *Youth Justice*, 0(0). https://doi.org/10.1177/14732254231156844.

Gibson, R.Vaswani, N. and Dyer, F. (2024) Supporting Practice in Scotland: Lessons from the Children and Young People's Centre for Justice. In: Price, J. and Creaney, S. (eds) *Knowledge and Skills Partnerships in Youth Justice*. Abingdon: Routledge.

Haines, K. and Drakeford, M. (1998) *Young People and Youth Justice*. London: Macmillan.

HM Inspectorate of Probation (2021) *An Inspection of Youth Offending Services in Cheshire Youth Justice Service*. Available from: https://www.justiceinspectorates.gov.uk/hmiprobation/wp-content/uploads/sites/5/2021/12/Cheshire-YJS-v1.1.pdf.

Hopkins Burke, R.D. (2018) *An Introduction to Criminological Theory*. 5th edn. Abingdon: Routledge.

McLaughlin, E. and Muncie, J. (2006) *The Sage Dictionary of Criminology*. 2nd edn. London: Sage.

Moore, R., Brazier, A. and Mercer, H. (2024) How the Inspectorate Works with External Academics/researchers. In: Price, J. and Creaney, S. (eds) *Knowledge and Skills Partnerships in Youth Justice*. Abingdon: Routledge.

Neary, M. (2019) Student as Producer and the Democratisation of Science. *Impact: the University of Lincoln Journal of Higher Education Research*, 1(4). ISSN: 2516–7561.

Neary, M. and Winn, J. (2009) The Student as Producer: Reinventing the student experience in higher education. In: *The Future of Higher Education: Policy, pedagogy and the student experience* (pp. 192–210.). London: Continuum. ISBN: ISBN: 1847064728.

Smithson, H. and Jones, A. (2021) Co-creating Youth Justice Practice with Young People: Tackling power dynamics and enabling transformative action. *Children and Society: The International Journal of Childhood and Children's Services*, 3(3), 348–362. ISSN 0951–0605.

Stout, B., Williams, B. and Yates, J. (2008) *Applied Criminology*. London: Sage.

Strudwick, K. (2017) Debating Student as Producer: Relationships, contexts and challenges for higher education. *PRISM: Casting New Light on Learning, Theory and Practice*, 1(1), 73–96.

Whyte, B. (2009) *Youth Justice in Practice: Making a difference*. Bristol: Policy Press.

Wigzell, A., Paterson-Young, C. and Bateman, T. (eds) (2024). *Understanding Children's Pathways away from Offending: Critical reflections on desistance and children from theory, research and practice*. Bristol University Press.

1 Enablers and barriers to the development of knowledge and skills partnerships in youth justice

Jayne Price and Sean Creaney

Chapter objectives

By the end of this chapter, you should be able to:

- Assess how knowledge and skills partnerships help to navigate the theory/practice nexus.
- Realise the importance of championing a unique synergy between academia and youth justice practice.
- Identify the key components of building and sustaining reciprocal relationships between academics and practitioners.

Knowledge and skills partnerships in youth justice services: Bridging the worlds of theory and practice

> There's an awful lot to be said for a local university evaluating services in terms of understanding the local context, getting to know the staff and the organisation as well … If you have a close relationship with those evaluating your service that obviously means that in some respects the information that researchers get can be more reliable because staff don't feel they are under scrutiny in quite the same way. But evaluators need to be in a position where they are sufficiently independent to be able to criticise as well.
>
> (Dr Tim Bateman, quoted in CYP Now, 2012)

The quote above from a leading academic, cited within a news report about a youth justice knowledge and skills partnership, provides a very good illustration of how joint working can assist in the application of theory and enable research-informed or evidence-based practice to be developed or progressed within youth justice services. It also underscores the important role of youth justice 'pracademics'[1] (Volpe and Chandler, 1999) and the realisation that partnerships of this nature between academic institutions and multi-agency youth justice services can build and maintain close working relationships, providing fertile ground to collaborate on initiatives, 'test out' new and mutually beneficial areas of interest, co-design resources and bespoke guiding frameworks, and/or open-up research opportunities for scholars and practice-focused academics alike (Case and Haines, 2014; Smithson et al., 2022). As will be illustrated within this chapter, these types of collaborations, consequent dialogue and interactions that result from these exchanges, can be beneficial to stakeholders for several reasons, including access to advice and training, data and placement opportunities (Hayes, 2018). The Youth Justice Board published guidance for academic and Youth Offending Team (YOT) partnership working in 2017 (Smith-Yau, 2017). The guidance

DOI: 10.4324/9781003411192-2

outlines key principles such as clarity over aims, power sharing arrangements, roles, leadership and resource allocation (Smith-Yau, 2017). Within the pages that follow, this chapter builds on this body of work and, in so doing, offers a nuanced account of how principles are applied into practice and the extent to which evidence/research and other factors, are considered and utilised to inform discussions about the care and treatment of justice-involved children at one particular and unique multi-agency service.

The **Knowledge and Skills Partnership** (**KSP**) between Cheshire Youth Justice Service, Edge Hill University and the University of Chester has no additional financial support and there is an informal rather than formal agreement in place. There are benefits and limitations to this. On the one hand, it can reduce opportunities with there being no funding for specific work or projects; on the other hand, due to there being no reporting requirements (which can be requested as part of conditions attached to funding) such bureaucratic tasks are avoided, allowing those involved in the project to innovate and unleash creativity. Crucially, the latter has enabled the execution of a 'critical edge' as part of a criminological and pedagogical approach. In other words, academics have the space and scope to cast an 'analytical gaze over the processes of criminalisation, crime enforcement, and the criminal justice system' (Canton and Yates, 2008:6). As Posner (2009:14) notes in a discussion around the nature of the academic/practitioner nexus, issues can be 'addressed through a shared community of thoughtful practitioners and academics, each contributing unique perspectives but learning from each other through meetings, conferences, exercises and informal discussions'.

Whilst raising issues, problematising terminology (especially language that is in common parlance) and system responses remains a key feature of the work of academics involved in the KSP, the underpinning approach or driving philosophical perspective is likened to a form of applied criminology (Canton and Yates, 2008). There is a noticeable commitment amongst group members to explore tangible ways in which empirical evidence and criminological theories can be applied in practice or used to inform or influence policy developments across and within multi-agency child and youth justice services. Whilst maintaining academic freedom is a necessity, there is a clear focus on listening to and seeking to address the needs or concerns of practitioners through a problem-solving methodology likened to an appreciative type of inquiry. This is key. as Posner (2009:13) notes: 'While theory can be self-contained, the impact of our research and teaching arguably finds its most compelling and highest audience when it addresses the agenda items and concerns of practitioners'.

There is also a focus on practitioner experiences and expertise and how frontline perspectives from workers influence research/academic agendas. As alluded to, reciprocity is at the heart of the KSP, where practitioners and academics hear and understand one another (receptive of somewhat differing environmental contexts and organisational priorities), and the principle of power-sharing and the spirit of mutuality are respected and enacted. These are key elements underpinning forms of joint working within the partnership arrangement. These guiding principles are set out and discussed in detail in other chapters within this edited collection. Whilst there may be differing expectations or world views (Huey and Mitchell, 2016:303), over many years the academic leads and practitioners within the service have worked hard to maintain reciprocal relationships, acknowledging differences of opinion but seeking a degree of consensus through striking a balance between different perspectives or viewpoints on matters (Posner, 2009).

Prior to discussing the details of the programmes of work undertaken, at this point it is necessary to briefly discuss how and why the KSP came into fruition. Gareth Jones, Tom

Dooks and Dr Sean Creaney met in 2017 to formalise partnership arrangements between the service and the university, which initially prioritised research and practice placement opportunities for students and guest lectures. Following this, Gareth originally approached Dr Katie Hunter whilst liaising with the University of Chester to explore opportunities for extending the existing knowledge and skills partnership arrangement. Katie was moving on from the university and handed over responsibility to Dr Jayne Price. When students request research or practice placements, meetings are held to discuss and consider the proposal and to decide upon resource implications (see Chapter 2 for more detail). The placements allow students to shadow practitioners, learn systems, attend and observe various multi-agency meetings. Students also learn about how professionals undertake assessments and supervise children and young people undertaking court order requirements or diversionary measures. Students also learn about the roles and responsibilities of multi-agency youth justice services and develop insight into the reasons why children enter the system and are supported throughout the process. The academic leads[2] attend regular research meetings organised by practitioners, as discussed later in this chapter. The value of such partnership working is highlighted and recognised by the Youth Justice Board (Smith-Yau, 2017) and HM Inspectorate of Probation (Smithson and Gray, 2021). Projects that have resulted from such links have contributed to the development of knowledge about how to improve children and young people's participation by co-creating projects and activities. This has informed the Child First agenda in England and Wales (Smithson and Gray, 2021).

As Case Study 2 illustrates, as part of the KSP, colleagues within the University of Chester conducted research to investigate the impact of Covid-19 on practice within Cheshire Youth Justice Services. Through interviews with staff members and creative participatory measures with children and young people, the service obtained a clear understanding of both groups' experiences of the service during this challenging operational time. The study also provided a set of recommendations relevant to flexible working principles: their advantages and disadvantages from practitioner perspectives. The findings of the research were disseminated to senior managers within the service. This has helped to bolster forms of creative practice with the introduction of more socially prescribed psychosocial therapeutic interventions, including a music group and spoken word, to work with children and young people (Cheshire Youth Justice Service, 2023).

Practitioners may be reticent to participate in studies of this nature due to a perceived fear of being scrutinised or judged. They may be of the view that there is little benefit to them in becoming a research participant. Indeed, this is understandable when we consider that 'they are frequently the providers/generators of data but receive no feedback or report of the work they have participated in' (Hine, 2008:31). However, practitioners within Cheshire Youth Justice Service are comfortable with and open to ongoing review and development of their practice (Cheshire Youth Justice Service, 2023). This chapter now proceeds to discuss how and why the KSP embraces the combined use of data, shared expertise and training. It presents the accounts and narratives of practitioners involved in the development of the academic/practitioner research group.

Case study 1: Practitioner perspective: Research group

> So how does the hard-pressed practitioner, faced almost daily with new research and a seemingly never-ending supply of facts and figures, 'findings', evaluations and recommendations, sort the wheat from the chaff?
>
> (Taylor, 2010:xvi)

Whilst it was decided that the Knowledge and Skills Partnership would be an informal arrangement via a type of quid pro quo exchange, in 2020 we jointly established a research group to help practitioners make sense of findings, evaluations and recommendations from relevant research studies (Taylor, 2010:xvi). The group, led by a practitioner, meet frequently throughout the year remotely, and often there are external guest speakers sharing practice and research insights, including new innovations, in an accessible way. Members of the group interrogate the evidence-base and scrutinise the principles of effective practice by reflecting on the development and efficacy of restorative practices, participatory initiatives and trauma-informed approaches. As part of this initiative, academics have been working with practitioners to develop or co-produce a relationship-based practice framework (Stephenson and Dix, 2017). This framework is deemed necessary to set out the key principles that should guide decision making and subsequently drive innovative practices in the field. This framework can be utilised as a heuristic/practical device to facilitate relationship building and forge quality partnerships between children and their practitioners, bolstering children's active involvement in supervision, reducing passive compliance, and preventing inauthentic transactional arrangements from forming (Creaney, 2020). It can also be used as a mechanism to provoke refection on how practitioners can navigate tensions between care and control or manage the dual role of enforcer and enabler (see Creaney and Burns, 2023) or overcome challenges with engagement, especially when working with children subject to court orders, who may have a tendency to feel obliged to engage in interventions as opposed to actively participate (CYCJ, 2022).

'Children First' as a philosophy and model of practice also aligns to the framework. It has been discussed during research group meetings as part of the KSP (Cheshire Youth Justice Service, 2023). This concept has been gaining recent currency in both the policy arena and as a strategy implemented within practice settings (YJB, 2021). As Hampson (2023:317) notes, 'The importance of giving the child a voice, listening to their views and actively collaborating with them is a central aspect of Child First (Tenet 3)'. At the research group meetings there have been discussions around incorporating the Child First principle into practice with children in or on the cusp of the justice system (Case and Hazel, 2023). Crucially, as part of these discussions, there is acknowledgment of the variety of factors that can influence how policy is formulated, or how services and interventions are conceptualised or developed. It can be difficult to advance evidence-based practice for several reasons, not least due to long-standing beliefs, ingrained mentalities and resource constraints that can act as barriers to the development of progressive or principled practices. Some of these matters are alluded to and concisely summarised by Smith (2006:79): 'lobbyists and pressure groups demand attention, habit and traditional ways of conceiving problems are hard to change, and political ideologies and considerations of electoral popularity will inevitably enter the decision making process' (Smith, 2006:79). For the purposes of this chapter, members of this group were invited to attend a focus group to discuss their perceptions of the partnership; attendees included case workers, managers and volunteers.[3] Within this, they reflected upon their experiences as part of the group and more generally within the service.

Knowledge and skills partnerships

Within the research group, discussions have centred around the academic/practitioner nexus and development of evidence-based practice. The research group have a detailed record of presentations delivered from April 2021. Speakers for future events are suggested by those on the research team. Remote working has better facilitated these talks which take place over Teams/Zoom. There are no financial payments made to speakers as their time delivering such presentations forms part of their engagement and impact. Many practitioners feel that these talks enable more reflection on their practice and discussion across the service:

> 'we've always done it this way' ... No, no one says that at all anymore.
>
> (Mark, restorative justice worker and chair of research group)

> I think things are a lot more meaningful now.
>
> (Jez, manager)

When initially asked about knowledge and skills partnerships and their meaning to them, attendees alluded to the concept being a bridge between the worlds of criminological theory and youth justice practice (Taylor, 2010). Whilst highlighting the importance of academic scholarship and empirical research, they also acknowledged the experiences and expertise of frontline practitioners alongside their values and principles as being 'equally valid and valuable evidence for practice' (Whyte, 2009:48). It was also recognised that practitioners at all levels in various roles within the service, including volunteers and mental health workers, offer crucial and equally important contributions:

> ...sharing our knowledge with other organisations but vice versa as well [...] They are the extended part of our service, so they come with a wealth of knowledge and understanding of their local communities. So, it's being able to hear and listen to what they've got to say, but not only that, incorporate their thoughts and feelings into the way that we shape our service.
>
> (Chris, manager)

> I always framed it in that sort of academic way. And I think that's a really interesting point, isn't it, about looking at it in the different ways with academia, but also the other services that you have involvement with.
>
> (Miriam, divert team practitioner)

> I just thought it was really interesting the way that [research] gets transformed into practice.
>
> (Ann, senior management team admin officer)

> I've been volunteering with the Youth Justice Service of 20 years now and [have] met a lot of young people and so on and in other areas of things that I do. We have quite a lot of in-service training and new ideas coming in.
>
> (Michael, volunteer)

> I remember when we had [information/training] a few weeks ago about autism and my knowledge of autism suddenly blossomed from what I thought I knew about from years of working with autistic kids and things, and it's sudden ... I saw it all quite differently and [it] helped me to understand much better the things I'm reading

in the kind of reports that we get before meeting young people and I think opportunities for that kind of sharing [of knowledge and information].

(Michael, volunteer)

There were discussions around the importance of relational and non-hierarchical relationships. Such considerations contribute to building organisational cultures. Crucially, these are some of the foundations that allow for knowledge and skills partnerships to develop, providing the scope to acknowledge and value a greater range of expertise (Social Care Institute for Excellence, 2022). Numerous examples were provided for the ways in which such partnership working had helped to direct the principles of effective practice:

If we have any students or if we have any mentors or volunteers, it's always healthy from my point of view to try and you know get their knowledge about life in some respects, which actually you know, you can link in with youth justice in regard to whether it be relationship-based practice or whatever.

(David, divert team practitioner)

[Student] was on placement and I was her placement supervisor as such, and she was able to like shape our understanding of suicide [and] of working with females and bringing her learning and her understanding and the academic lecturers [she attended] into our thoughts.

(Chris, manager)

Michael [volunteer] puts his hands up to everything but has helped us to shape our service and Michael comes from an academic background [...] he was a teacher he was head of pastoral care of a high school and so some of his community understanding and knowledge of that level helped us shape [the service]. Michael created, with myself and another volunteer, the changes in the referral order panel processes for the reviews and the finals; he also came back to me and said, 'oh, paperwork isn't good enough for rehabilitation of offender leaflet – let's change it'. And so, you know, I could always say, '[...] no, you're all right. I'm happy with what I'm doing' but he comes from an understanding of this background but also listens to families and young people that are experiencing our service, and so it would be foolish not to listen and not to do something about it.

(Chris, manager)

Volunteers within the service are drawn from a range of backgrounds. They are valued team members who are encouraged to feel a sense of belonging within the service by attending and participating in staff forums and training sessions. As the accounts of focus group attendees illustrate, their experiences and perspectives are of importance and value to how the organisation operates or functions. Knowledge and skills partnerships were described by practitioners to 'work'. In other words, it was dubbed an effective vehicle to facilitate research-informed practices. The KSP had inspired several attendees to further engage with their own research, of benefit to themselves personally and professionally:

I think like doing, what we've done, it raises a lot more questions for us as practitioners and it sort of allows us to develop as a team, as a service ... because we do have our own like little separate teams and I think it's a positive way of developing really and it's also helped us.[...] The knowledge that comes from outside services, that comes into our service just allows us to develop really positive interventions with young people.

(Rea, support worker)

I knew nothing about [knowledge transfer partnerships] when I first joined the service [...] I remember [Sean] coming and doing something about desistance. I [remember] thinking, 'gosh, that's interesting! I must look that thing up, whatever that means'. And then I did my effective practice certificate and it got me really fired up about research.

(Mark, restorative justice worker and chair of research group)

As alluded to by Mark, one of the academic leads delivered a session on desistance to practitioners as part of a training day. It was explained that desistance as a concept is contested but can be understood as the cessation of crime by those previously engaged in criminal activity (HMIP, 2016; Creaney and Smith, 2023). The talk then focused specifically on how constructive child–practitioner relationships can be a *medium for change*. In other words, relationship-based practice is necessary to promote both primary and secondary desistance (non-offending) and key to helping the child live a fulfilling life (Burns and Creaney, 2023). This presentation helped the workforce to 'think through' the application of desistance theory to practice. Key principles were identified (i.e. identity transformation) and discussed. Ideas were put forward in a collaborative way that essentially 'shaped the thinking of those with the power and authority to bring about change – policy makers and practitioners' (Hine, 2008:32).

I'm in the fifth year of my six years of university at the minute and I would never have thought I would have gone to university because I do not read books, I hate doing the research and that sort of stuff, Well, I did. But through doing this job and doing the research that I've been doing for university, it does sort of bring about things. And something sort of clicked in my brain. And I was like that is the reason why we do what we do is because of all this research.

(Rea, support worker)

A lot of really good research and you know, proven research that will inform their practice. So, I'm getting feedback when we do that, that actually, you know, my colleagues are actually becoming more confident in their practice because of what we've actually brought to the forefront of the youth justice service.

(David, divert team practitioner)

Some focus group participants also described reparative activities being a useful mechanism through which relationships can be built and discussions facilitated around the child's interests and needs. This is especially so when non-threatening spaces have been forged, allowing children the opportunity to supply input positively and creatively in a meaningful process. Whilst it is important to guard against the risk of reparation becoming a tokenistic exercise where those involved gain little from the process, some members of the research group were of the view that community-based reparation can assist in the promotion of positive outcomes and reduce re-offending (Pamment, 2016).

Members of the management team were described as supportive of the partnership. It is worth noting that attendees highlighted how they had previously felt some distance from the partnership as they perceived it to be a management-led or inspired initiative. However, they then realised that it is a project that is designed to be inclusive of different or diverse perspectives from various workers across the multi-agency services. A key element of effective partnerships and knowledge exchange is said to be strong leadership and buy-in from practitioners (Peer Power and Youth Justice Board, 2021). This was reflected in the following quote relating to the growth of the research group:

> I think that there might have been about five people in the very first one. But it's grown and grown to the point where it's fabulous, it's amazing. But what has created that? What's created the curiosity and what's created people's interest to want to attend those things? ... and we need to emulate that in other areas as well with research [...] everyone's so interested in the way that [Mark, the research group lead] shares these things and the people [guest speakers] that you get in, which is amazing as well.
>
> (David, divert team practitioner)

The practitioners, however, were mindful that knowledge and skills partnerships required relevant professional investment. Certain systems and processes, including factors such as workload pressures, can create barriers to developing knowledge and skills partnerships due to limiting the ability of practitioners to engage in different ways of working:

> But we have to create opportunities to do that, and sometimes there isn't the energy or the appetite to make that possible. [...] we're so busy that we think [oh] there's a change in our service that we think sometimes it's an add-on, but in my opinion it's an essential add-on because if we continue to work in the same manner that we worked last year, the year before, the year before that and not bring anybody else's fresh ideas in, then we're never going to improve or change or shape ourselves and I think that's the reason why I actually brought in the volunteers.
>
> (Chris, manager)

There were some notable challenges in championing the synergy between academia and practice, across agencies and internally. Access to resources seems to be a challenge and research, at times, being seen as an 'add-on' rather than core to the organisation. This was highlighted by Huey and Mitchell, (2016:301) in a thought piece about research-informed practice within policing, who argued that 'research experience is not (always) valued within organisations'. The practitioners who participated in the focus group research for this chapter identified a need for time set aside for learning, as work for the KSP was 'outside of our real jobs' needing 'service motivation' through allocated time to engage. There was also a requirement for personal motivation and support, as academic content could be challenging, which could lead to some practitioners feeling disengaged or disempowered:

> I really struggle sometimes with some of the language that's used. I mean, I'm in university myself at the minute and I have to read over and over and over again because I just don't understand it. It's only when someone explains it in the sessions that we have that I sort of understand what's being said and that. It takes more than

just one person or a book for me to understand that information really. But that's just from a personal standpoint. But I'm sure I'm definitely not on my own in that.

(Rea, support worker)

...when we have guest speakers coming in and explaining it in layperson's terms rather than me reading the book, me reading that information, it's much easier to process for me and I imagine that's quite similar to a lot of people in the service.

(Rea, support worker)

I think a lot of people still hear the words research books, papers, journals, articles and go oh that's not for me, you know like that universe is not for me. Whereas they'd probably be fine with it, you know it's just the confidence in it. So how do we open it up to people who wouldn't necessarily be open to it, but also the new staff we get, you know, how do we bring them on board? What makes them want to do it, make them want to go to events, read the research. Because it's really important that we do that and don't frighten people off. And the young people as well. I think getting them to take part in it, I'm trying to always bring the children I work with to take part in it because their voice is so important, but they haven't got the confidence or don't feel like they've been listened to.

(Miriam, divert team practitioner)

Miriam, a member of the research group, alluded to the difficulties creating and sustaining meaningful relationships with children to maximise their participation in processes, including in research studies. Creaney and Burns (2023) have detailed barriers to achieving youth participation in practice which can include children experiencing a sense that their views are not being taken into account. Other barriers include persistent bureaucracy (i.e. time consuming assessments or excessive attention paid to updating systems), which can limit contact time with children and families. However, in spite of these constraints, as some of the accounts from practitioners allude to, workers have room for manoeuvre to work creatively, using and exercising judgement to respond carefully to identified need in a way that is compatible with a participatory rights discourse. They are capable of invoking and nurturing a culture that values research and the need to facilitate evidence-based practice. More recently, the Lundy (2007) model has been discussed at the research group meetings as a way to not only take account of children's perspectives, but as a mechanism to promote children's participatory rights throughout their contact with the youth justice system. Members of the research group are open to reflective practice and considering ways to improve their work. In response to Laura Lundy's presentation regarding participation, practitioners acknowledged that this could be improved and had set up an online database where children could document their experiences to inform practitioners how to enable them to participate and achieve personal goals. This has recently been established and is thus in development. Whilst practitioners are acutely aware of the importance of relationship-building, the theory and practice of participation and co-production is one example of an area for development that has been identified and is being addressed through a series of discussions, training and talks co-ordinated collaboratively through the research group (Cheshire Youth Justice Services, 2023). Practitioners are receptive to ideas on how to approach practice from many different perspectives, including the voice of the child. This attention has led to fascinating discussions around ways to initiate participatory principles and progressive models of practice to maximise children's involvement in decision making processes.

Whilst there is not a universal or widely accepted definition of participation used across the youth justice sector, encouraging or motivating children to engage in discussions is nevertheless a key focus of practice (Burns and Creaney, 2023). Notwithstanding that it is a concept that varies in definition, arguably it is morally and ethically right to seek children's views and involve them in decision making, especially about topics that relate to their life and lived experiences. This is both a central tenet of the United Nations Convention on the Rights of the Child (UNCRC) and a key element of effective practice within a Child First justice model (Burns and Creaney, 2023; CYCJ, 2022:3; Lundy, 2007). These perspectives are also reiterated and included within the evidence-based Lundy model (2007) of space, voice, audience and influence. Whilst, according to Lundy, *influence* is the 'holy grail of child participation', before explaining how pivotal this principle is, there are other important somewhat interrelated concepts and considerations to reflect upon (see Box).

The Lundy model

First, creating safe or non-threatening *spaces* is key, where children feel able to exercise 'freedom of thought' through being awarded meaningful opportunities to exercise agency/ choice (Article 12 of the UNCRC), engage in friendly and important conversations, sharing their perspectives on matters. This includes facilitating discussions around the extent to which children want to have control over the agenda-setting and decision-making (Peer Power and Youth Justice Board, 2021).

Second, and relatedly, for this intention to be realised in practice, they must have a sense that they have authority to *voice* their opinions, 'speak truth to power' and be reassured by power holders that there will be no adverse consequences for them in 'speaking out' on various matters related either to their own lives or how institutions operate and exercise power over others (Lundy, 2007; Creaney and Burns, 2023; Creaney, 2020). Creating such a welcoming environment that is conducive to a diversity of voices being expressed is especially important given that a high number of children have experienced traumatic childhoods that can impact on levels of engagement (Spacey and Thompson, 2021; Thompson and Spacey, 2023).

Third, a defining feature of this model is the redistribution of power (see also Arnstein, 1969). Whilst power dynamics are difficult to navigate and will be a constant struggle, it is necessary to create access to power holders, where children can offer a candid view about situations or circumstances that affect them, and be listened to by those in authority and provided with responses to their questions or concerns.

Fourth, *influence* is a principle that is of equal importance to the other parts of the model. Practitioners or 'power holders' have responsibilities to communicate clearly with children about the influence and/or impact of their participation, which can improve their experiences and potentially bolster their involvement in similar processes in the future. It is crucial that they are treated in a way that is perceived to be legitimate, which includes a clear explanation for why certain decisions are being made and/or responses to recommendations for improvement.

Research into practice

The research group meetings and presentations have enabled practitioners to recognise or reflect upon the binary categorisations of care and control, the use of 'victim' and 'offender' labels, the emergence of desistance-informed practice, and ways to balance risk management with an emerging emphasis on promoting wellbeing and personal development (Creaney and Smith, 2023). A primary example was following a presentation regarding 'The Relationship-Based Model' (by Martin Stephenson, Chief Executive of Unitas, and Heidi Dix, University of Suffolk). This model is informed by psychological evidence and principles of trauma-informed care focused upon developing trusting relationships, acknowledging harm, and nurturing desistance. An attendee at the talk, David, a divert team practitioner, called the model a 'lightbulb moment' of work he was already doing which gave him the confidence to continue it. Following this presentation, Mark Hamill, chair of the research group, led a seminar and round table discussion at an away day informed by this work which led to it being embedded in practice within the service. A manager, Jez Brown, highlighted the value of this to him:

> So for me, I think the way relationship-based practice has been introduced and reinforced with us has been done really well here because we've had this talk and then Mark has taken the framework away and then what we've done is it's been presented at an away day and that was excellent, [what] really strengthened that for me, and I know a lot of other practitioners as well, was that we also had a former service user who was saying about the importance of it. I distinctly remember this young person saying that, you know, the one thing that he remembers most of all was his keyworker, just sending in messages to say, how are you during the week and that sort of thing really, it was hearing it in a few different ways, you know, so you got the research underpinning what you're doing first, you've got that license to do it. We've got our own framework which is then sort of reinforced with practitioners to say yes, this is the way we want to go forward. This is how we can do it.
>
> (Jez, manager)

Members of the research group have also engaged in critical reflection, especially around identity and labels following a presentation from Dr Ali Wigzell and Dr Tim Bateman about the theory and practice of desistance. The research group recognised the limitations of some practices such as a focus upon identity that were part of their day-to-day work and reinforced by new divert assessment. However, the presentation opened up discussions about what identity does mean for them within the service and how they could maintain a child-first focus:

> ...but actually do you know what – looking at both sides of the argument, isn't that healthy to be able to look at both sides and then where does it fit with that young person if that young person actually wants to, you know, talk about their identity. Well, who are we to say if it's about the young person? It's about what they want and if they wanna talk about it, they want to, you know, identify as being something that they need to discuss and converse about and understand who they are. We're there to actually help provide those sort of platforms for them to have those discussions.
>
> (David, divert team practitioner)

These considerations led back to a discussion of relationship-based practice and how practitioners could support children in the development of new identities (e.g. transitions) to other people in their lives. One key challenge with regard to relationship-based practice is finding a balance between 'risk management' and 'child first practice', as highlighted by Dr Anne-Marie Day as part of a presentation to the research group (see also Day, 2022). Practitioners acknowledged that risk formed part of their day-to-day role and felt that, despite their attempts to shift this language to that of 'wellbeing', 'harm' or 'safety', wider embedding of this language is limited as the concept of risk is retained in surrounding services including the police. Notwithstanding the problems (including ethical and moral) of managing risk through a deficit-based lens, and despite it lacking integrity (see Case and Hazel, 2023; Creaney and Case, 2021), this approach continues to be used – to an extent – in practice, especially in relation to harm and safety concerns.

Huey and Mitchell, (2016:302) raise issues around the extent to which practitioners are attuned to findings resulting from research, and query their levels of commitment to access and engage with research publications, which tend to be targeted at academic audiences, and at times, can contain jargon (complex terminology). Whilst there are noticeable challenges to using research and data to improve practice, Miriam highlighted the importance of accessing and reading research papers and attending webinars (especially those online, which were felt to be much more accessible). Nevertheless, time pressures and other admin tasks have made this difficult. It was felt that this hindered knowledge and skills sharing by those engaged within the research group. Time and accessibility were key components to build and sustain reciprocal relationships between stakeholders with due consideration for children:

> I think the struggle is time. I know a lot of other people have said it, but from a personal point of view, it's probably the last thing on your mind, even if you did it on a Friday. Friday is your last thing before the weekend. It's sort of put to the back of your list of things to do unless you have got an invested interest in a particular thing. […] When you're forced into that situation of being in academia, say if you are going to university or you're having to do something [that's] part of it, I think that's … that sort of promotes it, but I do think that can hinder it as well because I think then when it's a forced situation, I do think it can sort of put a barrier there as well.
>
> (Rea, restorative justice worker)

> I think we do try and make it accessible for staff or at least try and push the door that may be closed a little and push the door open a little to them [through inviting guest speakers to research group meetings] and we try and encourage colleagues to attend them by teams, and at least get them to just start to think outside the box really, if anything.
>
> (David, divert team practitioner)

At this point, it is important to note that a manager within the Service, Chris, collated a list of actions. This set of actions included alerting staff members to the research group and the purpose of the KSP as part of an induction process, creating opportunities for staff to learn from other agencies, such as the child and adolescent mental health services, and engage with other learning expertise sharing opportunities. This illustrates that the service is a 'learning organisation', receptive to new ideas. There is a clear willingness of practitioners within the service to continually engage with knowledge exchange activities and enhance their practice. An area that practitioners also wanted to improve, was knowledge and skills exchange between services:

> There was a practice that happened in [service] where there was a particularly complex young woman that couldn't cope with a number of specialists that were involved. So, another professional meeting took place, and it was only two people that delivered the interventions and the specialists fed in what they should do and they also through high-risk meetings, the professionals are actually in attendance there. […] We just got to create an opportunity to emulate that across Cheshire.
>
> (Chris, manager)

> … CAMHS workers, and they've got huge amounts of knowledge. And actually they seem to be at some sort of arm's length from us and maybe there should be more knowledge transfer partnerships happening all over the place.
>
> (Mark, restorative justice worker and chair of research group)

> I think then it just needs to be more support and transfer of knowledge from our embedded workers rather than being the experts.
>
> (Mark, restorative justice worker and chair of research group)

Practitioners felt that they obtained specialist insight from the specialists and agencies they work alongside:

> We do so much now with the children who work with it. It's just we're basically you know, personal assistant, education workers, CAMHS, everything. You know, we do some speech, language [support], we do some [substance] misuse [support], we do health [care], we do everything … And like I say The Box [speech and language] training was really good for that reason. We had 10 online sessions to do, which opened up a whole new world of speech and language therapy, and then a follow up with the specialists and it really helped us understand a bit more about what they do and then how it helps with the children we work with.
>
> (Miriam, divert team practitioner)

Information about The Box training can be accessed here: https://www.rcslt.org/learning/the-box-training/. However, this type of knowledge exchange activity was not felt across all agencies, with some said to be limited to 'information sharing' which hindered practitioners' ability to understand differing thresholds for entering services such as CAMHS. Focus group participants outlined the need for more emphasis on practitioners exchanging 'underpinning' skills and practical expertise, as a way to 'shine a light' on particular challenges, reflect upon the benefits of working in partnership, and essentially better meet the needs of children and their families (Taylor, 2010). In other words, they were keen to create and nurture distinct forums whereby several practitioners could engage with broader knowledge and skills exchange. At this point, it is important to note that Youth Offending Teams (YOTs) or youth justice services in England and Wales are multi-agency organisations. Indeed, justice-involved children have complex needs that can more effectively be addressed through multi-agency responses (Pamment, 2019). However, this approach can be challenging to execute. For example, children may find it difficult to engage in any meaningful way with multiple professionals, and experience of a sense of frustration if having to repeat or retell their stories (Byrne and Brooks, 2015).

Nevertheless, practitioners from various backgrounds, including education, health and social care, work with children on the cusp of entering formal criminal justice systems and those who are mandated to attend appointments. They seek to address underlying issues in order to help prevent offending by children and young people. Professionals conduct assessments, facilitate strengths-based and inclusionary participatory practices, alongside authoring reports and making relevant referrals to ensure access to necessary support services (Creaney and Case, 2021).

As Taylor (2016:9) uncovered as part of a detailed review of the youth justice system in England and Wales:

> It is a considerable disappointment that time and again during the review the provision of mental health services for children has been criticised by YOTs and by schools. They consistently report difficulties in getting support to those children and families who need it most. The thresholds for involvement from Child and Adolescent Mental Health Services (CAMHS) appear to be impossibly high in some areas, and children who are showing signs of palpable distress, both in their presentation and their behaviour, are not meeting the criteria for specialist mental health support.

As Buck and Creaney (2020) note, many YOTs do have CAMHS workers seconded to teams in an attempt to ensure children are assessed at the earliest opportunity and have access to sufficient levels of support to prevent problems from escalating (see also HMIP, 2017:37). Through engagement in knowledge and skills exchange activities, mental health workers can train other (non-specialist) practitioners within the multi-agency service 'to understand and look out for mental health' (Taylor, 2016:10).

Case study 2: Academic perspective: Impact of Covid-19 on youth justice practice

The Knowledge and Skills Partnership (KSP) has facilitated knowledge exchange through research opportunities. In 2020 Dr Jayne Price was interested in exploring the impact of the pandemic on Cheshire Youth Justice Service. Along with colleagues from the Institute of Policing at the University of Chester (Dr Dean Wilkinson and Charlene Crossley), she was successful in securing funding through the University of Chester QR funding 2019/20 and, subsequently 2020/21, to conduct this research. Ethical approval was received from the University of Chester Institute of Policing ethics committee and the fieldwork was undertaken between October and November 2020 with staff, and up to March 2021 with children and young people. The research aimed to capture and understand the implications of the Covid-19 pandemic on practitioners and young people involved within the service and to consider the immediate and future implications of the changes.

At this point, it is necessary to provide some context. Youth Justice Services had moved away from face-to-face contact with children and young people, and this was gradually reintroduced when government guidance allowed, and determined by judgements on individual risk and needs. Owing to restrictions, the research had to be conducted remotely. Differing approaches were taken with children and young people and staff members. The research with the staff followed two stages: the first using InVision (an app/webpage) with a central question: 'What has been your experience of working for the service during Covid-19?' Practitioners could anonymously post their responses on the page. This approach allowed the researchers to identify themes which were drawn out for discussion within focus groups/interviews. Eight staff members were recruited, two focus groups were held and two one-to-one interviews conducted remotely via Microsoft Teams. Staff members were recruited from across the service, offering a range of perspectives. Their responses were all transcribed and analysed by the research team. Four core themes were found across the responses: changes to service delivery, homelife working, perceptions of engagement and future practices. Practitioners were positive about senior management flexibility and decision making during the pandemic to a working from home model, and many felt supported, although they missed the community of working together in-person. The staff members who participated prided themselves on their service delivery to children and young people but struggled with the lack of opportunity to work alongside them face-to-face, particularly due to the inability to recognise any concerns children may present with. They recognised the importance of flexibility to future working for areas such as external meetings, given the vast area covered by the service, but felt that there was no substitute for face-to-face engagement with children and young people. A focus of our recommendations from a staff perspective was upon their well-being and future ways of working. This included relationships with children and young people and their participation within the service, particularly the long-term impacts for those who may return to the service.

The research with children and young people employed a creative arts-based methodology, using an artist who worked with them via Microsoft Teams to devise lyrics about their experiences within the service during the pandemic. The approach reflected child-first participatory methods that sought to allow children and young people to lead the narratives about their experiences. It also provided key learning for the service about the benefits of the relationship-based practice model (discussed earlier) and greater creative/participatory socially prescribed psychosocial therapeutic interventions. For more detail about the value of the methods see Wilkinson, Price and Crossley (2022) and Price, Wilkinson and Crossley (2023). The lyrics were co-produced with an experienced artist who identified with the young people (n=4, aged 15 years and above) involved within the service and built a strong rapport with them upon meeting virtually. They co-produced lyrics of rap and grime genre to the interests of participants, ensuring the young people led the narrative about their experiences. The findings reflected two core themes of identity and relationships. For further detail about the research, methods and findings see Price, Wilkinson and Crossley (2023). In line with government guidance at the time, each youth justice service led their own contingency plan and examples of best practice were uploaded to the Youth Justice Board resource hub. The research team produced findings, reports and recommendations for both aspects of the research, which informed the Cheshire Youth Justice Services recovery plan from the pandemic and their annual plan. The partnership has also led to a subsequent funding bid application to understand the longer-term implications of changes to the service during the pandemic. Having the KSP established ensured that the time constraints of such an application were eased due to the existing relationships, established networks and contacts within the field.

Concluding thoughts: Interpreting and applying research in youth justice services: Turning rhetoric into action?

> To what extent does the work of criminologists, particularly empirical research, actually influence the decision making of policy makers or the delivery of criminal practice?
>
> (Hine, 2008:18)

This chapter has examined the phenomena of knowledge exchange in one particular multi-agency youth justice service, premised upon the notion that *the decision making of policy makers or the delivery of criminal practice* (Hine, 2008:18) should be guided by theoretical/conceptual and empirical considerations. Using a case study approach, it offers a comprehensive, research and practice-based overview of a unique knowledge and skills partnership between Edge Hill University, the University of Chester and Cheshire Youth Justice Services. The authors have provided a nuanced account that can be likened to a form of *applied criminology* (Hine, 2008:18), arguing cogently that academic/practitioner knowledge exchange can lead to innovative and progressive practices. More specifically, the chapter has affirmed the value of such partnership arrangements and related initiatives that seek to assist applications of criminological theory/evidence into practice. It has presented two case studies. The establishment of a research group created the space for knowledge and skills exchange especially between academia and practice whilst also making academic work feel more accessible to practitioners. The research group lead, a youth justice pracademic who combines a practice mindset with an interest in the role and use of empirical research, has worked tirelessly to foster a climate in which criminological research is 'valued, understood, produced and consumed' (Huey and Mitchell, 2016:301). Of course, it is essential that any approach to practice or intervention decided upon is informed by the most reliable evidence, ideally guided by insights from significant or substantial empirical research. There are other considerations at play, however, that impact on the extent to which evidence-based practices can be formulated, such as the child's wishes and professional intuition or practice expertise. Alongside a high degree of relationship-based practice, and positive pro-social identity development, it is necessary to ensure the views of children are systemically taken into account at strategy/policy level and at the point of service delivery.

The KSP is continuing to co-develop innovative methods to promote more active participation of children, seeking to explore ways to maximise children's participation in decision making and embed forms of co-creation across the organisation. This includes ideas around ways to utilise creative approaches to participatory practice, to facilitate children's involvement in the design, delivery and evaluation of services. Peer Power's Voice and Influence Charter is one mechanism that can be drawn upon to guide discussions on how to navigate dynamics of power within relationships and advance strengths-based cultures within settings (Peer Power and Youth Justice Board, 2021; see also Creaney et al., 2023). Despite a focus on collaboration, co-production can be quite difficult to achieve in practice, for a range of reasons, not least a distrust of professional authority or paucity of incentives and rewards for participating in a joint decision-making process. As part of the KSP, stakeholders have been conscious of the need to monitor the extent to which policy and practice considerations are evidence-led, informed by theory, or underpinned by frameworks or guiding principles that are supported by empirical research (findings from studies that are valid and reliable) (Hine, 2008).

The chapter has challenged any notion that evidence can be easily interpreted and applied into practice, at least in a perceivable 'rational or linear' style (Hine, 2008:24; see also Goldson and Hughes, 2010:220–221). For example, factors such as public protection concerns, values, and other guiding principles, influence the decision-making process and shape attitudes towards how phenomena are viewed, understood and responded to (see Smith, 2006; Hine, 2008). Moreover, it is recognised that there are some practitioners within the service who are not actively engaged in discussions around knowledge and skills partnerships and the role of evidence-informed practice, owing to time constraints and workload pressures. Whilst there are key benefits for the partnership, it is important to find ways to engage staff members by setting aside time and creating an accessible space to facilitate dialogue around expectations and opportunities. Practitioners wished to build upon this, recognising that their partnerships with wider services have greater scope for knowledge and skills exchange to the benefit of children and young people.

As Case Study 2 presented, as part of the KSP an exploratory study into the impact of the pandemic on Cheshire Youth Justice Services was undertaken. This case study provided insight into how the partnership allowed for research to take place quickly at a time when the service required an understanding of the impacts of the pandemic. The research has led to improved practice beyond that time. The research team co-developed creative/participatory socially prescribed psychosocial therapeutic interventions. These prosocial pursuits can be worthwhile opportunities for children and young people who have frequently been bereft of legitimate opportunities for self-expression (see Creaney et al., 2023). The organisation has capitalised on this finding and advanced a strategy to further develop socially prescribed interventions within the service. Other creative interventions have been used as a vehicle or 'hook' to engage young people in collaborative discussions.

As the following chapter outlines and illustrates, students as researchers or volunteers play a key role in the knowledge and skills partnership. When undertaking a placement within the field, they have opportunities to utilise and apply requisite theoretical or subject-specific knowledge combined with critical thinking skills (learning and understandings accrued in academic environments). As part of the 'Building Professional Skills for Youth Justice' (BPSYJ) programme, students are able to enhance their technical skills or graduate attributes, and develop and demonstrate reflexivity, key aspects of personal and professional development.

Notes

1 Whilst this concept has been subjected to critique and thus can be described as being diverse and fluid (see Dickinson and Griffiths, 2023), it is employed here as a way to depict the role of practice-focused academics who have field-specific or tacit knowledge of the 'real world' (Huey and Mitchell, 2016), thus a unique grasp of the likely implications of research-informed practice.
2 Dr Creaney and Dr Price
3 This research was approved by the University of Chester Social and Political Science Research Ethics Committee.

References

Arnstein, S.R. (1969) A Ladder of Citizen Participation. *Journal of the American Institute of Planners*, 35(4), 216–224.

Barton, A., Davis, H. and Scott, D. (2019) Quiet Silencing: Restricting the criminological imagination in the neoliberal university. In A. Diver (ed.) *Employability via Higher Education: Sustainability as scholarship*. Cham: Springer. https://doi.org/10.1007/978-3-030-26342-3_34.

Bond-Taylor, Sue and Davies, Ceryl (2019) Youth Justice Live! Flexible pedagogies in an online/offline community of practice. In *Flexible Pedagogies in Practice: Implementing flexibility in higher education through online learning communities*. Rotterdam: Sense Publishers.

Buck, G. and Creaney, S. (2020) Mental Health, Young People and Punishments. In P. Taylor, S. Morley and J. Powell (eds) *Mental Health and Punishments: Critical perspectives in theory and practice*. Abingdon: Routledge.

Burns, S. and Creaney, S. (2023) Embracing Children's Voices: Transforming youth justice practice through co-production and child first participation. In S. Case and N. Hazel (eds) *Child First: Developing a new youth justice system*. London: Palgrave Macmillan.

Byrne, B. and Brooks, K. (2015) *Post-YOT Youth Justice*. What Is Justice? Working papers. London: Howard League.

Cadet, N. and Griffiths, T-L. (2023) Embedding Employability in the Social Sciences Curriculum: Reflections from an applied university. *Journal of Perspectives in Applied Academic Practice*, 11 (2), 121–134.

Canton, R. and Yates, J., (2008) Applied Criminology. In B. Stout, B. Williams and J. Yates, *Applied Criminology*. London: Sage.

Case, S. and Hampson, K. (2019) Youth Justice Pathways to Change: Drivers, challenges and opportunities. *Youth Justice*, 19(1), 25–41.

Case, S. and Hazel, N. (eds) (2023) *Child First: Developing a new youth justice system*. London: Palgrave Macmillan.

Case, S.P. and Haines, K.R. (2014) Reflective Friend Research: The relational aspects of social scientific research. In K. Lumsden (ed.) *Reflexivity in Criminological Research*. London: Palgrave.

Chadwick, K. and Scraton, P. (2006) Critical Criminology. In E. McLaughlin and J. Muncie (eds) *The Sage Dictionary of Criminology* (pp. 97–100). London: Sage.

Cheshire Youth Justice Services (2023) *Youth Justice Plan, 2023–2024*. Available at: https://moderngov.cheshireeast.gov.uk/ecminutes/documents/s110010/Appendix%201%20-%20Cheshire%20Youth%20Justice%20Service%20Plan.pdf.

Children and Young People's Centre for Justice (CYCJ) (2022) *Children and Young People in Conflict with the Law: Policy, practice and legislation*. available at: www.cycj.org.uk/resource/youthjusticeinscotland/.

Crawford, K., Horsley, R., Hagyard, A. and Derricott, D. (2015) *Pedagogies of Partnership: What works*. York: HEA.

Creaney, S. (2020) Game Playing and 'Docility': Youth justice in question. *Safer Communities*, 19(3), 103–118.

Creaney, S. and Burns, S. (2023) Freedom from Symbolic Violence? Facilitators and barriers to participatory practices in youth justice. *Youth Justice*, 0(0). Online. https://doi.org/10.1177/14732254231156844.

Creaney, S., Burns, S. and Day, A.-M. (2023) Guest editorial. *Safer Communities*, 22(3), 149–155. https://doi.org/10.1108/SC-07-2023-054.

Creaney, S. and Case, S. (2021) Promoting Social Inclusion: Participatory rights alternatives to risk discourses in youth justice. In P. Liamputtong (ed.) *Handbook of Social Inclusion Research and Practices in Health and Social Sciences*. Singapore: Springer.

Creaney, S. and Smith, R. (2023) Social Work and Youth Justice. In J. Parker (ed.) *Introducing Social Work*. 2nd edn. London: Sage.

CYP Now (2012) Youth Offending Team and University Partnership Unveiled. https://www.cypnow.co.uk/news/article/youth-offending-team-and-university-partnership-unveiled.

Day, A-M. (2022) 'It's a Hard Balance to Find': The perspectives of youth justice practitioners in England on the place of 'risk' in an emerging 'child-first' world. *Youth Justice*, 23(1). https://doi.org/10.1177/14732254221075205.

Dickinson, J. and Griffiths, T.L. (2023) Introduction. In J. Dickinson and T.L. Griffiths (eds) *Professional Development for Practitioners in Academia*. Knowledge Studies in Higher Education, vol. 13. Cham: Springer. https://doi.org/10.1007/978-3-031-33746-8_1.

Freire, P. (1996 [1970]) *Pedagogy of the Oppressed*, London and New York: Penguin.

Giroux, H. (2000) *Impure Acts: The practical politics of cultural studies*. London: Routledge.

Goldson, B. and Hughes, G. (2010). Sociological Criminology and Youth Justice: Comparative policy analysis and academic intervention. *Criminology & Criminal Justice*, 10(2), 211–230.

Hampson, K. (2023) Cementing Child First in Practice. In S. Case and N. Hazel (eds) *Child First: Developing a new youth justice system*. London: Palgrave Macmillan.

Hayes, D. (2018, 31 July) YOTs and Universities Link Up. *CYP Now*. https://www.cypnow.co.uk/features/article/yots-and-universities-link-up.

Hine, J. (2008) Applied Criminology: Research, policy and practice. In B. Stout, B. Williams and J. Yates, *Applied Criminology*. London: Sage.

HM Inspectorate of Probation (HMIP) (2016) *Desistance and Young People: An inspection by HM Inspectorate of Probation*. Manchester: HM Inspectorate of Probation.

HM Inspectorate of Probation (2017) *The Work of Youth Offending Teams to Protect the Public*. Manchester: HM Inspectorate of Probation.

Huey, L. and Mitchell, R.J. (2016) Unearthing Hidden Keys: Why pracademics are an invaluable (if underutilized) resource in policing research. *Policing (Oxford)*, 10(3), 300–307. https://doi.org/10.1093/police/paw029.

Lundy, L (2007) 'Voice' Is Not Enough: Conceptualising Article 12 of the United Nations' Convention on the Rights of the Child. *British Educational Journal*, 33(6), 927–942.

Neary, M. and Winn, J. (2009) The Student as Producer: Reinventing the student experience in higher education. In *The Future of Higher Education: Policy, pedagogy and the student experience* (pp. 192–210). London: Continuum. ISBN: ISBN: 1847064728.

Pamment, N. (2016) Community Reparation for Young Offenders: Perceptions, policy and practice. In *Youth Justice Community Reparation in Practice* (pp. 56–74). London: Palgrave Macmillan.

Pamment, N. (2019) The Decline of Youth Offending Teams: Towards a progressive and positive youth justice. In A. Pycroft and D. Gough (eds) *Multi-Agency Working in Criminal Justice: Theory, policy and practice*, pp. 271–286. Bristol: Policy Press. https://doi.org/10.56687/9781447340270-020.

Peer Power and Youth Justice Board (2021) *Co-Creation and Participation in Practice Project*. London: Peer Power/YJB.

Posner, P.L. (2009) The Pracademic: An agenda for re-engaging practitioners and academics. *Public Budgeting & Finance*, 29(1), 12–26.

Price, J., Wilkinson, D. and Crossley, C. (2023) Children and Young Peoples' Lyrics and Voices Capturing Their Experiences within Youth Justice Services. *Safer Communities*, 22(3), 186–199. https://doi.org/10.1108/SC-08-2022-0029.

QAA (2022) Subject Benchmark Statement for Criminology. https://www.qaa.ac.uk/quality-code/subject-benchmark-statements/criminology.

Smith, D. (2006) Youth Crime and Justice: Research, evaluation and 'evidence'. In B. Goldson and J. Muncie (eds) *Youth Crime and Justice: Critical issues*. London: Sage.

Smithson, H., Gray, P. and Jones, A. (2020) 'They Really Should Start Listening to You': The benefits and challenges of co-producing a participatory framework of youth justice practice. *Youth Justice*, July. https://doi.org/10.1177/1473225420941598.

Smithson, H., Lang, T. and Gray, P. (2022) From Rhetoric to Reality: Participation in practice within youth justice systems. In S. Frankel (ed.) *Establishing Child Centred Practice in a Changing World, Part A* (pp. 111–122). Emerald Studies in Child Centred Practice. Bingley: Emerald.

Smithson, H. and Gray, P. (2021) *Supporting Children's Meaningful Participation in the Youth Justice System*. HM Inspectorate of Probation Academic Insights 2021/10, August. https://www.justiceinspectorates.gov.uk/hmiprobation/wp-content/uploads/sites/5/2021/08/Academic-Insight-%E2%80%93-Supporting-childrens-meaningful-participation-in-the-youth-justice-system.pdf.

Smith-Yau, W. (2017) Academic/YOT Partnership Working Guide. Youth Justice Board for England and Wales. https://yjresourcehub.uk/research-guidance/item/download/513_155aef7190608f feb0e549726e30a56d.html.

Social Care Institute for Excellence (2022) Co-production in Social Care: What it is and how to do it. Available at: www.scie.org.uk/co-production/what-how.

Spacey, M. and Thompson, N. (2021). Beyond Individual Trauma: Towards a multi-faceted trauma-informed restorative approach to youth justice that connects individual trauma with family reparation and recognition of bias and discrimination. *British Journal of Community Justice*, 18(1), 18–35.

Stephenson, M. and Dix, H. (2017) *Relationship-based Practice in Youth Justice*. London: UNITAS.

Stout, B., Williams, B. and Yates, J. (2008) *Applied Criminology*. London: Sage.

Strudwick, K. (2017) *Debating Student as Producer: Relationships, contexts and challenges for higher education. PRISM, Casting New Light on Learning, Theory and Practice*, 1(1), 73–96.

Taylor, C. (2016) *Review of the Youth Justice System in England and Wales*. London: Ministry of Justice.

Taylor, W. (2010) Introduction: A handbook of youth justice? In W. Taylor, R. Earl and R. Hester (eds) *Youth Justice Handbook: Theory, policy and practice*. Cullompton, Devon: Willan.

Thompson, N. and Spacey, M. (2023) 'I would want to see young people working in here, that's what I want to see …' How peer support opportunities in youth offending services can support a child first, trauma-informed, and reparative model of practice for youth justice. *Safer Communities*, 22(3), 200–216. https://doi.org/10.1108/SC-08-2022-0031.

Volpe, M.R. and Chandler, D. (1999) Resolving Conflicts in Institutions of Higher Education: Challenges for pracademics. CNCR-Hewlett Foundation Seed Grant White Papers, 8. https://readingroom.law.gsu.edu/seedgrant/8.

Whyte, B. (2009) *Youth Justice in Practice: Making a difference*. Bristol: Policy Press.

Wilkinson, D., Price, J. and Crossley, C. (2022) Developing Creative Methodologies: Using lyric writing to capture young peoples' experiences of the youth offending services during the COVID-19 pandemic. *Journal of Criminological Policy and Practice*, 8(2), 105–119.

Youth Justice Board (YJB) (2021) *Strategic Plan 2021–24. Report*. London: YJB.

2   Criminology placements and work experience opportunities in youth justice

Sean Creaney and Jayne Price

Chapter objectives

By the end of this chapter, you should be able to:

- Appreciate the knowledge and skills acquired as part of a practice or research-based placement.
- Analyse the benefits of work placement opportunities in youth justice teams and examine their impact.
- Explore how work placement opportunities contribute to developing knowledge and skills.
- Outline key principles necessary to facilitate rewarding and fulfilling Criminology placements.
- Explore how 'Student as Producer' as a concept can be utilised to open up opportunities for meaningful collaboration between educators, students and professionals in the production of knowledge.

Introduction

> Undertaking work experience and volunteering are great ways to improve your employability and demonstrate motivation and enthusiasm both for developing yourself and learning about different occupational roles and sectors ... Ideally, the best way for employers to recruit a future graduate can be to see them in the workplace and observe how they perform undertaking tasks and managing deadlines or pressure on a daily basis.
>
> (Ragonese et al., 2015:48)

Alongside identifying and progressing principles of effective practice through the research group (see Chapter 1), the knowledge and skills partnership between Edge Hill University, University of Chester and Cheshire Youth Justice Services has founded the Building Professional Skills for Youth Justice (BPSYJ) programme. Likened to an initiative, it is a useful mechanism to maximise criminology placements for students, further enhancing opportunities to develop skills and knowledge and apply theory into practice. The benefits of these experiences cannot be overstated. In addition to helping to negotiate access to the setting for the students, academic leads promote student independence and help to facilitate imaginative (potentially transformative) thinking in students about the state of criminal justice practice (Bond-Taylor and Davies, 2019). The purpose of this chapter is to explain how and why this knowledge and skills partnership has provided

DOI: 10.4324/9781003411192-3

valuable opportunities to advance graduate attributes, through promoting skills acquisition. Drawing on the rhetoric and practice of 'Student as Producer', it presents insights into the types of practice and research placement opportunities available as part of the partnership arrangement. Some students have benefited from participating in guest lectures delivered by youth justice professionals, and thus been exposed to 'real-world phenomena' (Usherwood, 2015) alongside having access to expert advice and guidance around career development, including subject-specific knowledge needed to work in the field and graduate attributes that need to be deployed or drawn upon to 'negotiate the complex realities of youth justice practice' (Taylor, 2010:189). The practitioners delivering these sessions and interacting with students are motivated to inspire others, garner respect and credibility due to their identity as 'pracademics' (Posner, 2009), a term which reflects both practice experience and academic knowledge. These professionals also have contacts in industry and useful networks that can be tapped into by students seeking to advance their careers in this multi-agency sector or conduct research on interesting topics. As the accounts of students and alumni confirm,[1] academic leads and youth justice professionals work collaboratively with the students and treat them as capable, knowledgeable independent learners, who are then enabled to engage in a process of deep learning, and through their active participation, are able to tap into or draw upon subject-specific knowledge and apply criminological theory to practice. As the accounts from students indicate, these experiences can be rewarding and fulfilling. As the chapter proceeds to discuss in more detail, 'Student as Producer' is also part of the discourse and practice of the BPSYJ programme.

Student as producer

The student–university relationship appears to have been the subject of much debate and discussion in recent times. External forces that are beyond a student or graduate's ability to control or influence, including economic factors and structural transformations, can impact on career choices and limit or restrict opportunities for students to acquire industry experience. Moreover, if a service is experiencing budget constraints or staffing issues this can jeopardise the continuation of placement schemes, as resources are required for them to operate smoothly and sustainably. Furthermore, the neo-liberal lexicon of students as 'consumers' has continued to influence how learners are to be perceived and treated. This is perhaps unsurprising given the public and political pressure placed upon Higher Education Institutions (HEIs) in the UK to ensure courses offer students 'value for money' (Cadet and Griffiths, 2023:121). Nevertheless, this view of students as 'customers' or 'consumers' has been critiqued by critical criminologists and others (McCulloch, 2009). They have also questioned the extent to which employer agendas, or even the mantra of 'employability' (despite it being ill-defined) is applicable or appropriate to the academy (at least within the discipline of critical criminology). In other words, criminology-related courses tend to subject criminal justice agendas to critique, exposing inequalities and confronting injustices (Barton, Davis and Scott, 2019). If university courses seek to satisfy employer needs and priorities as a primary focus, opportunities for knowledge production and meaning may be diminished or occupy a limited role and ultimately contribute to a perception that degree-level courses are affirming a system that they appear to critique (Barton, Davis and Scott, 2019). What is more, when students are viewed as consumers, this can lead to them becoming passive in their learning, especially when there is little attention given to how a student's skills, experience and knowledge can be utilised in creative ways or if there is a lack of focus on how they can apply critical thinking skills to real work-place scenarios (McCulloch, 2009). As Bunce, Baird and Jones (2017: 1959) note, 'students who identify as consumers may have little interest in what is actually being taught and show reduced responsibility for producing their own knowledge'. In response to such concerns, the Student as Producer concept has gathered momentum and began to gain traction as an evidence-based concept in criminology and criminal justice courses.

Bond-Taylor and Davies (2019) utilised this concept, which formed a key element of a comprehensive pedagogic framework, as part of the *Youth Justice Live!* project. This scholarship and wider body of work around use of the concept (see Neary, 2019; Strudwick, 2017) inspired the academic leads to adopt and subsequently embed Student as Producer as part of a strategy around the work-based learning element of the knowledge and skills partnership.[2] It has been utilised or mobilised to maximise opportunities for deep learning and to reiterate the importance of students participating in (research-engaged) extra-curricular activities (such as work-related learning schemes), whereby students 'share knowledge, skills and information… [and] take ownership of their learning experiences' (Bond-Taylor and Davies, 2019:100, see also Strudwick, 2017).

The academic leads[3] have periodically (re)stated the narrative that students have knowledge and skills that can be harnessed and mobilised through research and placement opportunities within youth justice services. Opportunities such as these also provide added value in the form of 'graduate attributes' (variously defined and understood but generally relate to a blend of relevant and useful subject specific knowledge and practice-based skills), which aligns to the Office for Students' (2022) metrics around students/graduates achieving positive outcomes from their studies. In other words, students involved in the knowledge and skills partnership are in receipt of, and actively contribute to, learning activities that seek to boost employability skills. This was illustrated during discussions with Emma Day, who participated in the BPSYJ programme. Emma is a former student who previously worked in support services in residential childcare and now works in a clinical therapeutic setting as an assistant psychologist (see 'In Focus' case study A).

'In Focus' case study A

Emma Day, who is currently an assistant psychologist, postgraduate researcher, and a member of the Criminology Professional Advisory Group at Edge Hill University, reflects on her experiences undertaking a research and practice placement at Cheshire Youth Justice Services.

SEAN: What did your research and practice-based placement entail?
EMMA: I started my placement in the second year of my degree with Cheshire youth justice service and during my time there I got to experience all aspects of how the justice service works. I also got to work directly with young people whilst delivering interventions with the substance misuse worker, and attending court hearings at Cheshire magistrates. I was also asked to conduct an internal research project with employees of the service to consider what it was like to be a female working within the organisation. This, in particular was great for my own development because being an undergraduate, it's rare to have the opportunity to devise and conduct your own research project. In the course of this research, I set up a focus group with female

workers of the youth justice service to find out what their experiences had been and whether they faced any gender specific difficulties in terms of their personal and professional lives. That piece of research was actually taken to the board, where I had the opportunity to deliver my findings to some key stakeholders in the sector, which was such a fantastic experience considering my academic level at the time. I hadn't even began my dissertation, so to have had the chance to do primary research, with real participants, it really set me up to be able to do really well in my final year.

SEAN: What was it like to present your findings to people in positions of power?

EMMA: I remember that the chairman and other delegates of the city and borough councils had attended, also high ranking officers from the police, people from the youth justice board, there were other well known and respected people in the sector there that I got to present to as an undergraduate. It was a fantastic chance to be able to showcase what I was capable of and for my own progression as well, particularly being able to make those kind of connections in the industry. Leading on from that, the fact that I was able to access those professionals for my dissertation really helped to facilitate that research in a meaningful way. My dissertation focussed on the experiences of bereavement and loss for young people in contact with youth justice services and also the effect of vicarious trauma on professionals who work with these young people day to day. Having access to those practitioners and having working relationships with those who work directly with young people in these circumstances was perfect for what I was doing my research on.

SEAN: why did you focus on the relationship between childhood trauma and offending?

EMMA: So initially for the dissertation, I was looking to do the research directly with young people as I believe that bereavement, loss and grief have been significantly under researched in relation to their impact on offending behaviour. However, I didn't realise at the time that there are a lot of barriers to that for an undergraduate researcher and having access to those participants. Luckily the relationships I'd built through my placement gave me the chance to talk to key professionals who through their work with young people had plenty of experiences to share with me at the focus group. This is also where the theme of vicarious trauma began to develop in the research and that was something that the Head of service was really interested in because it wasn't something that they had particularly thought about on that level. That's the beauty of the nature of this type of research, you can be surprised at what comes up and it can bring a new perspective to your work. When you sit and think about it, of course you would expect professionals to experience vicarious trauma on some level when working in these situations with young people who have experienced so much...

SEAN: Did you receive any training before starting the placement?

EMMA: So for my placement at the youth justice service I'm not sure if they had done this sort of thing before. I think it was a learning curve for us both. I think it was quite new what they were approaching but they were organised and open to challenging me and themselves. It must be a challenge to have somebody come in who is looking at it from a different point of view in terms of purely the academic theory behind what it is that they are doing. The professionals, a lot of them are very qualified, but you do have people who haven't got that university background and don't necessarily link in the underpinning theory in the day to day nature of their work. So, it worked really well. It was interesting for both sides to have those two-way conversations from those different points of view, to create new ideas and better, more informed ways of working, in particular for me to get first-hand experience of the practical aspects of the theory that I knew so well and that I was so invested in. To have that practical experience was second to none. Being at uni you don't often get to do that, you are not doing a vocational subject, it is very academic, so it is great to have that different perspective. I got to speak to mental health nurses, practitioners and caseworkers. I got to go to court regularly as well. You can see the judicial system in action, in process. You get to see their job on a day-to-day basis. You're not just reading out of a textbook; you are seeing it in real life and you are talking to real people who are actually doing these roles and progressing in these careers. As an undergraduate, you do your theory work and without actually seeing it in practice it's useless, because you need to have that first hand experience of what actually goes on in the real world.

SEAN: What are some of the challenges implementing theory/research into practice?

EMMA: It's all well and good sitting down as an academic or researcher and reading and writing about everything that there is to know, but you can only ever really know something from seeing it, from feeling it from being in it. It's what it is to know something, isn't it? It's to experience it for ourselves in the real world.

Subject- or discipline-specific skills include the ability to initiate motivational interviewing techniques or utilise the principle of pro-social modelling when working with justice-involved children (Trotter and Evans, 2023). The former can be a useful way of building on a child's strengths by encouraging positive steps. The latter is a way to enact change through being a positive influence on the life of a child who may have experienced adversity. Students develop subject-specific knowledge about the purpose of and issues associated with the concept of rehabilitation. They also have opportunities to critique types of 'treatment' and reflect on the efficacy of types of surveillance and control within public protection agendas. Essentially, this academic study helps students to become cognisant of and knowledgeable about the 'core knowledge and skills required to understand young people's offending behaviour, explain it, make well-founded judgements, plan appropriate interventions and communicate their knowledge and decisions to others clearly' (Baker et al., 2011:1). The importance of volunteering and putting theory into practice was illustrated during discussions with Amanda Rush, a postgraduate researcher (see 'In Focus' case study B).

'In Focus' case study B

Amanda Rush, a postgraduate researcher who is currently volunteering with Cheshire Youth Justice Services, provides insight into her experiences of conducting fieldwork and working directly with children and young people as part of her undergraduate studies.

SEAN: Describe your experience of placement and putting theory into practice.

AMANDA: Doing the volunteer work alongside the studies has helped massively. Getting an insight of what happens within the roles. I do think it's invaluable. Without it, I don't think I'd have done as well as I did. Learning about theories and models within the classroom, I can then take them into practice. But in practice it doesn't always work as it should on paper. So, you have to adapt.

SEAN: How can these experiences help with career development?

AMANDA: If other students were to do it, they would get so much out of it. I think they need to experience what it's like out in the field, in jobs that they're applying for. They should do work experience. I think it should be part of the curriculum. I don't think all students fully understand what's expected of them and what they're going to face once they leave university and go into the job role itself. Yeah, it's not just what they're going to face, it's what they're going to feel as well. Because I didn't expect to feel the way I do feel. I thought I was quite controlled in my emotions. I could go in there almost robotic and not be affected by what's being said to me. However, I am affected by what I'm hearing and what is coming from these young people and the parents or carers. Everyone has affected me in some way. And I just wasn't expecting that. I wasn't prepared for that. But I do think a placement would help them be more prepared for what they're going to face in reality.

SEAN: What are some of the benefits and challenges to implementing theory/research into practice?

AMANDA :Doing the trauma informed approaches section of the course has been absolutely invaluable. I'm able to see in the reports where the trauma has come from. Areas where trauma could have occurred, that the panel members haven't picked up on.

SEAN: Can you tell me about your research?

AMANDA: I don't think I'd have created the piece of research that I was able to do if I had not had the contacts that I did. Chris Dunn (supportive gatekeeper) has been absolutely outstanding. I couldn't have asked for anybody better. To put me in touch with the people that I needed to speak with and the opportunities to go out and meet them in person as well. After I've submitted my work, I've been able to go and meet professionals, either at panel or in the office. We've started planning for my master's in terms of what research I'm going to undertake.

SEAN: How important are contacts/networks?

AMANDA: I've got a multitude of people that I can turn to now and say, 'I'm interested in doing this. Any chance you can arrange it for me?' I emailed somebody about the youth court as I am going to court on Thursday to observe. They said 'yeah. This is where you want to be. We'll sort it out. This is what you have got to wear'. I'm building up my network through volunteering. I was also asked to provide advice and guidance to a youth justice worker who was writing a pre-sentence report. I had access to a full history of what has happened and what was going on in the child's life. I put forward an argument that an alternative to custody was the most appropriate sentence.

At this point, it is necessary to note that each person holds a specific (somewhat differing) 'frame of reference' that guides or influences their responses. Whilst each decision concerning responses to justice-involved children should be defensible, at times it may be difficult to notice and separate out certain beliefs or assumptions that can unintentionally affect how a person is to act in a given moment (Creaney and Burns, 2023). This is why it is important for students to be reflective, using models or certain techniques as guidance. This task is needed to help placement students participating in the BPSYJ programme to uncover/detect or understand driving forces behind certain feelings and emotions.

There are challenges to obtaining placement opportunities, as Cadet and Griffiths, (2023:122), highlight, including 'employer access, course capacity, and student readiness'. Regarding the latter, there may be a degree of reluctance on the part of learners to embrace independence or they may be of the view that they are ill-equip-ped to undertake placement activities. Indeed, it takes time to prepare students to engage in such learning and development opportunities. In relation to the BPSYJ programme, there are also certain selection processes to judge suitability for the role and/or vetting procedures in place; requirements that need to be adhered to. Whilst such conditions or requirements are necessary at least for safeguarding reasons, if the recruitment process is too bureaucratic or demanding this can act as a barrier, pre-venting students from applying for such roles (Flanaghan, 2005). In addition to this concern or challenge, employer access may be denied. Child and youth justice services may not have the capacity or resources necessary to provide placement or volunteer-ing opportunities. For these reasons, higher education institutions need to create 'alternative forms of engagement alongside placement opportunities' (Cadet and Griffiths, 2023:123). For example, at Edge Hill University, a research assistant role[4] has been created for students who have selected the work experience module and are required to undertake placement hours. This research placement opportunity is mod-elled on the Student as Producer concept[5] to enhance research skills and provide a unique opportunity for them to share insights through collaborative relationship-building with academics (co-investigators including Dr Jayne Price, and external col-leagues within the public and/or voluntary sectors) and contribute to the process of producing knowledge related to the development of peer support practices in a youth justice context. The research project also seeks to explore the extent to which peer support can contribute to a Child First approach and be designed in accordance with the collaboration principle, centred around the needs, interests and perspectives of those in receipt of interventions, alongside maximising opportunities for lived experienced mentors to nurture self-confidence and personal growth. The research assistant role may be more appealing for students who are not able to undertake a traditional work placement due to caring responsibilities or other commitments. Moreover, the student-led Criminology Society at Edge Hill is premised on the idea of 'Student as Producer', resulting in academic staff and students working collabora-tively on various educational projects to cultivate and enhance key skills and crimin-ological knowledge including opportunities to explore the theory/criminal justice practice nexus (**see Appendix A and B for student reflections on this experience**).

Moreover, there are other challenges to maximising positive outcomes for students, including an underdeveloped infrastructure or lack of key personnel with required expertise to advise students on work-based learning opportunities. What is more, when the term 'employability' is used in an uncritical manner, this may limit a truly reflective scholarship (Schön, 1987) alongside restricting opportunities for a deep 'criminological imagination' (Goldson and Hughes, 2010) that involves independent thinking and critical scholarship to critique and challenge oppressive structures and power dynamics. A critical criminological ethos or approach is at odds, or at least in conflict with, a strategy that seeks to confirm, consciously or otherwise, existing ways of working and satisfy the needs of powerholders (Stout, Williams and Yates 2008). We concur with Cadet and Griffiths' (2023: 123) informed perspective that such enriching opportunities should invoke in the student a desire to interrogate current practice, 'as well as observing and participating' in relevant and useful activities.

Within lectures and seminars, students do engage in discussions around how to present (non-confrontational) perspectives to challenge the status quo. Relatedly, likened to a critical criminological ethos, learners are taught the importance of disclosing and disseminating discoveries (especially related to the consequences of symbolic violence) however 'troubling' or disconcerting these accounts of practice appear and in spite of any uncertainty about 'speaking truth to power' (Scraton, 2007:14–15). Within the work experience module, for instance, workshops are facilitated to enable 'students to make meaningful connections between their academic knowledge, policy and practice, and their personal values, which will shape their futures' (Cadet and Griffiths, 2023). Within lectures and seminars, students have reflected upon how a pro-social approach can be drawn upon when identifying and addressing the wide-ranging needs of children and when navigating challenging times (Cherry, 2017). This involves being attentive to circumstances and underlying issues, alongside sufficient attention placed on structures necessary to maximise positive child outcomes.

Skills and knowledge

As stated within the Subject Benchmark Statement for Criminology (QAA, 2022:6), students should be in receipt of adequate assistance from tutors and be gently encouraged 'to reflect on how their own experiences may be shaping their views'. Student participation in the process of reflection on learning and professional development is more likely to be meaningful when there is a commitment to the creation of a safe learning environment to foster forms of collaboration and positive relationship-building (acknowledging each other's knowledge and skills), in which the students feel supported to participate without feeling judgement (Light, Cox and Calkins, 2009; Bond-Taylor and Davies, 2019).

In relation to the BPSYJ programme, there are clear and transparent recruitment and selection processes in place. When a student has an interest in undertaking a practice placement, they submit an application, setting out their suitability for the role to the academic leads (Dr Sean Creaney and Dr Jayne Price). If a student is proposing a research project, they are expected to explain the purpose of the research study and demonstrate competency in research skills, along with a brief narrative regarding the potential benefits to the service if their study was to be commissioned. Following shortlisting, applications are then submitted to the youth justice service, which considers submissions at a management meeting, and if agreement in principle is achieved, the student begins work on an application for ethical clearance. Students who undertake a placement have access to a supervisor who can oversee their progress and monitor their professional development. There are also prerequisites such as undertaking relevant and useful training and participating in supervision meetings with mentors in the setting. During seminars, as part of the work placement module, there is also a focus on dispelling any preconceived ideas or myths about reflection being unimportant or likened to a self-indulgent navel gazing exercise (Cadet and Griffiths, 2023). Whilst evidencing academic ability remains an advantage when seeking employment in this field, it is necessary for students to demonstrate skills and attributes, including evidence of engagement in reflective practice (Flanaghan, 2005, Ragonese et al., 2015). Professionals must be acutely aware of why they think and act in certain ways. This includes reflection on the extent to which responses are compatible with their vision and values or in line with organisational cultures (Haines and Drakeford, 1998).

Not only can work placement experiences enhance skills and attributes, but undertaking such a role can also be useful for acquiring industry relevant capital/ power, opening up connections and professional networks. As Amanda notes (see 'In Focus' case study B), being active in the field, and becoming immersed in relationship building and decision making at various stages can result in students acquiring insider knowledge of organisational culture, gaining a sense of how the service operates. This insight accrued within the setting can be drawn upon and be of value when seeking similar experiences or graduate level employment. The networks and contacts built up can be utilised to facilitate access to potential participants as part of a proposed research project.

Volunteering or undertaking a practice placement can be a diverse role; tasks can be many and varied, from mentoring and advocating for children to acting as an appropriate adult. The latter includes monitoring the extent to which police officers act in a way that is respectful of children's rights, especially the welfare principle (see Appendix A, where a student reflects on her role supporting vulnerable children and adults). Volunteers play a vital role ensuring children receive adequate and necessary support and access to timely provision. Moreover, it can be argued that volunteers may be more likely to build authentic relationships with those children who perceive paid workers as agents of the youth justice system preoccupied with initiating types of social control to contain perceived threats (Flanaghan, 2005). Another volunteer role includes referral order panel member, which was created through the Youth Justice and Criminal Evidence Act 1999. To undertake this role volunteers must have the ability to relate and connect with children and young people – not dissimilar to the requirements of other positions on the front line.

Moreover, when shadowing professionals or co-facilitating group work sessions, students have a degree of discretion regarding how they proceed or act towards others. As part of the assessment requirements for the work-related modules, students must document their experiences of undertaking a placement or volunteer experiences, alongside keeping a record of evidence of continuing professional development (CPD) to be included as appendices in the portfolio assessment. They are also expected to make links to relevant criminological theory, criminal justice policies or evidence-based practices. Emily Bourque, a former criminology student, provides insight into how the work experience module prepared them for a criminology placement within a multi-agency child and youth justice service (see 'In Focus' case study C).

'In Focus' case study C

Emily Bourque was awarded a 1st class honours degree in Criminology and is now undertaking paid work within the criminal justice sector. During her undergraduate studies she secured a 60-hour work placement with Cheshire Youth Justice Service and was able to gain first-hand experience of the justice system and how it has adapted during the Covid-19 pandemic.

SEAN: What is your experience of doing a work placement?

EMILY: I loved it. Due to Covid restrictions, I undertook some work from home. I initially met with my placement supervisor who provided a good overview of the work I would be doing. I then had a meeting with other professionals, including the speech and language therapist and members of the Child and Adolescent Mental Health team. In addition to meetings with these colleagues and members of the diversion team, I also met with court officers and the restorative justice workers. I also attended the youth court. I sat with a court worker, and I had quite a few cases for that one. So that was quite a long day. When I completed my work placement I applied for a volunteer role, was interviewed and offered the position. I have completed training courses and I now do the referral order panels as well. I think it's really nice because I see some of the practitioners that I met during my placement. These experiences open so many doors as well because I can add this to my CV and include in a job or course application.

SEAN: Does this experience link with your criminology degree studies?

EMILY: In addition to doing the placement, I did the youth justice module as well. Doing the placement helps in understanding the application of theory to practice. More people should definitely seek to gain relevant work experience. I think it just opens up so many more doors as you get opportunities to network, build contacts and relationships with professionals. I messaged my placement supervisor with Cheshire Youth Justice Service to inform them of my 1st Class Honours degree classification. The service then included this information in the newsletter.

SEAN: What is your experience of doing the work experience module?

EMILY: As part of the work experience module, we had support from the careers officer, and guidance on how to write cover letters and prepare a CV. We learned how to do all of that as well, which is obviously really good. It was a lot of admin bits like you did have to write a placement diary. So it would be like every single thing that I'd done in the day, I'd have to go home and write up in this diary. And then I'd then have to use that as part of the portfolio assignment. It was about what we learnt by being on the placement and how this links with criminology. For example, the labelling theory was a useful concept that I studied in the classroom. When on placement, I was mindful of the need to work in a positive and constructive way with children and their families to ensure they did not feel stigmatised or labelled. There were other theories or concepts I learned about that I could see being put into practice when on placement. These experiences and skills have also helped with my career development. I am now undertaking paid work within the criminal justice sector.

As alluded to, as part of the Building Professional Skills for Youth Justice programme, students have opportunities to acquire and apply a blend of technical knowledge and interpersonal communication skills. This includes being an observer during a youth court hearing or facilitating reparative activities, and in so doing, gaining a sense of the environment that professionals operate within alongside an understanding of how the service functions. It is worth noting here that the students undertaking the work experience module have timely and necessary opportunities to provide updates on their experiences through appropriate mechanisms and channels. Students are also taught within the degree programme about factors affecting offending and ways to identify and manage risk.

As alluded to in Chapter 1, the concept of risk has fallen into abeyance as a result of the Child First Offender Second model being favoured and adopted by the Youth Justice Board for England and Wales (Case and Hazel, 2023), The risk-based model of practice has been phased out, and the Youth Justice Board (YJB) has introduced a Child First strategy. The YJB is the body responsible for devising policy and monitoring the implementation of principles of effective practice. The importance of involving children in decision making processes cannot be overstated. In recent times there has been a marked focus on the necessity to include the child's voice in systems, alongside maximising opportunities for their skills, knowledge and experience to be recognised and valued (Peer Power and Youth Justice Board, 2021). Whilst there are problems detecting factors affecting offending or determining a child's 'risk status', professionals do need to be mindful that young people are likely to present at least a degree of harm to others as well as themselves. Whilst it is ethically and morally right that minimising harm remains a priority, it is also necessary to facilitate legitimate opportunities for healing and growth. To achieve such aims, a 'children first philosophy' should be embraced, according to Haines and Drakeford (1998:89). This framework should 'inform, guide and shape all that youth justice workers do in and for children in the criminal justice system' (Haines and Drakeford, 1998:89). This includes, for instance, ensuring that children and young people are not labelled (explicitly or implicitly) as 'offenders' by professionals or others. This philosophy has been mobilised more recently. As a principle it has been operationalised and incorporated into plans and methods of practice at strategy level and at the point of service delivery (Case and Hazel, 2023; Youth Justice Board, 2021).

This subject knowledge is most certainly of use to students. It can be utilised as part of the placement opportunity to help them understand the difficulties between care vs control, welfare vs justice, rehabilitation vs risk management (see Goldson and Hughes, 2010), and to reflect upon where there are differences between rhetoric and reality, or other factors (in addition to academic research) impacting upon decision making processes (also see Chapter 1). For example, students may observe practitioners engaged in multi-agency conversations about techniques and measures necessary to manage potential harm a child may cause to others (Baker et al., 2011). Furthermore, as part of a focus on enhancing graduate attributes, within certain modules, students are introduced to key concepts and empirical research highlighting key principles and skills, including role clarification, pro-social modelling, problem solving, cognitive and relationship skills (Trotter and Evans, 2023). Students are also introduced to the different mechanisms and frameworks that can be utilised to formulate interventions or encourage children's participation.

Students become aware of key issues within youth justice through teaching and learning activity, such as concerns regarding racially discriminatory practices and a lack of support for disadvantaged and marginalised groups (Creaney and Smith, 2023). They also learn about the extent to which justice-involved children have experienced adversity and forms of social harm. It is through direct practice experience that students can experience workload pressures and understand how practitioners navigate the demands of high caseloads and the consequences of insufficient resource or budget constraints (see 'In Focus' case studies). Chloe Hill, Alumni and member of Edge Hill's Criminology Professional Advisory Group, has delivered talks to current students on job opportunities in the criminal justice sector and provided guidance on how to boost employability skills, gain relevant work experience and navigate job application processes. Chloe Hill provides an enlightening account of their experiences, alluding to it being a satisfying and meaningful experience (see 'In Focus' case study D).

'In Focus' case study D

SEAN: What is your experience of doing a work placement?

CHLOE: During my undergraduate degree in Psychological Analysis of Offending Behaviour, I sourced and completed a placement project with Cheshire East Youth Offending Team between 2017 and 2018. This placement offered the ability to gain first-hand experience of volunteering within the criminal justice system as part of the Youth Offending Team which supported the theoretical work we were completing in our studies. I knew I wanted to pursue a career within the criminal justice system, and I had an interest in youth crime and rehabilitation. I began by meeting with management to discuss the placement, what experience I wished to gain from my time volunteering with them and seeing how I can be of help to the service. Throughout this placement, I became involved in many different areas of the service. I supported the delivery of different reparation and summer projects in the community. I have always had an interest in the court system and therefore was able to attend Youth Court to observe and shadow members of the team. This was my first experience within court and was something I really enjoyed and knew I wanted to pursue. I also started setting up my own community reparation project for future use. A common interest with the young people I worked with was animals, and therefore I began to establish a professional link between dog shelters and the Youth Offending Team, for young people to give their time to help in the shelters. Additionally, I helped the successful completion of the Safer Lives Survey with young people in the Cheshire East and West area exploring youth violence, weapon use and lived experiences which would impact upon future research and knowledge. Conducting the survey with the young people really opened my eyes as to the real-life experiences of some of those I interviewed.

SEAN: What are the benefits of undertaking a practice placement?

CHLOE: I thoroughly enjoyed my time with the Youth Offending Team and felt that I was able to add value to the service through my volunteering and put what I had learnt in my studies into practice. The experience I gained was invaluable and paved the way for my career within the justice system. I believe it is important for future students to continue volunteering for the Youth Offending Team to continue to make an impact on the service and the young people we work directly with. I believe the placement module of any undergraduate degree is so important for students to undertake to seek an opportunity to gain experience in a field of interest to them, as well as this experience reflecting well when applying for jobs in the sectors after graduation.

As Chloe alluded to, reparative activities can be a useful mechanism through which relationships can be built and discussions facilitated around the child's interests and needs. Moreover, it can be argued that placement students are able to provide much-needed support to hard-pressed practitioners, necessary during times of austerity or reduced budgets to workforces.

Discussion and conclusion

This purpose of this chapter was to explain how and why the Building Professional Skills for Youth Justice (BPSYJ) programme, created through the knowledge and skills partnership, provides valuable opportunities to advance graduate attributes, facilitate and nurture skills acquisition. Drawing on the rhetoric and practice of Student as Producer, the chapter has presented insights into the types of practice and research placement opportunities available as part of the BPSYJ programme. Some students have benefited from participating in guest lectures delivered by youth justice professionals, and thus been exposed to 'real-world phenomena' (Usherwood, 2015) alongside having access to expert advice and guidance around career development, including subject-specific knowledge needed to work in the field and graduate attributes that need to be deployed or drawn upon to 'negotiate the complex realities of youth justice practice' (Taylor, 2010:189). Each academic year, Gareth Jones, former Head of Cheshire Youth Justice Service, delivers several guest lectures to criminology students on the causes of knife crime/youth violence and ways to address these issues from a practitioner's per-spective. He also provides useful advice and guidance in terms of career opportunities within the youth justice sector, and ways to enhance graduates' attributes and employ-ability skills through volunteering opportunities within Youth Justice Services. The practitioners delivering guest talks and interacting with students are motivated to inspire others, and garner respect and credibility due to their identity as 'pracademics' (Posner, 2009), a term which reflects both practice experience and academic knowledge. These professionals also have contacts in industry and useful networks that can be tapped into by students seeking to progress their careers in this multi-agency sector or conduct research on interesting topics.

Other students have either undertaken research *with* and *for* the service. As some of the accounts from students and alumni also indicate, the effort and commitment of practice supervisors within Cheshire Youth Justice is particularly noteworthy, cultivating learning and development opportunities for students, nurturing their employability skills. For example, students have had worthwhile opportunities to read referral order panel reports, and developed insights into how the youth court operates. The knowledge and skills partnership is reciprocal in the sense that practitioners have been able to showcase their own leadership qualities, hone mentorship skills and project empathy when building professional relationships with students (see Bramford and Eason, 2021 for more discus-sion on these reciprocal benefits). Cheshire Youth Justice Services can be described as a 'learning organisation' (Taylor, 2010:194), receptive to innovative ideas for navigating the complex terrain of knowledge transfer. This multi-agency service values learning and development opportunities for its workforce, especially but not exclusively related to the theory-practice nexus.

Conversations with students and alumni have been integrated within the chapter to illustrate the points. The knowledge and skills partnership 'recognises both the student role and also that of the service professionals, and foregrounds the different elements brought by the different actors to the learning process together with the achievement of jointly held goals and objectives' (McCulloch, 2009:180). In other words, and as the accounts of students and alumni confirm, academic leads and youth justice professionals work collaboratively *with* the students and treat them as capable, knowledgeable and independent learners, who are then enabled to engage in a process of deep learning and, through their active participation, are able to tap into or draw upon subject-specific knowledge and apply criminological theory to practice.

Students undertaking research placements have been actively involved in their own learning journey, discovering fresh insights, and disseminating their work to relevant stakeholders within the setting. Through capitalising on work experience opportu-nities, students have been able to acquire relevant sector experience that can be drawn upon and included in future job applications. They have also been able to observe how organisational culture and vision can shape attitudes to decision making, detecting factors that can influence the development of participatory or inclusive approaches to practices, identifying differences between the rhetoric and reality of the application of criminological theory into practice. This learning includes the relevance and usefulness of psycho-social perspectives when seeking to understand the under-lying factors affecting a person's behaviour or when assessing and 'making sense' of how childhood trauma or adverse experiences impact life chances (Cadet and Grif-fiths, 2023; Bramford and Eason, 2021).

Drawing on insights from other university–industry collaborations (Berbegal-Mirabent et al., 2020; Aizpun et al., 2015), at this point it is necessary to reiterate the importance of students being able to acquire skills and apply them in a multi-disciplinary criminal justice setting. These skills include, but are not limited to, being a reflexive practitioner capable of building relationships, with an ability to exercise discretion and use professional judgement when necessary, plus be able to think creatively or imaginatively, and able to work within a team and independently when designing and delivering interventions or updating assessments and recording contacts (Aizpun et al., 2015; Baker et al., 2011; Taylor, 2010). Whilst thinking in a Child First way is increasingly becoming the bedrock of youth justice practice, what must be understood are the ways in which practitioners seek to 'broker multi-faceted hybrid fusions' of different methods or models of practice (Goldson and Hughes, 2010:212). There are also other factors impacting on decision making, complicating the 'translation of official policy into operational practice' (Goldson and Hughes, 2010:215) that therefore must be taken into account by students and educators alike (see Chapter 1). To help students guard against adopting a stance likened to a reductive practice that locates the identified or perceived problems within the individual inducing blaming mentalities, a context sensitive approach that is receptive to the role of outside influences on behaviours is described as necessary. Thus, in-depth technical knowledge is needed, especially in relation to navigating the youth court process, report writing and assessment, management of risk, intervention planning, components of a relationship-based practice, the dichotomy of desistance vs Child First, and participatory principles. Whilst this knowledge can be taught and learned through interactive modular content and be subject-specific, engaging guest lectures delivered by industry experts, cultivating meaningful opportunities for students to 'transfer learning to real-world settings', must also remain a key objective of educators (Cadet and Griffiths, 2023:131).

Notes

1 This research was approved by the University of Chester Social and Political Science Research Ethics Committee.
2 Student as Producer has also been utilised as a guiding principle and underpinning philosophy of the Edge Hill University student-led Criminology Society.
3 Dr Jayne Price and Dr Sean Creaney.
4 This project was co-designed by Jessica Gallagher, work-related learning officer, and Dr Nicholas Longpre, Psychologist.
5 Students have the unique opportunity to engage with an ongoing research project funded by Edge Hill University, under the Research Investment Fund, strand 3. The present research project aims to explore the design and development of participatory peer support interventions in youth justice, which involves the recruitment and training of young people to undertake peer mentor roles, supporting children involved in care or justice systems. Students have the opportunity to learn how to conduct a systematic literature review and narrative synthesis. Semi-structured interviews with peer mentors and practitioners were conducted and thematic analysis used to explore participants' opinions, attitudes, and beliefs regarding the design and development of a peer mentoring scheme. The researchers adopt an appreciative inquiry and a reflective process within the study to discuss the main findings and to set out some key principles to advance peer mentoring in youth justice, by reflecting upon what challenges lie ahead and how this principled and progressive practice can help transform youth justice services. The research assistant role will involve analyses of secondary data, reflection, and research writing. Furthermore, students will be invited to join meetings with external collaborators, which includes local charities, and co-investigators working at Edge Hill University, University of Chester, and Durham University.

References

Aizpun, M., Sandino, D. and Merideno, I. (2015) Developing Students' Aptitudes through University-Industry Collaboration. *Ingeniería e investigación*, 35(3), 121–128. https://doi.org/10.15446/ing.investig.v35n3.48188.

Baker, K., Kelly, G. and Wilkinson, B. (2011) *Assessment in Youth Justice*. Bristol: Policy Press.

Berbegal-Mirabent, J., Gil-Doménech, D. and Ribeiro-Soriano, D.E. (2020) Fostering University-industry Collaborations through University Teaching. *Knowledge Management Research & Practice*, 18(3), 263–275. https://doi.org/10.1080/14778238.2019.1638738.

Bramford, K. and Eason, A.L. (2021) Criminology Placements: Work-based learning and organisational 'buy in'. *Higher Education, Skills and Work-Based Learning*, 11(2), 317–329. https://doi.org/10.1108/HESWBL-10-2019-0133.

Barton, A., Davis, H. and Scott, D. (2019) Quiet Silencing: Restricting the criminological imagination in the neoliberal university. In A. Diver (ed.) *Employability via Higher Education: Sustainability as scholarship*. Cham: Springer. https://doi.org/10.1007/978-3-030-26342-3_34.

Bhui, H.S. (2001) New Probation: Closer to the end of social work? *British Journal of Social Work*, 31(4), 637–639. http://www.jstor.org/stable/23716231.

Bond-Taylor, Sue and Davies, Ceryl (2019) Youth Justice Live! Flexible pedagogies in an online/offline community of practice. In *Flexible Pedagogies in Practice: Implementing flexibility in higher education through online learning communities*. Rotterdam: Sense Publishers.

Bunce, L., Baird, A. and Jones, S. (2017) The Student-as-Consumer Approach in Higher Education and Its Effects on Academic Performance. *Studies in Higher Education*, 42(11), 1958–1978.

Cadet, N. and Griffiths, T-L. (2023) Embedding Employability in the Social Sciences Curriculum: Reflections from an applied university. *Journal of Perspectives in Applied Academic Practice*, 11 (2), 121–134.

Canton, R. and Yates, J., (2008) Applied Criminology. In B. Stout, B. Williams and J. Yates, *Applied Criminology*. London: Sage.

Case, S. and Hampson, K. (2019) Youth Justice Pathways to Change: Drivers, challenges and opportunities. *Youth Justice*, 19(1), 25–41.

Case, S. and Hazel, N. (eds) (2023) *Child First: Developing a new youth justice system*. London: Palgrave Macmillan.

Chadwick, K. and Scraton, P. (2006) Critical Criminology. In E. McLaughlin and J. Muncie (eds) *The Sage Dictionary of Criminology* (pp. 97–100). London: Sage.

Cherry, S. (2017) *Transforming Behaviour: Pro-social modelling in practice*. 2nd edn. London: Taylor & Francis.

Crawford, K., Horsley, R., Hagyard, A. and Derricott, D. (2015) *Pedagogies of Partnership: What works*. York: HEA.

Creaney, S. and Smith, R. (2023) Social Work and Youth Justice. In J. Parker (ed.) *Introducing Social Work*. 2nd edn. London: Sage.

Creaney, S. and Burns, S. (2023) Freedom from Symbolic Violence? Facilitators and barriers to participatory practices in youth justice. *Youth Justice*, 0(0). Online. https://doi.org/10.1177/14732254231156844.

CYP Now (2012) Youth Offending Team and University Partnership Unveiled. https://www.cypnow.co.uk/news/article/youth-offending-team-and-university-partnership-unveiled.

Flanaghan, T (2005) Working with Volunteers in the Youth Justice System. In T. Bateman and J. Pitts (eds) *The RHP Companion to Youth Justice*. Lyme Regis: Russell House.

Freire, P. (1996 [1970]) *Pedagogy of the Oppressed*, London and New York: Penguin.

Giroux, H. (2000) *Impure Acts: The practical politics of cultural studies*. London: Routledge.

Goldson, B. and Hughes, G. (2010) Sociological Criminology and Youth Justice: Comparative policy analysis and academic intervention. *Criminology & Criminal Justice*, 10(2), 211–230.

Haines, K. and Drakeford, M. (1998) *Young People and Youth Justice*. Basingstoke: Macmillan.

Hayes, D. (2018, 31 July) YOTs and Universities Link Up. *CYP Now*. https://www.cypnow.co.uk/features/article/yots-and-universities-link-up.

Hine, J. (2008) Applied Criminology: Research, policy and practice. In B. Stout, B. Williams and J. Yates, *Applied Criminology*. London: Sage.

Light, G., Cox, R. and Calkins, S.C. (2009) *Learning and Teaching in Higher Education: The reflective professional*. 2nd edn. London: Sage.

McCulloch, A. (2009) Student as Co-Producer: Learning from public administration and the student-university relationship. *Studies in Higher Education*, 34(2), 171–183.

Neary, M. (2019) Student as Producer and the Democratisation of Science. *Impact: the University of Lincoln Journal of Higher Education Research*, 1(4). ISSN: 2516-7561.

Neary, M. and Winn, J. (2009) The Student as Producer: Reinventing the student experience in higher education. In *The Future of Higher Education: Policy, pedagogy and the student experience* (pp. 192–210). London: Continuum. ISBN: ISBN: 1847064728.

Office for Students (2022) About the Teaching Excellence Framework (TEF). Available at: https://www.officeforstudents.org.uk/advice-and-guidance/the-tef/about-the-tef/.

Peer Power and Youth Justice Board (2021) *Co-Creation and Participation in Practice Project*. London: Peer Power/YJB.

Posner, P.L. (2009) The Pracademic: An agenda for re-engaging practitioners and academics. *Public Budgeting & Finance*, 29(1), 12–26.

Price, J., Wilkinson, D. and Crossley, C. (2023) Children and Young Peoples' Lyrics and Voices Capturing Their Experiences within Youth Justice Services. *Safer Communities*, 22(3), 186–199. https://doi.org/10.1108/SC-08-2022-0029.

QAA (2022) Subject Benchmark Statement for Criminology. https://www.qaa.ac.uk/quality-code/subject-benchmark-statements/criminology.

Ragonese, E., Rees, A., Ives, J. and Dray, T (2015) *The Routledge Guide to Working in Criminal Justice: Employability skills and careers in the criminal justice sector*. Abingdon: Routledge.

Schön, D.A. (1987) *Educating the Reflective Practitioner: Toward a new design for teaching and learning in the professions*. San Francisco: Jossey-Bass.

Scraton, P. (2007) *Power, Conflict and Criminalisation*, Abingdon: Routledge.

Smithson, H., Gray, P. and Jones, A. (2020) 'They Really Should Start Listening to You': The benefits and challenges of co-producing a participatory framework of youth justice practice. *Youth Justice*, July. https://doi.org/10.1177/1473225420941598.

Smithson, H., Lang, T. and Gray, P. (2022) From Rhetoric to Reality: Participation in practice within youth justice systems. In S. Frankel (ed.) *Establishing Child Centred Practice in a Changing World, Part A* (pp. 111–122). Emerald Studies in Child Centred Practice. Bingley: Emerald.

Smithson, H. and Gray, P. (2021) *Supporting Children's Meaningful Participation in the Youth Justice System*. HM Inspectorate of Probation Academic Insights 2021/10, August. https://www.justiceinspectorates.gov.uk/hmiprobation/wp-content/uploads/sites/5/2021/08/Academic-Insight-%E2%80%93-Supporting-childrens-meaningful-participation-in-the-youth-justice-system.pdf.

Smith-Yau, W. (2017) Academic/YOT Partnership Working Guide. Youth Justice Board for England and Wales. https://yjresourcehub.uk/research-guidance/item/download/513_155aef7190608ffeb0e549726e30a56d.html.

Stout, B., Williams, B. and Yates, J. (2008) *Applied Criminology*. London: Sage.

Strudwick, K. (2017) Debating Student as Producer: Relationships, contexts and challenges for higher education. *PRISM, Casting New Light on Learning, Theory and Practice*, 1(1), 73–96.

Taylor, W. (2010) Reflective Practice in Youth Justice. In W. Taylor, R. Earl and R. Hester (eds) *Youth Justice Handbook: Theory, policy and practice*. Cullompton, Devon: Willan.

Trotter, C. and Evans, P. (2023) Developing Evidence Based Practice Skills in Youth Justice. *European Journal of Probation*, 15(2), 147–161. https://doi.org/10.1177/20662203231185088.

QAA (2022) Subject Benchmark Statement for Criminology. https://www.qaa.ac.uk/quality-code/subject-benchmark-statements/criminology.

Usherwood, S (2015) Building Resources for Simulations: Challenges and Opportunities. *European Political Science*, 14, 218–227. https://doi.org/10.1057/eps.2015.19.

Wilkinson, D., Price, J. and Crossley, C. (2022) Developing Creative Methodologies: Using lyric writing to capture young peoples' experiences of the youth offending services during the COVID-19 pandemic. *Journal of Criminological Policy and Practice*, 8(2), 105–119.

Youth Justice Board (YJB) (2021) *Strategic Plan 2021–24. Report.* London: YJB.

Appendix A

Lucy Baines reflects on her experiences of working in the criminal justice sector as both a criminal justice assistant and as an appropriate adult, and provides a fascinating insight into the theory/practice nexus. She is also studying the LLB (Hons) in Law with Criminology and is co-president of the Criminology Society.

What is the Criminology Society and what does your role involve?

When helping to support an open day on campus, Isabella and I were talking about why a criminology society is important and how we can set it up. I'm in the Law Society and I organise the events for them, and we've received feedback from students about how it has enhanced their sense of belonging and their experiences. All students within the School of Law, Criminology and Policing can apply to become members of the Society. I'm a co-president with responsibility for Academic Events & External Opportunities. We are currently organising a social event, as well as making plans for academic-type events including a guest speaker series. We are also in the process of applying for funds through the Student Opportunity Fund to enable a prison visit, to enrich student experiences and help them make sense of links between theory and practice. I recently co-chaired an alumni panel, where former students shared knowledge and insights into their careers working within the criminal justice sector and related fields. Since the society was re-launched, we have over 70 students become members and we have created committee roles, which include Treasurer, Social Media Manager, Inclusion Officer, Alumni Relations, Social Events Co-ordinator, and year representatives. These roles are beneficial for students to enhance their CV and evidence graduate attributes.

What are the key features of the Criminology Society?

In other institutions there can be a separation between the teachers and the students. This involves the teacher in an 'expert role' with little collaborative practice. Whereas at Edge Hill, there is a commitment to form a partnership, an agreement that each person is capable of sharing their own knowledge and experiences. During the open day, when discussing the courses with prospective students, I was able to share my knowledge around career options because I did a lot of research in that area before I started my course. I helped the students to feel 'listened to' and 'understood'. The lecturer can talk all about the course. They can tell you about the structure, what you're going to study, how many days a week you'll be in. They can tell you all that, but they can't really tell you how it's going to be actually doing it. That's where I think it is amazing to get students involved in these conversations.

And they really want to hear from students, because obviously at the end of the day, that's what they're going to be doing if they choose that course. So it's having someone to tell them that they're going to be all right, you're going to be able to do it. You'll get the help that you need from the lecturers. They kind of see you as a peer. It's very insightful, I think.

What did your work experience involve and did this help to understand the theory/ practice nexus?

I originally started as a criminal justice assistant in an administration role and then I became an appropriate adult having completed a training course. This work involves supporting vulnerable adults and young people in police custody. I will attend and support them, making sure that their rights are upheld, that they're getting everything that they need because due to their vulnerability, obviously being young is an automatic vulnerability for them. And I feel like it did definitely help with my criminology modules, especially when we were talking about the criminal justice process, looking at the agencies like prisons and courts and things like that and how they treat determining contexts. And obviously, I'd seen in person through my own eyes how these determining contexts were treated. And I'm not saying it was like bad or good, but it just did give me that insight into real life rather than just looking at a journal article about what someone else's opinion was. I could kind of form my own opinion and have a better understanding when I went to write an essay.

And seeing how someone's age impacted their outcome in police custody, it was extremely insightful for me, because I had no idea it was like that. So obviously it helped with critically analysing criminal justice responses for the assignment. Obviously as a student, you'll hear the term 'cycle of crime' a lot. But I'd never actually physically seen it until I was an appropriate adult.

Appendix B

Isabella Fitzsimmons, who is co-president of the Criminology Society and studying the B. A. (Hons) Criminology and Law programme, shares insights into experiences of work-related learning and participating in extra-curricular activities.

What is the Criminology Society and what does your role involve?

The Criminology Society is premised on the idea of 'Student as Producer' as a framework to coordinate academic and social events. Students and tutors work together to plan and develop activities. This involves each person being respectful of each other's perspectives, embracing different insights and treating contributions as of equal value. For example, the Society is in the process of setting up a lecture series and has been promoting involvement in extra-curricular activity (alumni events) to help students develop key skills and graduate attributes. At the alumni event, I encouraged former students to reflect on their work experiences and asked them to provide guidance to current students related to professional development. As part of my co-president role, I helped to create year representative roles and appointed students to these positions to act as role models and mentors to others.

We have set up a committee and promoted events through the social media accounts. It is about collaborative working. It is based on the principle that both lecturers and students have areas of expertise and knowledge that can be shared when working together. I co-chaired the recent alumni and networking event, and it was fascinating to hear about routes into different careers and key skills needed to work in specific fields. As part of my role as co-president of the Criminology Society, I have participated in extra-curricular activities, and this can help to develop graduate attributes, especially leadership skills and networking. I have also assisted during open days and provided insight into career opportunities.

What is your experience of work-related learning?

I spoke with tutors and the work-based learning team about networking and different work experience opportunities. I've been shadowing another barrister in the Crown Court on a high-profile case. I had the opportunity of going down to the cells to meet some of the defendants. It is eye-opening and has given me a fascinating insight into the court process and different roles of professionals. This has led to reflections around how the jury view defendants on the stand. This work experience opportunity has also helped me to 'think through' theoretical perspectives, such as the labelling theory and the self-fulfilling prophecy.

3 How the inspectorate works with external academics/researchers

Robin Moore, Andrea Brazier and Helen Mercer

In summary, this chapter sets out:

- how the inspectorate promotes an evidence-informed approach in youth justice
- the differing ways in which the inspectorate collaborates with academics and external researchers
- how the inspectorate seeks to overcome the challenges to building and utilising evidence.

Introduction

HM Inspectorate of Probation seeks to promote excellence in youth justice services across England and Wales, having led the inspection of youth justice work, both on its own and jointly with other inspectorates, since 2003.[1] It is a strategic aim of government that services should reduce reoffending,[2] while also taking all reasonable steps to keep the public safe (Ministry of Justice, 2019), and the inspectorate's position is that this is most likely if practice is aligned to evidence, and if the evidence base grows over time. The inspectorate – which is independent of government – thus starts with the principle that services should be evidence based (Baker, 2008) or else evidence led. The latter requires approaches which are guided by the best available research findings (incorporating a broad range of research methods) alongside practice knowledge and lived experiences, and which are underpinned by clear theories of change, assisting with further evaluation. Once validated through robust evaluation, specific approaches and interventions can then be described as evidence based.

Bearing in mind that the inspectorate also inspects probation services, its stated vision is of 'high-quality probation and youth justice services that change people's lives for the better'. Elaboration upon the inspectorate's role is provided through its purpose statement, which makes explicit reference to both research and evidence-based judgements and guidance:

> HM Inspectorate of Probation is the independent inspector of probation and youth justice services in England and Wales. We set the standards that shine a light on the quality and impact of these services. Our inspections, reviews, research and effective practice products provide authoritative and evidence-based judgements and guidance. We use our voice to drive system change, with a focus on inclusion and diversity. Our scrutiny leads to improved outcomes for individuals and communities.

DOI: 10.4324/9781003411192-4

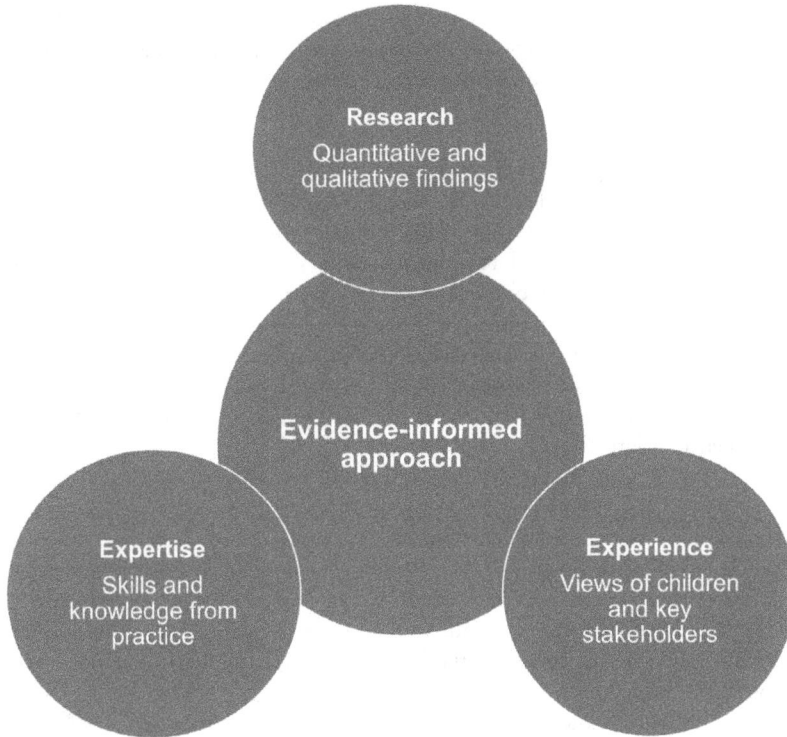

Figure 3.1 An evidence-informed approach

To help meet this purpose, the inspectorate has a stated commitment to reviewing, developing and promoting the evidence base for high-quality services. A key source of evidence is research evidence, which is used alongside inspection findings (encompassing the views/experiences of both children and practitioners) to inform understanding of what helps and what hinders youth justice services, to develop the inspection programmes, guidance and effective practice products, and to consider system-wide change that could change lives for the better.

How the inspectorate benefits from working with external academics and researchers

To help review, develop and promote the evidence base, the inspectorate collaborates with academics and external researchers in numerous ways, looking to utilise and maximise the knowledge, experience and skills across the research community. As can be seen across the following types of knowledge generation/exchange, the aim is to produce as rounded and balanced a view as possible, avoiding partiality, while also recognising that the evidence base never stands still – it continually evolves – and that we should never expect to find all the evidence by looking too narrowly in one place. Careful thought is also paid to both 'knowledge translation' and 'knowledge mobilisation' (Health Service Executive, 2021), so not simply one-way dissemination but also seeking to connect those who produce research and those who use it, with a focus on trying to make research evidence as usable and practical as possible, encouraging meaningful engagement and interaction with research findings and its implications, and building a common understanding of what helps and what hinders service delivery.

Advisory group

A number of prominent academics are members of the inspectorate's Probation and Youth Justice Expert Advisory Group. This group – which meets at least twice a year – provides advice on current and developing issues in service delivery and practice which could/should be reflected in the core inspection programmes or could be the focus of the thematic and research programmes or effective practice guides. The members are appointed based on their specific knowledge and expertise, and they can also be asked to contribute to specific pieces of work on an ad hoc basis; an example being the provision of advice in relation to the development of the core youth justice inspection programme due to commence in late 2024.

Commissioned research

It is beneficial to all that youth justice services are grounded in reliable and robust evidence, and the inspectorate considers where it can most helpfully fill evidence gaps or improve the quality of the current evidence. Account is taken of any recent changes to policy, service delivery or caseloads, the latest inspection findings, and what would be helpful for future inspections.

High-quality research studies and evaluations can assist with policy (and inspection) developments and enable services and delivery to be improved, maximising positive outcomes for children and others. When designing new studies, the inspectorate seeks to make full and effective use of its internal research team resource and then commissions or involves external researchers/analysts where they have specialist up-to-date knowledge, expertise and/or skills, and/or where there is insufficient internal capacity to meet the required timescales. Flexibility is maintained, identifying the most efficient way of completing any research to a sufficiently high standard and balancing the need for findings to be robust, relevant and timely.

The inspectorate has recently commissioned research projects on the topics of knife crime, community resolutions, contextual safeguarding, effective management, and care-experienced children. To increase interest and value for the frontline, practice examples are included in the published reports where possible. Two such examples, from the report on the implementation and delivery of community resolutions (Marshall et al., 2023), are as follows:

Community resolutions interventions including restorative justice

A group of young people had caused damage to a storage facility which contained motor vehicles. They were caught on CCTV and identified, and all admitted that they were involved in the incident. They were all then referred into the youth justice service (YJS) and because the victim wanted the matter to be dealt with in this way, it was dealt with by a community resolution with a restorative justice element. All the young people involved realised what they'd done was wrong and they agreed, as per the YJS suggestion and assessment, that they would go and make right the damage. They worked with the victim to repair the damage, supervised by some members of YJS staff. They all did their bit to repair the damage. The victim was really happy about that, and everybody got something out of it. It was considered a very good outcome on the part of the YJS, the victim, and the young people involved.

YJS-led scrutiny panels

Although not yet implemented, some YJSs were in the process of setting up a promising area-wide, YJS-led initiative which would allow them to scrutinise each other's implementation and delivery of out-of-court disposals (OOCDs) and evaluate each other's performance. A motivator for setting this up is to have a YJS-led scrutiny panel alongside the police-led scrutiny panel. The intended process will include a review of each of YJS's policies and a sample of cases to share practice, reflect and learn from each other. This will help to ensure that OOCD's were delivered as intended, and according to the YJS OOCD policy and guidance. It will further review consistency of decision-making throughout the OOCD process, to improve local support for young people.

When commissioning research (and when undertaking inspections – see later sections), careful consideration is given to how to give a stronger voice to those children who are supervised by youth justice services, with a clear focus on their experiences. The importance of 'voice' is emphasised in the Lundy model of child participation (Lundy, 2007). The model provides a helpful way of conceptualising a child's right to participation, as laid down in Article 12 of the UN Convention on the Rights of the Child (Pleysier and Kilkelly, 2023). The four elements of the model have a rational chronological order: space, voice, audience, influence.

Two approaches which have been adopted within commissioned projects are as follows:

- In the project examining the implementation and delivery of community resolutions (Marshall et al., 2023), focus groups were undertaken with young people using Ketso Kits,[4] which are portable kits laid out on tables with participants writing their ideas (in written or visual format) on specially made 'leaves' before placing them on a central felt to create clusters of ideas.
- In the project on the supervision of care-experienced children, appropriate ways of engaging with the children were discussed with a care-experienced young person's research group, obtaining views on the questions to ask and the most appropriate format for conducting the research. A Mobile Instant Messaging Interviewing (MIMI) approach, using WhatsApp, was then adopted as a core method (alongside an interview option) because of its accessibility and familiarity to young people, providing the option for participants to record voice notes if preferred, and to use other features such as emojis, gifs, photos and music.

Thematic inspections

There are many similarities between research projects and thematic inspections. As Shute (2013) has recognised, 'the techniques employed by the inspectorates are, broadly

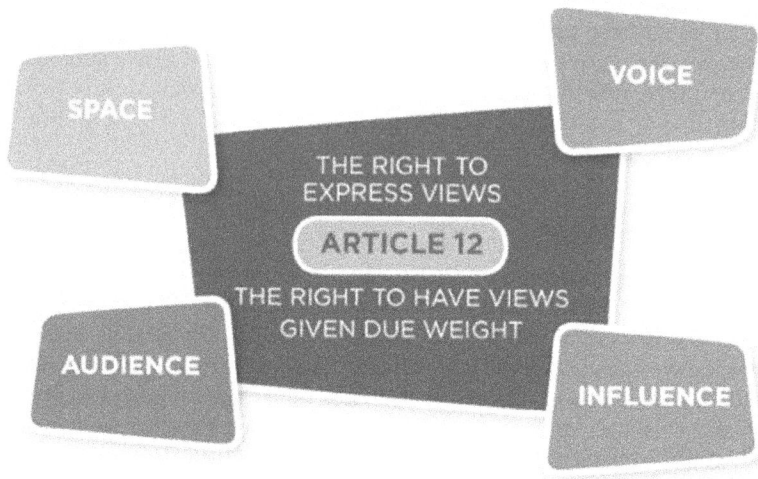

- **SPACE**: Children must be given safe, inclusive opportunities to form and express their view
- **VOICE**: Children must be facilitated to express their view
- **AUDIENCE**: The view must be listened to.
- **INFLUENCE**: The view must be acted upon, as appropriate.

Figure 3.2 Lundy model of child participation[3]

speaking, the same as those used by social scientists in other settings, drawing on quali-tative and quantitative approaches'. Many of the principles and considerations are also alike, with a need to think about rigour, impartiality, credibility and transparency. Simi-larly to research projects, rigour requires that inspection findings are 'robust and sup-ported by a verifiable evidence base assembled using a sound methodology' (Shute, 2013). Recognising the need for thematic inspections to be both informed by the current research evidence and to be undertaken in a way which is aligned to the scope and goals of the inspection and the agreed inspection questions, academics are involved as advi-sors – either on their own or as part of wider steering groups – when this would be beneficial, identifying and utilising academics with expertise in relation to the specific thematic topic.

External organisations are also commissioned within thematic inspections to help give a stronger voice to children supervised by youth justice services. By developing open and trusting relationships with children, the commissioned partners are able to provide con-fidence and reassurance that creates the space for children to be active participants within the inspection process. For example, User Voice (which undertakes peer-led action research) was commissioned to hear directly from children and present their unfiltered feedback in the recent thematic inspections examining (i) the experiences of black and mixed heritage boys in the youth justice system; and (ii) education, training and employment services. Alongside the published reports, User Voice played a key part within the accompanying online launch events, further prompting the voice of the child.

Action plans have since been implemented to take forward the recommendations from the thematic inspection reports, and the User Voice reports have been distributed beyond Youth Justice to wider government representatives.

To maximise interest and value, case studies are included in the reports where possible. For example, the User Voice report (2022) on children's experiences of education, training and employment services included the following positive case study.

Case study

One child stated that the YJS were 'doing an amazing job' after she was 'kicked out of mainstream school'. She spoke of how she was supported by the YJS through 'thick and thin'.

She had been assessed for learning difficulties and **felt that she had been involved in the process. Subsequently, she was transferred to a specialist school** that 'covers people with ADHD and learning difficulties'. She felt that she was **given ETE options,** that she was **included in the decision and supported at every stage.** What really shone through was the YJS's ability to advocate for her educational needs and support her 'through the rough times I have had throughout my journey'.

She had **regular check-ins regardless of Covid-19** via phone or face-time and stated that 'support carried on even if I couldn't have anyone round my house due to restrictions'.

She was **currently completing a number of different courses that covered academic, behavioural, and life skills.** She was also completing a course designed for those with learning disabilities. She had **high aspirations for her future** and wanted to move on from her offending behaviour and 'get good grades to get myself a good job'. She reported **positive outcomes in the form of 'better behaviour'** and said 'I have improved so much since having YJS behind me.'

The Behavioural Insights EAST framework – easy, attractive, social, timely – is helpful when thinking about communicating findings, and for the thematic inspection on education, training and employment services, the inspectorate commissioned KeyRing[5] to produce an easy-read version of the final report, with simplified text and drawings (HM Inspectorate of Probation, 2022). An example of the content of this report is set out in Figure 3.3.

Partnerships

The inspectorate has been involved in a range of collaborations and partnerships with academic institutions, ranging from placements for undergraduate students to fellowships for experts. For a number of years, support has been provided to Manchester Metropolitan University's Q-Step programme[6] which provides quantitative social science training to students, equipping them with relevant knowledge and skills. Each year, a number of students use inspection data to answer agreed research questions. The inspectorate has a further link to the Midlands Graduate School,[7] an accredited Economic and Social Research Council (ESRC) Doctoral Training Partnership involving six universities with a focus on widening access to postgraduate funding. Through this partnership, the inspectorate is collaborating on a Ph.D. studentship with the University of Nottingham on 'co-action plan

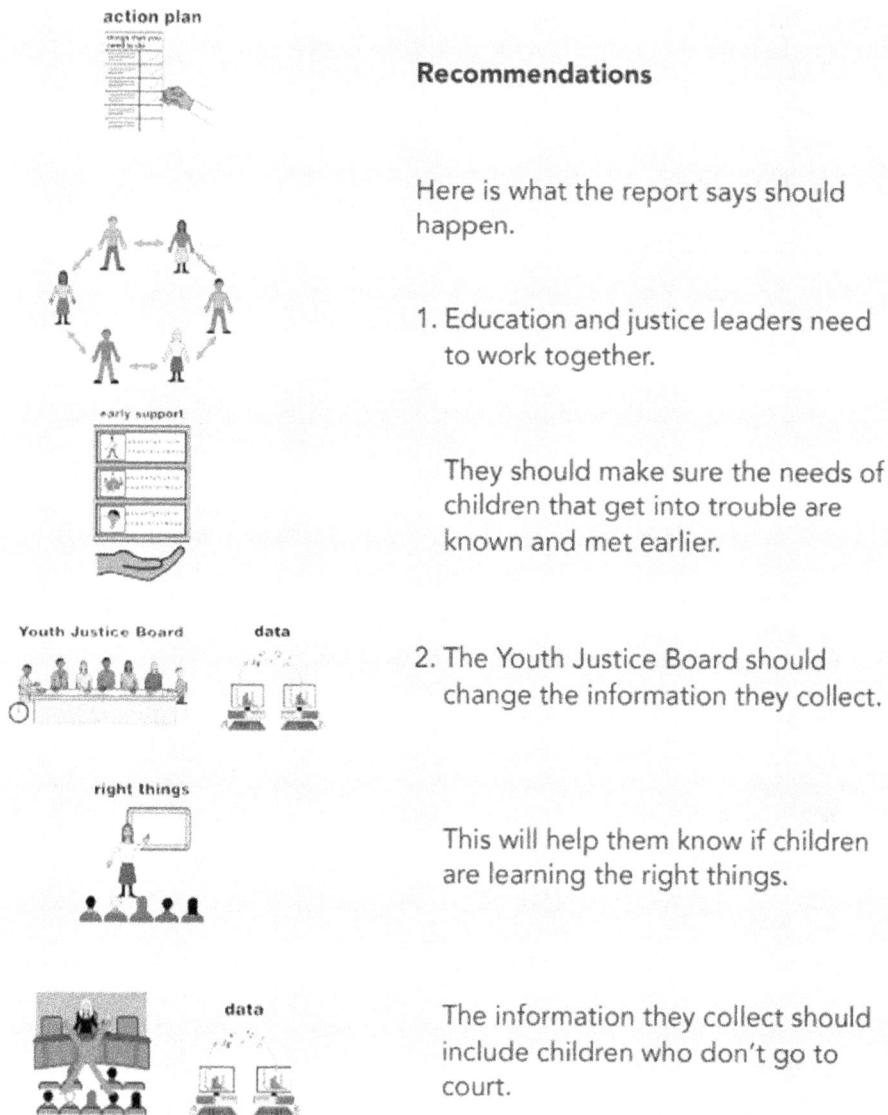

Recommendations

Here is what the report says should happen.

1. Education and justice leaders need to work together.

They should make sure the needs of children that get into trouble are known and met earlier.

Youth Justice Board   data

2. The Youth Justice Board should change the information they collect.

right things

This will help them know if children are learning the right things.

data

The information they collect should include children who don't go to court.

Figure 3.3 Extract from thematic inspection easy-read report on education, training and employment

production and inspection', beginning with the theories and discourses that have informed the development of co-production within public services and within the work of probation and youth justice inspection specifically, before focusing on the practicalities of co-produced inspections and the experiences of those involved.

Another link to academia was established through Capabilities in Academic Policy Engagement (CAPE)[8] which is a knowledge exchange and research project that explores how to support effective and sustained engagement between academics and policy professionals. It is funded by Research England and is a partnership of five universities, in collaboration with the Government Office for Science, the Parliamentary Office for Science & Technology, Nesta, and the Transforming Evidence Hub. Through CAPE, the inspectorate joined up with the Ministry of Justice to support a policy fellowship exploring the range of outcome measures needed to better understand desistance and (reductions in) reoffending.

External research projects

Youth justice research projects are supported and commissioned by a range of key stakeholders and funders, and the inspectorate's research team is often asked to assist or provide advice to external projects. This can be to assist with initial scoping and/or a funding application, or longer-term involvement such as through a project steering group or advisory group. For example, the inspectorate provided input through the steering/special advisory groups for the Nuffield Foundation commissioned projects on: (i) understanding preventative interventions; and (ii) exploring racial disparity in diversion.

Academic Insights papers

Another approach adopted by the inspectorate for reviewing and promoting the evidence base is through commissioning Academic Insights papers, which were launched in 2019. Around 50 papers have now been published,[9] authored by a wide range of academics and researchers across different institutions and organisations, with different areas of expertise and backgrounds, and from both England and Wales and also some other jurisdictions. Some are by very well-known and established academics, while some are by academics at an earlier stage in their career.

In one of these Academic Insights papers, Smithson and Gray (2021) summarise recent work across Greater Manchester which enabled the co-creation with justice-involved children of a transformative framework of practice, termed Participatory Youth Practice (PYP). The PYP principles are grounded in children's rights and an ethos of meaningful participation, highlighting the need to help children to problem solve, to find better options, and develop their ambitions. The paper concludes with a 'How to Guide' for co-creation and participation; essential ingredients being the fostering of equitable relationships, gaining trust, creating safe spaces, ensuring clarity of purpose, and investing the necessary time and resources. Notably, all of this work was enabled through a knowledge transfer partnership project between Manchester Metropolitan University and the ten Greater Manchester youth justice services, funded by the Economic and Social Research Council (ESRC) and the Arts and Humanities Research Council (AHRC). To help embed the principles, training was delivered to each of the services, with each service identifying a 'participation champion' to provide support to their colleagues.

In another of the Academic Insights papers, Fox and Albertson (2020) highlight the importance of research and evaluation to supporting continuing innovation in the delivery of services, requiring networks and relationships both at the individual and organisational level. They highlight how there are natural links between innovation and (i) approaches which involve co-creation with service users, (ii) localised approaches that focus on the development of shared values, and (iii) the concepts of evidence-led and evidence-based practice.

'Five-minute reflections from research' videos

More recently, the inspectorate launched 'five-minute reflections from research' videos,[10] which are also aimed at all those interested in the key lessons from probation and youth justice research. Reflecting upon their work, leading academics set out their top pieces of advice for the delivery of high-quality probation and/or youth justice services. In one of the first videos, Professor Hannah Smithson highlights the importance of (i) letting young people participate, (ii) adopting a public health approach, and (iii) learning from the impact of the Covid-19 pandemic. She advocates 'a whole system approach to addressing children's needs because disjointed services ultimately result in disjointed approaches'.

The key challenges

Both research and inspection activities can influence and drive positive change at the individual practitioner, operational delivery and/or policy levels. The impacts can be immediate or longer-term, and they are not always transparent, making them difficult to monitor and measure. However, the most beneficial and impactful projects and activities tend to be those which satisfy the following three criteria (Belcher et al., 2016):[11]

- **robustness**: projects which are well-designed and well-executed, with an appropriate approach and methodology for addressing the specified questions
- **relevance**: projects which provide learning and findings of relevance to current policy and delivery priorities and which can be implemented relatively easily by key stakeholders
- **timeliness**: projects which produce useful, usable outputs at the right point in time.

Notably, there are challenges in relation to all three criteria.

Robustness

There remains much to learn, and the focus needs to be upon ensuring that all research, whatever its type, is as robust and rigorous as possible, maximising its full potential. Over the years there have been disagreements and conflicts within the research community regarding the relative value of differing approaches, models, disciplines and types of research, which can lead to knowledge hierarchies rather than an embracing of knowledge equity and diverse perspectives (Harriott, 2023), and can ultimately result in a reduced focus upon the shared goal of changing children's lives for the better. As research questions vary markedly in nature, a wide range of research methods are required, with a recognition that differing approaches can be highly complementary. There is room for action-based research, in-depth case study work and longer-term experimental designs, while always being aware and fully transparent about the differing strengths and limitations of all approaches (see the *Magenta Book* (HM Treasury, 2020) for a wide range of evaluation methods and their key pros and cons). Crucially, attention then needs to be given to merging the differing types of evidence together as therein lies the real promise for evidence-informed and evidence-based practice.

All research proposals and designs need to pay special regard to the resource demands that will be placed upon the frontline. Research projects often require the support and time of practitioners and also senior staff and engaged gatekeepers who can facilitate the necessary access (to both people and data). Bearing in mind that the work demands placed upon those on the frontline can already be high, consideration should always be given to whether the proposed approach is proportionate and whether there are less resource-intensive ways of obtaining the necessary evidence.

Relevance

Research projects can be most impactful if they provide learning and findings of relevance to current policy and delivery priorities. However, this is extremely difficult if the priorities themselves are unclear or not communicated well. A lack of transparency led the 2015 Nurse review of the UK Research Councils to recommended that government departments should adopt a more strategic approach to research and development programmes, and a more sophisticated dialogue with academia. Following on from this review, departments have started publishing documents entitled 'Areas of Research Interest' (ARIs), with the Ministry of Justice having published two iterations. Their most recent iteration was published in 2020, summarising the department's evidence needs over the next three to five years and also highlighting the need for multi-disciplinary methodologies, encompassing modelling methods, data science techniques, ethnographic methods, behavioural science insights, and data mapping and linking. The ARIs can be seen as one step towards increased transparency and academic engagement.

Providing learning and findings of relevance to current policy and delivery priorities is further complicated when these priorities continually change. The political dimension needs to be recognised; within the lifetime of a government there can be quick and unexpected ministerial changes, which can in turn lead to significant changes in ministerial priorities. In April 2023, Alex Chalk was appointed Secretary of State for Justice, becoming the tenth Conservative MP to hold the position over a ten-year period (with Dominic Raab holding the position on two separate occasions). A general election is also on the horizon, raising the prospect of further change.

Timeliness

In a 2021 National Audit Office report, the heads of policy profession across government concluded that the biggest barriers to using evaluation to inform policy decisions were: (i) a lack of timely evidence; and (ii) an inaccessible knowledge base. The importance of timely evidence is further emphasised in the Ministry of Justice's 'Evaluation & Prototyping Strategy' (2023), which states as follows: 'Our vision is to deliver a world class justice system that works for everyone in society. Improving the quality, timeliness and accessibility of our evidence is essential to realise these strategic outcomes and deliver a justice system that works for everyone in society.'

It is certainly true that the timescales for delivery on policy priorities and change programmes can be tight, putting pressure on policy leads who may conclude that they do not have the time to wait for new research findings or even to engage with research experts. So whilst research projects should seek to satisfy all three criteria of robustness, relevance and timeliness, a balance often needs to be sought between them. For any specific project, clear communication and engagement with key stakeholders, including a management of expectations, is essential from the outset for the appropriate balance to be struck.

Key requirements for an evidence-informed approach

A number of reports have considered the extent to which evidence is used across government and different policy areas, and how this can be maximised. For example, based on a review of the literature on effective strategies to increase the use of research evidence, Breckon and Dodson (2016) set out the following underlying mechanisms:

- **awareness**: build awareness and positive attitudes towards evidence use
- **agree**: build mutual understanding and agreement on policy-relevant questions and the kind of evidence needed to answer them
- **access and communication**: provide communication of, and access to, evidence
- **interact**: facilitate interactions between decision-makers and researchers
- **skills**: support decision-makers to develop skills accessing and making sense of evidence
- **structure and process**: influence decision-making structures and processes.

These mechanisms are reflected within this section which sets out five key requirements (see Figure 3.4) for an evidence-informed approach in youth justice.

Figure 3.4 Key requirements for an evidence-informed approach

Embed an evaluation culture

An evidence-informed approach is one which is guided by the best available research findings alongside professional knowledge and practice wisdom, and the lived experiences of children and their families. To ensure that there is a sufficient link between evidence and practice, ultimately helping to deliver positive outcomes for children and their families, leaders need to focus upon building a research/evaluation culture which is hardwired into the organisation. Continuous learning environments are a feature of the most effective organisations, with a culture of support and critical reflection, and staff continually looking for ways to develop and improve. Staff need to be encouraged and given sufficient time, space and resources to continually reflect upon their practice and to learn from others and apply findings from research and elsewhere. There should also be a commitment to upskilling staff where required so that they have a sufficient understanding of the role of research and evaluation.

Dix and Meade (2023) set out an IDEAS framework for effective practice in youth justice which comprises the five interlinked elements of influence, delivery, expertise, alliance and support. Crucially, knowledge is set out as a key component of expertise, which includes an understanding of theoretical models and approaches. Similarly, in the 2010 review of child protection, Munro states that 'good professional practice is driven by knowledge of the latest theory and research'. When considering the research literature, practitioners need to consider what the latest research findings actually mean for their work with children and how they might be able to implement them in their practice. Some refer to this as 'research-mindedness', and Everitt (2002) indicates that it is evidenced by practitioners who:

- consistently define and make their objectives and hypotheses explicit
- understand that their explanations of the world are merely hypotheses, as they are tentative and open to be tested against evidence
- are aware of their expertise and knowledge and those of others
- consider theories that help to make sense of social need, disproportionality, and resources and assist in decision-making
- are thoughtful, and reflect on data (which includes actuarial data and clinical assessments) and theory, contributing to their development and refinement
- scrutinise and analyse data and information
- are mindful of how their own perspective, values and identity influences the way they see and understand the world.

Other relevant concepts are those of having a 'growth mindset' and 'professional curiosity':

- Practitioners with a growth mindset have a desire to explore, learn and understand, and to keep up to date with new developments – they are curious. They will reflect on and review their thinking, persist in the face of setbacks and obstacles, recognise the need to make consistent efforts to continuously develop, embrace challenges, learn from constructive feedback and find lessons and inspiration in others' success. They recognise that there may be different ways of doing things and are willing to explore different options.
- Phillips et al. (2022) have noted how in fields such as nursing, the concept of professional curiosity is used to encourage practitioners to stay abreast of the

Figure 3.5 The reflective, learning practitioner

latest developments and to engage with academic research and professional development. This is linked to a broader appreciation of the value of engagement with knowledge.

When inspecting youth justice services, the inspectorate pays attention to the extent to which a service is adhering to the evidence base and supporting its development through evaluation, and how well learning is communicated. Consideration is given to whether the service is explicit about the evidence base which underpins its vision and its plans and practices, and whether there is any work (actual or planned) to build on existing research, including opportunities for engaging researchers.

Relevant inspection standards

1.1.1 Is there an effective local vision and strategy for the delivery of a high-quality, personalised and responsive service for all children?

    a Does the YJS Management Board set the direction and strategy for the YJS, prioritising the quality of service and adherence to the evidence base?

1.4.4 Are analysis, evidence and learning used effectively to drive improvement?

    a Are service improvement plans supported through evaluation and development of the underlying evidence base?

    b Are the views of the children, their parents or carers, and other key stakeholders sought, analysed and used to review and improve the effectiveness of services?

    c Is learning communicated effectively?

Recent inspection reports have included examples where it was deemed that there was a strong use and application of evidence.

Use and application of evidence

Coventry

> The YJS approach to out-of-court work was based on a comprehensive analysis of the evidence-base, both national and local, in order to build a way of working which is integral to the city's long-term success in improving outcomes for children and protecting the public.
>
> (HM Inspectorate of Probation, 2023a)

Lincolnshire

> We were particularly impressed by in-depth understanding of the issues and challenges facing YJS children, predicated on the strong use of data and evaluation from internal and external sources and reports.
>
> (HM Inspectorate of Probation, 2023b)

Identify the critical evidence gaps

The evidence base should continually evolve, and to maximise the potential impact of research findings upon future policy and delivery, attention should be given to the critical evidence gaps. Research resources need to be maximised, which requires a strategic, joined-up and holistic approach to monitoring research activities – so who is doing what and when – and collating the evidence, identifying the most critical gaps and considering which questions can be answered in the short, medium and longer term, and who may be well placed to answer them, including any opportunities for collaboration. One of the challenges is keeping an eye on all the latest developments across the entire research community, so identifying the new, up-and-coming academics, while also being alert to relevant findings from other sectors. Alongside monitoring key publications and social media, it is important to build and maintain relationships across the research ecosystem, thinking about individuals, groups/networks, and organisations.

While the evidence base underpinning high-quality youth justice services has strengthened over time, it is notable that most research and evaluation studies within youth justice have lacked an economic component, with the consequence that robust evidence on both the costs and benefits of differing approaches and interventions is generally lacking. Progress is clearly required in terms of obtaining and using robust costs data, not least because resource pressures make it even more vital that funds are spent on approaches that provide the greatest possible economic and social return. More generally, there is scope for more projects with increased collaboration across analytical professions – potentially involving social researchers, economists, statisticians, operational researchers and data scientists.[12]

Consideration should also be given to the most appropriate outcome measures for impact evaluations, bearing in mind the limitations with proven reoffending data and the wide range of other measures that have been promoted and/or used. Attention needs to be paid to ensuring that these outcome measures are sufficiently timely, can be sufficiently tailored to the individual child (bearing in mind all the factors linked to desistance and pro-social development) and the support provided, and, ideally, are able to support robust claims of attribution.

Tailor methods and pay attention to the voice of the child

Having identified the critical evidence gaps, a focus is then required upon ensuing that the specified questions can be answered through well-designed and well-executed projects, with appropriate methodologies adopted. As noted above, there is room for a range of research methods, recognising that differing approaches can be highly complementary, while also giving careful consideration to the demands that will be placed upon the frontline and whether there are less resource-intensive ways of obtaining the necessary evidence.

When designing research projects, particular attention should be given to the voice of the child, and creating inclusive spaces where all views and perspectives are respected and valued (Harriott, 2023). After all, it would seem nonsensical to try to improve services without engaging and learning from those who have been in receipt of those services. Having experienced the services directly, children have unique 'lived' experience, which importantly can differ from the 'learned' experience of others. There is clear value in speaking early with children to ask them which approaches and methods they would find preferable for engaging them. Notably, there is now growing evidence regarding the benefits to using technology to help engage children and obtain their views (e.g. Kaufmann and Peil, 2020; Gibson, 2022), while being mindful of potential limitations from the 'digital divide' and issues around accessibility, usability and well-being. Technologies do of course continually evolve, and it is thus worth continually monitoring any new opportunities which they may provide.

These points apply equally to inspection activity; the inspectorate has to be mindful of the demands which result from inspection – both real and perceived – and a focus is required upon hearing the voices of children within all inspections to be able to fully understand their experiences, as exemplified within this video produced by Peer Power (2023). Collaborating with Peer Power leaders and young partners has aided the inspectorate's understanding of active and empowered participation and how to create meaningful participation opportunities which enable children to talk openly about their experiences.

When inspecting services, the inspectorate also pays attention to the extent to which the service itself is seeking, analysing, and using the views of children (and their parents or carers) to review and improve the effectiveness of delivery. There are potential benefits for both youth justice services and the children themselves from such involvement; the benefits for children can include feeling more respected, learning skills like problem-solving, decision-making, negotiation, listening and communication, having more self-confidence and self-esteem, and becoming more motivated to engage and succeed (Youth Justice Board, 2016).

However, the benefits of involvement can be squandered, and even reversed if the form of participation is poorly implemented. Building upon Arnstein's 'ladder of participation' (Arnstein, 1969), Hart (1992) divided different approaches into non-participation and degrees of participation, with the former encompassing manipulation, decoration and tokenism (see Figure 3.6). If the involvement of children feels like a tokenistic effort, or if

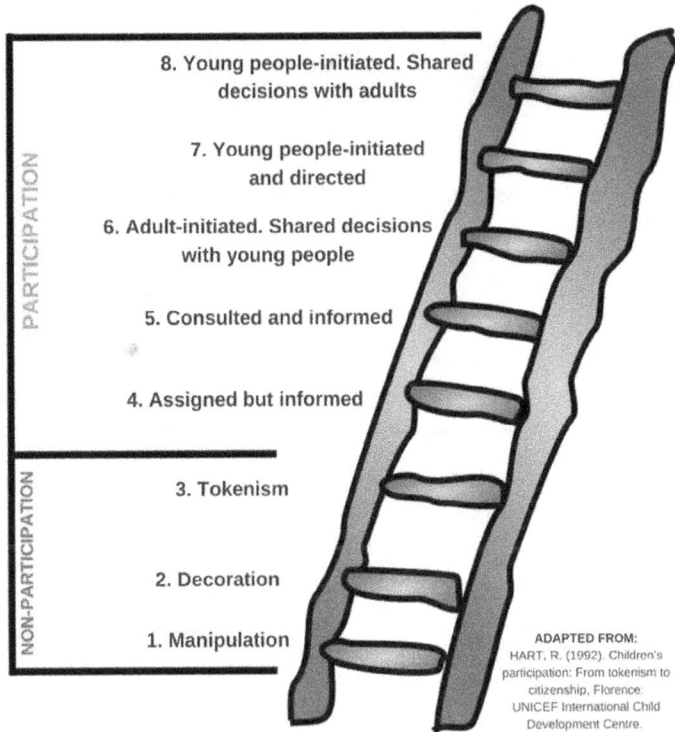

Figure 3.6 Hart's ladder of children's participation[13]

the process is frustrating and fruitless, then the initiative risks not just failing to achieve its aims but also alienating the children from potentially beneficial support.

There are now various guidance documents in place to help avoid such counter-productive impacts. For example, the Manchester Centre for Youth Studies has produced an engagement framework (2023) for the Participatory Youth Practice (PYP) framework highlighted previously. It is a strengths-based framework which sets out the following eight youth-led principles which were co-developed with children themselves:

- let them participate
- always unpick why
- acknowledge limited life chances
- avoid threats and sanctions
- help problem solve
- develop ambitions
- remember it's their choice
- afford them a fresh start.

Positively, the inspectorate has seen and reported on excellent approaches by individual youth justice services to involving children, and their parents or carers, and acting upon their feedback and input.

Involving children

Coventry

> The voice of children and their parents or carers is routinely gathered and features extensively in case work. A children's 'shadow' board (Through our Eyes) has been developed and the influence of this is evident in the work of the board.
>
> (HM Inspectorate of Probation, 2023a)

Swindon

> Swindon YJS values, collects, and proactively considers the views of children and their parents and carers. It gathers and captures their feedback in different ways, including an effective youth board, peer advocates, regular consultation events, surveys, audits, and end of intervention feedback. The service can show how, on many occasions, the contributions of children and their parents and carers have had a direct impact on informing service delivery. For instance, changes in the girl's intervention and the addition of a module in the weapons awareness programme. The 'village circle' initiative provides space for parents and carers to obtain support and provide insight into the quality of services their children are receiving. Irrespective of the number of parents attending, the sessions are never cancelled, and this is a credit to the service, its volunteers, and parenting workers.
>
> (HM Inspectorate of Probation, 2023c)

Support internal and external researchers

It was noted above that a research/evaluation culture is important for aligning evidence and practice, and that there should be a commitment to upskilling staff where required so that they have a sufficient understanding of the role of research and evaluation. Taking this further, it can be argued that supporting, co-producing or instigating research should be seen as a key part of the job, with clear links to professional learning, development and even career progression. After all, successful research projects involve much more than financial resources – they require: (i) the time of senior staff and engaged gate-keepers who can promote the research and facilitate access to practitioners, children, other key stakeholders and data; and (ii) a clear commitment from the research participants themselves.

In terms of data, greater regard should be given to ensuring that the data collated within core systems can support research activities, with a particular focus upon improving the availability and quality of costs data and a consideration of the potentially beneficial data held across agencies.

Focus on dissemination, engagement and impact

Expanding and strengthening the evidence base will of course be of limited value if no attention is then given to it. As Raynor (2018) states, 'finding evidence is not in itself the whole answer: persuading people that it is in their interests to pay attention to it is another challenge, and the nature of this challenge, and the uses and meanings of evidence, change over time'. It is certainly true to say that the importance given to research evidence can differ between individuals, between programmes of work, and over time. Furthermore, it needs to be recognised that while evidence and experience contribute to policy making, implementation and delivery, they sit alongside judgement, values, resources and political ideologies and interests. The complexities of these links have been highlighted by Baker (2008):

> The link between research and policy is complex. Evidence may contribute directly to problem-solving or may sometimes have a more indirect role in developing conceptual thinking. It is, however, only one of many influences on the formation of policy, and there will be times when political or financial imperatives take precedence ... Similarly, the link between evidence and practice is multifaceted rather than simply linear. The front-line delivery of services will be influenced by a range of factors, including practitioners' values, resource constraints and the responses of clients. Research can inform but not replace professional expertise – in fact, the latter will always be needed in order to determine how evidence can be best applied when working with individual young people.

Bearing in mind the differing drivers of change, there is a clear need to continually promote the value and importance of research evidence. After all, just because something

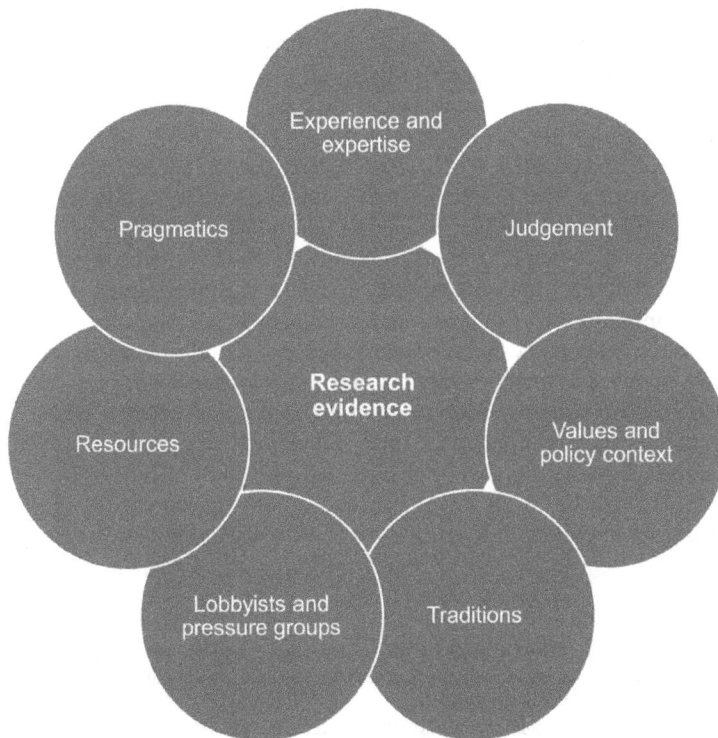

Figure 3.7 The drivers of youth justice policy and practice

makes intuitive sense and/or has political appeal, this does not mean that it will necessarily work, and there could even be unintended consequences. For successful 'knowledge translation' and evidence to be meaningfully used, impacting upon policy and practice, it needs to be reported in clear and accessible ways,[14] with tailoring to the specific audience and a focus on the key considerations and implications. A range of dissemination methods can be considered, including one-page summaries, factsheets, videos, animations, blogs, social media posts, workshops and training events. Further opportunities may also arise through technological advances, notably through new AI tools, while also thinking carefully about the potential limitations and dangers of such tools.

Going one step further, the concept of 'knowledge mobilisation' recognises the need for more than one-way dissemination and to think carefully about opportunities for meaningful engagement and interaction, helping to break down any divisions between 'evidence producers' and 'evidence consumers' (Boaz et al., 2023), and further embedding the evaluation culture highlighted above. To maximise the impact of research, Reed (2018) highlights the importance of engaging with empathy and humility to build connections, and trusting two-way relationships which then endure over time.

Conclusion

This chapter has set out the differing ways in which HM Inspectorate of Probation collaborates with academics and external researchers to review, develop and promote research evidence. Alignment between evidence and delivery is most likely to lead to improved outcomes for children, their families and the wider community; and the inspectorate looks to maximise the knowledge, experience and skills across the research community and produce as rounded and balanced a view as possible of the current evidence (combining research evidence with inspection evidence, and thinking about 'knowledge translation' and 'knowledge mobilisation'). These endeavours have been commended by key stakeholders (Phillips, 2022), with specific praise for the inspectorate's 'consistent combination of academic credibility and accessibility' (Raynor, 2022).

There are a number of challenges to building and utilising evidence, including a lack of practitioner time and resources, the unavailability of data, disjoints within the research community, and differing/competing drivers of change. To help overcome some of these challenges, the inspectorate examines whether individual youth justice services have an embedded research/evaluation culture, demonstrated through adherence to the evidence base, its further development through evaluation, and the communication of new learning and knowledge. To further drive an evidence-informed approach across the whole system, the inspectorate uses its voice to promote the value and importance of evidence, and to highlight the latest findings. Looking ahead, attention needs to be given to further opportunities for collaboration, and whether continuing technological developments open up new ways of filling evidence gaps, engaging children, and communicating/promoting research findings.

Notes

1 For more information on the history of the inspectorate and the types of youth justice inspection, see https://www.justiceinspectorates.gov.uk/hmiprobation/wp-content/uploads/sites/5/2023/10/The-history-of-HMI-Probation.pdf.
2 Section 37 of the Crime and Disorder Act 1998 states: 'It shall be the principal aim of the youth justice system to prevent offending by children and young persons'.
3 Figure adapted from Lundy, 2007.

4 For more information about Ketso Kits, see https://ketso.com/
5 For more information on KeyRing easy read reports, see https://www.keyring.org/cjs/easy-read-examples.
6 For more information about the Manchester Metropolitan University Q-Step programme, see https://www.mmu.ac.uk/qstep/
7 For more information about the Midlands Graduate School DTP, see https://warwick.ac.uk/fac/cross_fac/mgsdtp/
8 For more information on CAPE, see https://www.cape.ac.uk/
9 All the Academic Insights papers can be accessed here: https://www.justiceinspectorates.gov.uk/hmiprobation/research/academic-insights/.
10 The videos can be accessed here: https://www.justiceinspectorates.gov.uk/hmiprobation/research/reflections-from-research/.
11 Belcher et al. (2016) propose four main criteria: relevance, credibility, legitimacy and effectiveness. Others have set out more discrete criteria; see, for example Tracy (2010).
12 Within government, the cross-cutting 'Analysis Function' is seeking to increase collaboration across professions and to assist with the development of best practices.
13 Figure taken from https://www.mefirst.org.uk/resource/arnsteins-ladder-of-participation/
14 For example, the inspectorate has produced online evidence webpages which summarise key research findings, presenting them as concisely as possible – see https://www.justiceinspectorates.gov.uk/hmiprobation/research/the-evidence-base-youth-offending-services/.

References

Arnstein, S.R. (1969). A ladder of citizen participation. *Journal of the American Planning Association*, 35(4), 216–224.
Baker, K. (2008). Evidence-based policy and practice (EBPP). In Goldson, B. (ed.) *Dictionary of youth justice*. Cullompton: Willan Publishing.
Belcher, B.M., Rasmussen, K.E., Kemshaw, M.R. and Zornes, D.A. (2016). Defining and assessing research quality in a transdisciplinary context. *Research Evaluation*, 25(1), 1–17.
Boaz, A., Fitzsimons, B., Meakin, B., Muirhead, S., Williams, C., Weatherley, M., Knapp, M., Smith, L., Langley, J., Kendrick, H., Malley, J. and Bauer, A. (2023). Do research–practice partnerships offer a promising approach to producing research that improves social care practice and outcomes? *Journal of Long-Term Care*, 13 October, pp. 241–248. doi:10.31389/jltc.190
Breckon, J. and Dodson, J. (2016). Using evidence: What works? A discussion paper. London: Alliance for Useful Evidence.
Creaney, S. (2014). The benefits of participation for young offenders. *Safer Communities*, 13(3), 126–132.
Dix, H. and Meade, J. (2023). The IDEAS approach to effective practice in youth justice. HM Inspectorate of Probation Academic Insights, 2023/05. Manchester: HM Inspectorate of Probation.
Everitt, A. (2002). Research and development in social work. In Adams, R., Dominelli, L. and Payne, M. (eds.) *Social work: Themes, issues and critical debates*. 2nd edn. Basingstoke: Palgrave/Open University, pp. 109–116.
Fox, C. and Albertson, K. (2020). Innovation and the evidence base. HM Inspectorate of Probation Academic Insights, 2020/01. Manchester: HM Inspectorate of Probation.
Gibson, K. (2022). Bridging the digital divide: Reflections on using WhatsApp instant messenger interviews in youth research. *Qualitative Research in Psychology*, 19(3), 611–631.
Government Office for Science (2013). *Engaging with academics: How to further strengthen open policy making*. London: Department for Business, Innovation and Skills.
Harriott, P. (2023). Getting ready for culture change: A personal narrative. *Prison Service Journal*, 269, 4–7.
Hart, D. and Thompson, C. (2009). *Young people's participation in the youth justice system*. London: National Children's Bureau.

Hart, R. (1992). Children's participation: From tokenism to citizenship. Papers inness 92/6. Innocenti essay. New York: UNICEF.

Health Service Executive (2021). *Knowledge translation, dissemination, and impact: A practical guide for researchers.* Dublin: HSE.

HM Government (2021). *Government Functional Standard. GovS 010: Analysis.* London: HM Government.

HM Inspectorate of Probation (2019). *Service user engagement strategy 2019–2022.* Manchester: HM Inspectorate of Probation.

HM Inspectorate of Probation (2021). Building the evidence base for high-quality probation services: The role of probation providers. HM Inspectorate of Probation Research & Analysis Bulletin 2021/01. Manchester: HM Inspectorate of Probation.

HM Inspectorate of Probation (2022). *Education training and employment in youth offending teams: Easy read report.* Manchester: HM Inspectorate of Probation.

HM Inspectorate of Probation (2023a). *An inspection of youth offending services in Coventry.* Manchester: HM Inspectorate of Probation.

HM Inspectorate of Probation (2023b). *An inspection of youth offending services in Lincolnshire.* Manchester: HM Inspectorate of Probation.

HM Inspectorate of Probation (2023c). *An inspection of youth offending services in Swindon.* Manchester: HM Inspectorate of Probation.

HM Treasury (2020). *Magenta Book: Central government guidance on evaluation.* London: HM Treasury.

Jørgensen, T., Seim, S. and Njøs, B.M. (2023). How children and young people understand and experience individual participation in social services for children and young people: A synthesis of qualitative studies. *European Journal of Social Work.* doi:10.1080/13691457.2023.2256490.

Kaufmann, K. and Peil, C. (2020). The mobile instant messaging interview (MIMI): Using WhatsApp to enhance self-reporting and explore media usage in situ. *Mobile Media & Communication*, 8(2), 229–246.

Lundy, L. (2007). 'Voice' is not enough: Conceptualising Article 12 of the United Nations Convention on the Rights of the Child. *British Educational Research Journal*, 33(6), 927–942.

Manchester Centre for Youth Studies (2023). *Participatory youth practice: Engagement framework.* Manchester: Manchester Metropolitan University.

Marshall, D., Nisbet, A. and Gray, P. (2023). The implementation and delivery of community resolutions: The role of youth offending services. HM Inspectorate of Probation Research & Analysis Bulletin 2023/01. Manchester: HM Inspectorate of Probation.

Maruna, S. and Mann, R. (2019). Reconciling 'desistance' and 'what works'. HM Inspectorate of Probation Academic Insights 2019/01. Manchester: HM Inspectorate of Probation.

Ministry of Justice (2020). Areas of research interest. London: Ministry of Justice.

Ministry of Justice (2019). Standards for children in the youth justice system 2019. London: Ministry of Justice.

Ministry of Justice (2023). Evaluation & prototyping strategy. London: Ministry of Justice.

Morgan, K., Steenmans, I., Tennant, G. and Green, R. (2022). *Engaging with Evidence Toolkit: A practical resource to strengthen capabilities for evidence use and expert engagement.* London: Nesta.

Munro, E. (2010). *The Munro Review of Child Protection: Final report – A child-centred system.* London: Department for Education.

National Audit Office (2021). *Evaluating government spending.* London: National Audit Office.

National Youth Agency (2011). *Participation in youth justice: Measuring impact and effectiveness.* Leicester: National Youth Agency.

Nurse, P. (2015). *Ensuring a successful UK research endeavour: A review of the UK research councils.* London: Department for Business, Innovation & Skills.

Peer Power (2023). *How do you feel about your youth justice service?* [Film]. Available at: https://f.io/6Pw8-Alq (Accessed: 8 April 2024).

Phillips, J. (2021). *Understanding the impact of inspection on probation*. Sheffield: Sheffield Hallam University Helena Kennedy Centre for International Justice.

Phillips, J., Ainslie, S., Fowler, A. and Westaby, C. (2022). Putting professional curiosity into practice. HM Inspectorate of Probation Academic Insights 2022/07. Manchester: HM Inspectorate of Probation.

Pleysier, S. and Kilkelly, U. (2023). The right to participation in youth justice research. *Youth Justice*. doi:10.1177/14732254231208323.

Raynor, P. (2018). From 'nothing works' to 'post-truth': The rise and fall of evidence in British probation. *European Journal of Probation*, 10(1), 59–75.

Raynor, P. (2020). Evidence versus politics in British probation. *Forensic Science International: Mind and Law*, 1.

Raynor, P. (2022). What works in promoting 'what works'? A comment on Sanders, Jones and Briggs. *Probation Journal*, 69(2), 235–244.

Reed, M. (2018). *The research impact handbook*. 2nd edn. Fast Track Impact. https://www. fasttrackimpact.com.

Sasse, T. and Haddon, C. (2018). *How government can work with academia*. London: Institute for Government.

Shute, S. (2013). On the outside looking in: Reflections on the role of inspection in driving up quality in the criminal justice system. *The Modern Law Review*, 76(3), 494–528.

Smithson, H. and Gray, P. (2021). Supporting children's meaningful participation in the youth justice system. HM Inspectorate of Probation Academic Insights 2021/10. Manchester: HM Inspectorate of Probation.

Smith-Yau, W. (2017). *Academic/YOT partnership working guide*. London: Youth Justice Board.

Tracy, S.J. (2010). Qualitative quality: Eight 'big-tent' criteria for excellent qualitative research. *Qualitative Inquiry*, 16(10), 837–851.

Ugwudike, P. and Morgan, G. (2019). Bridging the gap between research and frontline youth justice practice. *Criminology & Criminal Justice*, 19(2), 232–253.

User Voice (2021). *'Black is guilty in their eyes'. Experiences of black and mixed heritage boys in youth justice services*. London: User Voice.

User Voice (2022). *'They don't help with the real life problems': Children's experiences of education, training and employment in youth justice services*. London: User Voice.

Youth Justice Board (2016). *Participation strategy: Giving young people a voice in youth justice*. London: Youth Justice Board.

4   Youth Justice Still Live! The centrality of relationships to the maintenance of a youth justice community of practice in challenging times and beyond

Sue Bond-Taylor

Objectives

By the end of this chapter, you should be able to:

- Explore how knowledge and skills partnerships in youth justice can provide support for both partners through sector challenges.
- Appreciate how knowledge exchange collaborations can effectively bridge critical and applied criminologies.
- Understand how a community of practice model can be used to establish and maintain relationships within knowledge exchange initiatives.
- Reflect upon how collaborative delivery models can promote flexible pedagogies which enhance graduate employability.

Introduction

This chapter provides an account of an educational development project which was established in 2014/15 to test the potential of collaborative approaches to curriculum design and delivery involving staff, students and local youth justice professionals. The *Youth Justice Live!* project led to the creation of a second year undergraduate Youth Justice module, and to a sustainable and lasting relationship with the Youth Offending Service (YOS) in Lincolnshire. The project was designed to respond to the emerging contexts of the higher education sector as it became increasingly subject to government agendas around careers, employability and skills. It was grounded in the principles of 'student as producer' which have been institutionally embedded at the University of Lincoln (Strudwick, 2017), as a challenge to HE power hierarchies which position students as mere *consumers* of HE. Initially conceived as a community of practice (CoP), this initiative prioritised relational approaches to learning, grounded in slow scholarship, and has supported the development of flexible pedagogies.

Almost a decade on, this chapter provides some reflection upon the development of debates around graduate employability and skills, and considers how this looks for students of youth justice and Criminology/Criminal Justice more broadly. I explore the longevity of the outcomes of this project, how it has been embedded and sustained over time, and how it has been shaped by unforeseen contexts and challenges beyond our control. The chapter makes use of some small-scale survey data to consider the experiences of both the undergraduate students undertaking the module, and the youth justice

DOI: 10.4324/9781003411192-5

professionals who support its delivery, to reflect upon its value and potential for future development.

Flexible pedagogies in a community of practice

Youth Justice Live! was established through funding from the University of Lincoln's internal Educational Development Fund in 2014/15. There was no intention within the funding proposal to develop a formal partnership with the Youth Offending Service, such as a knowledge transfer partnership agreement or a memorandum of understanding. Rather they were invited to be part of a more malleable collaborative curriculum design approach. As the lead academic, I had already validated a broad skeleton Youth Justice module in order to meet the quality assurance processes and timescale, and this now needed some flesh on the bones. The engagement of key 'stakeholders', i.e. the YOS and University of Lincoln students (including undergraduate students from years 1–3 and a Ph.D. student), was therefore seen as integral to exploring how we might come together to develop and deliver the module.

The lead academic and Ph.D. student initially selected a Community of Practice model as there was evidence that this could be used to promote social and situated learning (Lave and Wenger, 1991) and to deliver learning experiences which generate shared meaning making in a higher education setting (Lea, 2005). We drew upon the conceptualisation of the Community of Practice produced by Wenger et al. (2002:4) as being 'groups of people who share a concern, a set of problems, or a passion about a topic, and who deepen their knowledge and expertise in this area by interacting on an ongoing basis'. This resonated with the knowledge exchange objectives of the project, so that the Community of Practice was constructed as a space for collaboration in designing the module, and for the ongoing learning in its subsequent delivery.

Hart et al. (2013) have explored the potential complexity in understandings of how the Community of Practice model maps onto knowledge exchange partnerships between universities and community organisations. They note the lack of clear consensus on what a Community of Practice is, how it should be formed (with membership orchestrated deliberately or organically), how power is manifested in the relationships within the CoP, and what effectiveness might look like. I have previously written in more detail about the development of the Youth Justice Live! module and the ways in which the Community of Practice model was central to this (Bond-Taylor and Davies, 2020). Of particular importance and worth reiterating here was the intention to foster non-hierarchical relationships, interdisciplinary and cross-sector understandings, and the co-production of knowledge, reflecting our commitment to a 'slow scholarship' (Mountz et al., 2015) based in an ethics of care (Bozalek et al., 2014; Keeling, 2014). Therefore, rather than an instructivist approach to knowledge creation, this encouraged a 'two-way' process for sharing knowledge, skills and information, and reinforced the development of a supportive and secure community environment within which students were also given the power to become the *producers* of knowledge rather than passive consumers of it (Neary and Winn, 2009).

The Youth Justice Live! Community of Practice model also provided fertile ground for embedding Ryan and Tilbury's (2013) *flexible pedagogies* (Bond-Taylor and Davies, 2020). They identified six 'new pedagogical ideas' for a flexible HE sector, which have particular resonance for criminal justice education contexts. Whilst these were not the focus of the original curriculum design process, we saw opportunities to embed these principles within the module and have used them as a point of reference during its ongoing development. These six pedagogical ideas were:

Learner empowerment, which sits at the centre of the other five ideas and refers to approaches which involve students in their own learning, including 'processes of co-creation that challenge learning relationships and the power frames that underpin them' (Ryan and Tilbury, 2013:5). Criminology as a subject is founded in questions of power and control. Criminal justice educators therefore need to be reflexive about their own contributions to power hierarchies and inequalities in ways which empower students to direct the learning within and beyond the classroom.

Future-facing education is described as refocusing learning in ways which emphasise the potential for change 'that help people to consider prospects and hopes for the future' (ibid.). The politicisation of criminal justice and youth justice in particular, means that policies can tend to go around in circles, regurgitating previous failed strategies because of their populist appeal, and resulting in a 'nothing works' pessimism (Martinson, 1974). Reflecting on the potential for alternative, more hopeful futures for the system as a whole, and for individual service users more specifically, is a valuable attribute for a criminal justice workforce.

Decolonising education advocates for 'deconstructing dominant pedagogical frames that promote only Western world views' (ibid.) so as to promote cultural sensitivity and to reflect upon how colonial structures have shaped the discipline and our taken for granted concepts and knowledge. This is of particular resonance for criminal justice education because the history of criminal justice runs in parallel to the history of oppression of minority groups, the use of criminal law to maintain social control and the exclusion and delegitimisation of certain voices and experiences from the dialogue (including notably those subject to punishment and incarceration) (Saleh-Hanna et al., 2023).

Transformative capabilities as a pedagogical idea refers to a 'whole person' (ibid.) emphasis on capabilities, agency and competence as graduate attributes, rather than the more narrow skills agenda. If students are to enter employment in a system which has a reputation for enacting harm, for eroding human rights and social justice, and for corruption and collective forms of neglect, it seems to be even more important that they emerge as graduates who can think independently, and envision how they can levy forms of resistance to harmful practice and make positive changes within the machinery of criminal justice processes. Critical criminological education therefore plays an important role in making visible the lived experiences of those subject to harm, emphasising the structural conditions producing such harms, an instilling a commitment to confronting and challenging systems of injustice (Barton et al., 2019).

Crossing boundaries promotes opportunities for greater 'interdisciplinary, inter-professional and cross-sector learning' (ibid.) which support collaboration rather than siloed working shaped by disciplinary or institutional bias and conflict. Failure to share information, knowledge and expertise across the public sector has been identified as a central factor in service delivery failure (Bundred, 2006), and was the primary criticism in the Audit Commission's *Misspent Youth* report in 1996 which informed the development of the 'new youth justice' via the Crime & Disorder Act 1998. Consequently, this is integral to youth justice education given the multi-agency settings, growth of the multi-agency nature of youth offending services, and the expansion of multi-agency partnerships in managing risk and preventing harm.

Social learning, finally, expands the spaces in which learning happens beyond the walls of the classroom and the formal curriculum, to promote learning through dialogue and interactions. These can happen 'in addition to (or in tandem with) the interactions triggered within the formal curriculum' (Ryan and Tilbury, 2013:26), and increasingly make use of digital as well as real world connections. These interactions can also provide students with an opportunity to *apply* their knowledge in a form of 'academic practice as learning' as Strudwick (2019:1) has described in relation to police involvement in curriculum design and delivery.

Through the establishment of the Community of Practice and the collaborative curriculum design process, which included academic staff, students and youth justice professionals, this facilitated learner empowerment through the decentering of the lecturer as 'expert' and the reordering of traditional knowledge hierarchies. Students witness their lecturer learning alongside them in an exchange of knowledge and perspectives (including valuing those of students) that also entails a crossing of boundaries between theory and practice, different disciplinary understandings, political positions and professional identities. It is inherently future-facing as we discuss current practice but also the horizons of service development, shifts in government policy, and the aspirations of our students to connect with this future in their career plans. The CoP offers a unique opportunity to challenge student preconceptions and assumptions about what 'youth' and 'justice' might look like and to collectively ask the question: how can *we* do this better? Through this, students come to see their transformative potential and identify opportunities for volunteering within the service, and in the longer term to work in the sector and effect important changes. By adopting this flexible curriculum design, developed jointly with key youth justice professionals, it has been envisaged that we might better prepare students for the reality of working within this form of dynamic, multi-faceted role.

Finally, the module has incorporated social learning opportunities for students as they network and connect in the classroom with YOS staff. For students learning about the practice of youth justice therefore, the opportunities afforded by YOS engagement in the classroom include the potential for students to learn vicariously from the accounts of those staff and the opportunity to experience directly the everyday tasks that YOS officers engage in, including completing risk assessments within certain tools, designing intervention plans, and identifying red flags for safeguarding and exploitation concerns.

Almost a decade later, the module has evolved and established a regular delivery format based on a collaborative approach to teaching. For nine out of the twelve teaching weeks, the Youth Offending Service provides a different member of staff (or sometimes two), who are working in a role relevant to that week's workshop theme, to co-deliver the session with the lecturer. The classes run as two-hour interactive workshops, with a hands-on practical element to them being provided by youth justice professional's input. The team also provides a case study based on their case files, which is examined weekly to explore relevant issues and bring to life the issues discussed through a real-world example. Beyond the module, this relationship has also facilitated support for final year dissertation projects, for example providing service data, or interview participants for student research. The service is able to advertise its volunteering or paid employment vacancies to an interested pool of students, and therefore to fill some gaps in its manpower.

Over the course of this period, this community of practice has faced unexpected challenges in the wider social contexts, political and economic conditions and sector-specific threats and opportunities. This next section details three such challenging contexts which have both shaped the partnership and benefited from this long-term relationship in addressing these challenges head on. These include:

1   The reform and localisation of youth justice practice
2   The employability agenda and programme regulation in HE
3   The Covid-19 pandemic.

Challenging times 1: Localisation and normlessness in youth justice practice

The period of time during which this knowledge exchange relationship has been operating has been characterised by considerable shifts and developments in policy and practice in the youth justice sectors. The last decade in youth justice has seen significant change as a result of the austerity politics ushered in by the Conservative-led coalition government in 2010. The financial constraints of austerity prompted cuts to local authority budgets resulting in a clear reduction in spending upon universal youth services and preventative work with those 'at risk' (Creaney and Smith, 2014). It also generated conversations about how youth justice spending could be reduced. This 'opened up space for dialogue around costly, net widening, criminalizing, counterproductive and damaging institutional practices' (Yates, 2012:436). These 'risk'-focused net-widening interventions have included, for example: police targets which encouraged the arrest of children for minor offences; the use of civil sanctions for tackling antisocial behaviour, which then left young people open to policing and criminalisation; and the development of the Scaled Approach to intervention planning which generated a ladder of sentence options that the courts used in an escalatory manner as a response to perceived increases in 'risk'. By contrast, these new discourses informed practices underpinned by decriminalisation, contraction of the system and the development of diversionary and decarcerative strategies (Yates, 2012). The introduction of the Legal Aid, Sentencing and Punishment of Offenders Act (LASPO) 2012 was a significant step in this direction, as it allowed for more localised approaches to delivering youth offending services. It also encouraged more flexibility in offering out of court disposals, importantly reforming the cautioning system to permit repeat cautioning in place of the more restrictive Reprimand and Final Warning scheme.

Alongside all of this there has been a growing movement in developing 'Child First' approaches to youth justice (Haines and Case, 2015; Case and Browning, 2021) which prioritise children's rights. This movement was initially seen more from the ground up within local youth justice teams, but more recently has been included in Youth Justice Board strategic planning as a guiding principle underpinning the standards for children in the youth justice system (YJB, 2019). Across England and Wales, therefore, Youth Offending Teams have taken the opportunity presented by these concurrent contexts to redesign their services for young people who come into conflict with the criminal law (Gray and Smith 2019). This has led to a period of increasing diversity and creativity of responses reflecting local priorities, politics and needs of the community, but it has also been described as a period of normlessness, producing a level of 'incoherence and divergence approaching chaos' (Haines and Case, 2018:145), with a lack of consistency across the jurisdiction, creating a postcode lottery for young people who come into contact with youth justice services.

In Lincolnshire, since the outset of the Youth Justice Live! Partnership, the service has shifted from being a Youth Offending Service located within the Community Safety team of the local authority, to the new expanded Future4Me service housed in the Children's Services team, providing wraparound early help support, outreach and diversion for children at risk alongside statutory youth justice services. In 2017, in response to the new opportunities for local variation created by LASPO 2012, and in collaboration with Lincolnshire Police, the Future4Me service developed a new way of responding to young people who come to the attention of the police as a result of their behaviour. The new Joint Diversionary Panel (JDP) provided an out of court decision-making forum, and the accompanying new Youth Restorative Intervention (YRI) provided a non-statutory disposal within the county to address the needs of the young person without unnecessarily burdening them with a criminal record (Bond-Taylor, 2021). Building upon this, they later devised a specialist decision-making panel for harmful sexual behaviours. More recently a flagship Complex Needs Services has been developed as an integrated partnership between Lincolnshire Partnership NHS Foundation Trust (LPFT), Lincolnshire County Council (Children's Services), as well as education and youth offending services. This aims to provide holistic, trauma-informed support to young people who are at risk of criminalisation, exploitation and homelessness. They were also selected under the Department for Education's (DfE) Children's Social Care Partner in Practice Programme as one of three local authorities to develop and pilot a new bespoke local assessment tool for their statutory as well as out of court cases, in place of the YJB approved AssetPlus (Bartasevicius et al., 2020).

The creativity and coherence of these local youth justice innovations within the service in Lincolnshire is clear to see. However, when compared to the diverse practices in other local authorities, it only serves to illuminate the inconsistencies in youth justice service design at a national level, and the 'hotchpotch of punitive and welfarist approaches' (Case et al., 2015:100) to youth justice that can be seen across England and Wales.

The Youth Justice Live! Partnership has proved to be valuable during this period of change in two ways:

First, the service has been able to draw upon the support of the academic researcher to provide consultancy and evaluation, to evidence the successful outcomes of the service developments (Bond-Taylor, 2021). In addition to more formal and contractual consultancy arrangements, the academic support can be characterised as a 'critical friend', discussing ideas, evidence and methods for developing and monitoring practice. This can be seen as an important means of anchoring the service within a clear set of values, principles and objectives, as an antidote to the 'chaos' and 'normlessness' that might lead to less clarity of direction during this period of significant change. It is also an opportunity to keep challenging the service to develop in progressive and exciting ways, even where it has been rated as Outstanding; for example, most recently in developing attempts to promote children's participation and voice as a core element of 'child first' justice, the service has developed more robust requirements to contact the young person and ensure their views are considered by the Joint Diversionary Panel, as well as introducing 'expert by experience' advisors.

Second, and from the educational perspective, the existence of this knowledge exchange partnership has been fundamental in ensuring that the content of the module and student learning remains up to date, and reflects the local variations in practice which do not necessarily appear in academic texts. Each year, as we prepare for delivery of the module, it requires reflection upon what is different, what changes are in progress, and the reasons and rationale for these. This is invaluable for the academic with research interests in youth justice, so as to keep up with these local developments. By being able to include this learning in the module, we are also better able to prepare students who would like to pursue a career in youth justice or other services that work in multi-agency settings within the local community.

Challenging times 2: Employability, capabilities and experiential learning in youth justice education

Universities have for some time now been subject to growing pressure to improve 'employability' outcomes of graduates, as a means to demonstrate value for money and thereby justify high levels of student debt. Jameson et al. (2012) highlighted this emerging trend and considered the implications this might have for maintaining academic integrity and autonomy. They describe the creeping cross-party expansion of an employability agenda for HE through a number of policies and practices, including the inclusion of 'key employability skills' within the Quality Assurance Agency for Higher Education (QAA) subject benchmarks for all undergraduate degrees following the Dearing Report in 1997, the linking of employability outcomes with funding provision in the Labour government's 2009 HE 'Higher Ambitions' framework published in November 2009, the Conservative/ Liberal coalition's Minister for Universities and Science requirement for universities to publish 'employability statements' and the targeted investment in priority subjects following the Browne Review in 2010 (Jameson et al., 2012).

More recently, under the Conservative government, the Higher Education and Research Act 2017 has established mechanisms for imposing tighter controls over the sector through its creation of the Office for Students, and the 'Securing student success: Regulatory framework for higher education in England' (Office for Students, 2022) which provides a set of registration requirements for HE programme providers that the OfS monitors, accompanied by the threat of licence withdrawal and course closure. The B.3. condition of registration requires programme providers to ensure good student outcomes, which means students 'progressing into managerial or professional employment, or further study' (Office for Students, 2022:109). However, this language remains ambiguous and the way in which this might be determined, the definitions of 'professional' and the extent to which these are related to graduate salaries are unclear at the moment. Universities UK have warned that graduate jobs are difficult to define and recommended that the OfS should also reflect graduate views of their own success, as well as considering the value of university courses to society (Dickinson, 2022).

The differences in the value of a programme of study to the economy, to society, to the individual's bank balance, compared to their wellbeing and satisfaction is particularly marked for programmes that tend to feed the public sector job market, where pay has remained stagnant during the period of austerity. And this may raise further ethical dilemmas for critical academics who have historically highlighted some of the oppressive aspects of state institutions. This is especially notable in Criminology, as Jameson et al. (2012:29) have identified:

> For these criminologists, who would see ethical and political dimensions as central to any criminological debates, Becker's (1967) call to arms, which challenged academics to consider 'Whose side are we on?' still resonates, making collaboration in the academic arena with some employers and practitioners potentially problematic.

As Barton et al. (2019) have explored, if the goal of critical criminology is the pursuit of social justice, then criminology graduates could bring huge value to the very criminal justice organisations that are the subject of criminological critique, and in particular to the often vulnerable people who are caught up within them, but only if they receive an education which goes beyond organisational training, and which allows them to develop critical understanding, empathy, imagination and the motivation to take risks and effect change.

If criminology academics have been wary of integrating too much practice material into their programmes, state appointed training providers have equally omitted some of the wider theoretical and historical contexts to the practice. Hester and Case (2010) have described the ways that youth justice education in particular has become dichotomised, with a clear distinction between the vocational training which developed alongside the Youth Justice Board's National Qualifications Framework, and the academic youth justice courses taught to undergraduates within university degrees. They accuse the former of having been atheoretical, managerialist, and practical/vocational in focus, failing to generate critical thinkers capable of reflecting on youth justice practice at the micro or macro levels. The latter, however conversely risks being overly critical of criminal justice agencies and institutions and inadequately incorporating the practice elements of youth justice practice which graduates would be faced with upon entry to the youth justice workforce. They therefore advocate a synthesised curriculum which facilitates both employer engagement and 'academic integrity'. Bringing together these two elements provides students with opportunities for both critical and reflective understandings of the contexts of youth justice, and applied knowledge and experience of current youth justice systems, models and practices. This, they argue, would create a workforce of 'informed practitioners' capable of meeting the challenges of the contemporary youth justice system, and to be well placed to help shape its future development.

Alternative models of delivering employability education are therefore advocated, based on more holistic and value driven approaches. Speight et al.'s (2013:123) Learner Development Model emphasises learning for employability through the academic discipline – as a capabilities approach, rather than more narrowly focused skills:

> Employability reconceptualized is preparation for life rather than a specific job, it is about capabilities rather than specific skills, and about being rather than having. Several studies have challenged the idea that universities can or should teach employability 'skills' (Cranmer, 2006). We would have sympathy with such arguments, but counter that it is in the fostering of 'epistemic values', qualities and dispositions or capabilities that higher education curriculum and pedagogy can contribute to the production of life-wide and -long learners.

The Youth Justice Live! module aims to provide this synthesised education, in which critical and theoretical perspectives are seen as the mechanism to develop reflective practice, and thus to improve outcomes for young people. Developing our graduates as future 'informed practitioners' and more broadly as life-long/life-wide learners who are curious and careful in their work, can therefore support us to meet the registration conditions of the OfS without losing the academic integrity of the programme.

One way that university programmes are encouraged to add employability dimensions to criminal justice education is through incorporating Experiential Learning Opportunities for students. George et al. (2015:471) have noted the particular relevance of this for more applied criminal justice programmes, arguing that 'Preparing students to become practitioners or researchers in the criminal justice system necessitates that they be actively involved with the field in a hands-on, meaningful way'. They provide examples of ELOs including internships, field trips, service learning and research projects (George et al., 2015). Yet there are logistical challenges in delivering these within undergraduate degree programmes with large numbers of students enrolled, and in the context of conservative approaches to risk assessment around student engagement with secure environments and 'dangerous' offenders.

Moreover, experiential learning relating to criminal justice institutions raises particular ethical challenges regarding the privacy and vulnerability of those in the space, who are subject to criminal justice interventions. This is especially prevalent in the context of prison visits, where the indignity of coming under the gaze of the student group has been identified (Meisel, 2008) and is particularly problematic for children in conflict with the law and the criminal justice system, given the additional safeguarding requirements and legal protections of their anonymity. There is also the potential for the visit to be highly scripted and regulated, merely reinforcing misconceptions about prison life and obscuring the experiences of prisoners (Piché and Walby, 2010). For some therefore, prison visits cannot be justified on the basis of their pedagogic value or potential to effect attitudinal changes (see Long et al., 2018, for further discussion of the evidence).

Miner-Romanoff (2014) helpfully suggests the educational potential of experiential learning *at a distance*, making use of digital technologies to generate proximity between students and criminal justice service users. Such vicarious learning experience avoids many of the logistical and ethical dilemmas, but still generates some of the benefits of direct experiential learning opportunities, including improved understanding, ability to connect theory and practice, and greater empathy for criminal justice service users (ibid.).

The Youth Justice Live! module has made use of the knowledge exchange partnership to establish opportunities for experiential learning within the classroom through the direct interactions with the visiting YOS professionals each week. Through the accounts they provide of challenges faced, cases they have worked on and the young people they have encountered, students can vicariously experience the reality of youth justice practice. What remain lacking from this learning to date are the voices and experiences of the young people themselves, and in future, as part of our collective efforts to promote children's voice and participation rights within our work, we hope to explore how this might be achieved, ethically and remaining at a suitable distance to safeguard young people.

Challenging times 3: Covid-19 pandemic and lockdown learning

From a HE perspective, the Covid-19 pandemic generated significant challenges which we needed to overcome in order to maintain our standards of education for our students during the lockdown periods, but also in responding to the long-lasting changes to education and student behaviour resulting from that period. The initial lockdown in the spring of 2020 resulted in the implementation of emergency remote learning approaches such as e-learning, distance learning and virtual learning, required to limit physical contact between teachers and students (Aristovnik et al., 2023), with the remainder of the academic year being delivered online. The academic year 20/21 began with some optimism that we might be able to return to the classroom, but with the need to plan for online provision in case of subsequent lockdowns. Even when we were permitted to be in the classroom, student rates of absence due to illness or self-isolation requirements meant that the format didn't work as planned. By the second semester when the Youth Justice Live! module was taught, it was clear that a digital delivery format was going to be needed, but that the existing timetable of sessions would not be effective.

At that point in time, students attended a one-hour in-person lecture in which the academic provided the theory and context for the module, followed by a two-hour workshop (repeated to two groups) co-delivered with a YOS colleague. For 20/21 this was changed so that the theory was delivered asynchronously via a bank of pre-recorded 'bitesized' video lectures for students to watch in their own time. These videos could also be shared with the YOS visitors, which proved valuable both in session preparations and in supporting the continuing professional development of the staff. This freed up the timetabled hour for an online lecture as the key contact time with the YOS professional each week, which made best use of their valuable time. Our case study, which we had previously discussed in the classroom each week to highlight aspects relevant to the week's topic, was instead hosted online in Talis Elevate, a collaborative reading software to share, annotate and discuss the case study remotely. YOS colleagues were able to access this and see what students were posting, as well as to add their own responses. Each week ended with an additional hour of online seminar for the lecturer to catch up with the students, check understanding and ensure they had completed activities set for their independent learning (see Bond-Taylor, 2021 for more on the detail of the digital re-envisioning of the module).

At the same time of course, the youth offending sector had its own Covid-19 crisis in the workplace to attend to, including prioritising complex safeguarding issues, with the inequalities experienced by the most vulnerable and 'high risk' children being exacerbated during the pandemic (Price et al., 2023). They also had to rapidly adapt their service delivery to accommodate social distancing and implement remote technologies for delivering supervision and interventions with young people on court orders (Gray et al., 2022). It is testament to the strong relationships established over the previous years that the youth justice professionals were willing to switch to our new digital remote learning platform, and adapt their usual session plans to new formats. They were unfazed by the challenges posed by students' poor attendance or reluctance to switch their cameras on. The Community of Practice at this point was committed to the shared goal of problem solving how to keep the module running, in its collaborative format, in these difficult circumstances. The legacy of the pandemic for HE has been in the form of both positive and negative impacts. The development of new digital competencies amongst staff and students has supported more creative, blended learning approaches that we have tried to retain where they add value to student's learning (the bitesized lectures and collaborative reading software have remained). However, the ongoing impact of the interruption of student education during the pandemic has been to negatively impact student's attendance rates and their confidence in class. These produce challenging contexts into which to bring visiting professionals on the module, and so collaborative approaches to find shared solutions have been vital and constitute an ongoing task.

Experiences of students and YOS professionals

Students' perspectives

Student reflections on the module highlight some of the benefits to them in terms of employability. A student-led survey of graduates and continuing students who had completed the module was undertaken in the summer of 2022, and although response rates were disappointing (13 responses including 4 just finishing the year 2 module, 6 graduating students and 3 alumni), they do reveal some of the benefits to students of this model of co-delivery. These included in the first instance learning that this career pathway even exists – 84% agreed that the module improved their awareness of youth justice careers.

> ...the module outlined the various settings that the youth justice sector work in, which I was previously unaware of such as secure children's homes and training centres.

> It allowed me to understand the system and discover avenues for careers I didn't know existed.

This appears to be at least in part as a result of the students reflecting upon the learning achieved from having the practitioners in the classroom, which would not have been acquired if delivered only by a university academic. 77% of participants were consequently interested in pursuing a career in youth justice.

> The youth justice module had a significant impact on my aspirations ... it has given me an appreciation towards youth services.

> I feel more comfortable working in the youth justice sector since the Youth Justice Live! module, the practitioners coming into the workshops reaffirmed my choice to work within this sector.

Whilst broadly speaking, most of the students (69%) felt that the module did a good job of being transparent about the realities of working within the Youth Justice sector, 23% disagreed, with one of the participants who is now working in the sector commenting:

> It made it seem very rewarding all the time and positive, didn't really show the hardships of the everyday job (such as when you can't help, help doesn't work, the young person doesn't want to be helped, if they face abuse from families or young people etc, emotional labour etc)

There were clearly some challenges highlighted as well, especially where time limitations means that co-delivery led to less time spent explaining theory, with students expected to acquire this knowledge independently from the bitesized videos and their reading. For some students, including those with no prior study of criminology, this was particularly challenging:

> Some of the visits I found difficult to understand the relevancy to the subject, whilst I was learning about their work there was too much focus on minute details and less on the theory of criminology.

This quote further illustrates the limits of the employability focus, in that students don't always want a criminal justice career, they may want to learn for the sake of learning itself and enjoy the theory more than the practice. Striking the balance between theory and practice in a way which suits all student needs is inevitably difficult, and this continues to be something for the Community of Practice to reflect upon as we strive to get the balance right.

YOS professionals' perspectives

Whilst there are clearly considerable advantages for undergraduate youth justice students to this kind of partnership approach to delivery, it is important that services consider the benefits of their participation too. If we were to focus primarily on the skills and employability issue, then we can see how integrating youth justice professionals in the classroom could translate into longer term benefits for youth justice services, by ups-killing graduates with sector specific knowledge and practice experiences, and encouraging them to think about a career in youth justice. Knowledge exchange partnerships could therefore potentially address gaps in the workforce.

But beyond this, the experience of current staff involved in the partnership delivery itself indicates the additional value that is directly and immediately beneficial to youth justice professionals and which enhances their practice. Six YOS colleagues provided anonymised feedback on their experiences of the module via an online survey in July 2022, and it was clear from the responses that for these colleagues at least, their involvement provides a valuable opportunity for practitioners to connect their practice with theory, to remain up to date about the developing research evidence base, and perhaps to be challenged in new ways by the conversations and questions from both staff and students, as this YOS professional described:

> There is a huge importance to practice having an academic base, a link between practice, theory and research is extremely valuable. The module is a live and interactive link that brings our theory base to the forefront.

The YOS professionals noted how it enhances their own reflexivity, because 'it encourages you to look reflectively at your own practice before running a session and then to consider the input and options of students after the session' and that it 'has helped to challenge some of the thinking around our practices and encouraged greater reflection on what we do and why at times.'

In a more practical sense, working together to design the workshop content for students has also generated ideas for the YOS staff to take back with them and incorporate into training activities. A significant example of this is the 'Intersectionality' card game that was co-created between the academic and the clinical psychologist to help students' understanding of complexity and to generate conversations about issues of diversity in relation to young people's offending behaviour and their support needs. This card game is now used in training and supervision within the service's Complex Needs team, and to support multi-agency working, in helping external agencies understand what they do.

For both students studying the module and youth justice professionals involved in delivery, therefore, the key to the partnership is effectively bringing together theory and practice in ways which reveal the connections between them, and generate critical ways of reflecting upon that practice and how it may be improved or developed over time.

Conclusion: The centrality of relationships to this youth justice knowledge exchange partnership

This chapter has considered the origins of this University/Youth Justice Service knowledge exchange partnership, conceived as a community of practice to first design and then deliver a dedicated youth justice module for the Criminology programme. It has successfully embedded some of the 'new pedagogical ideas' that constitute Ryan and Tilbury's flexible pedagogies, as well as a commitment to experiential learning, slow scholarship and a value driven approach to reflecting upon youth justice policy and practice. The durability of this partnership has supported and sustained the work of both the University and the Youth Offending Service through challenging times, and enhanced practice for both institutions. It is therefore important to conclude by restating the key principles underpinning our community of practice, which have enabled it to flourish over this period of time.

- **Relationships**: Establishing relationships of trust and respect is fundamental to the success of the knowledge exchange partnership. This includes respect for each other's professional standing and responsibilities, the existence of different priorities and commitments across the two industries, and the need for communication and conversations to find out where the middle ground might be. One of the challenges of this is that such a model is easier to run where there is some consistency of staffing, so as to provide continuity from year to year, taking the time to meet for coffee and catch up before each session, especially with colleagues who return year on year, and this might not be viable in all university departments.
- **Reciprocity**: A central means to developing strong relationships is the need for reciprocity – some give and take in both directions. In a formal sense this might include arranging for YOS colleagues teaching on the module to be able to access library resources, whilst informally looking for opportunities to support the needs of the service, offering advice and feedback on day-to-day service development plans and progress.
- **Flexibility and commitment**: this is hugely important on both sides of the partnership – remaining open to changing the way things might be delivered, revising and updating session plans based on latest service developments, student feedback, or timetabling requirements. We have needed to take on board the disappointment around low student attendance and consider what we might be able to do within the module to improve that, whilst also recognising and supporting each other to understand that our students are impacted by many of the same social and economic challenges and mental health contexts that justice-experienced young people also face. Being able to respond to a crisis, with goodwill and a commitment to making things happen nonetheless has been key.
- **Self-reflection**: for all involved. The cross-sector nature of the knowledge exchange partnership means that university academics, students and professionals are all confronted with opportunities to reflect on our own values, beliefs, and practices, and this is of immense value in developing critical thinking and reflective practice to improve our work. This includes reflecting honestly upon some of the challenging realities of working in youth justice services, rather than only sharing the success stories as a means to promote the employment opportunities within the sector.
- **Shared goals and values**: One of the features of the partnership is the importance of shared goals and values, which bridges the divide between academic and professional perspectives. In this case, the goals of improving outcomes for children, and the promotion of children's rights, wellbeing and participation are fundamental to the community of practice. The academic conducts research into this area and supports the service as a critical friend to help them improve practice in achieving these goals, whilst the service has been proactive in developing creative and progressive

mechanisms for supporting children in conflict with the law, and this has been recognised within service inspections.

The essence of a community of practice is that the *practice* is always ongoing, the work is never done. This partnership therefore, along with the module which keeps it *live* from year to year, continues to evolve so as to address the latest challenges, introduce improved working practices and explore new opportunities for joint ventures which can support the aims and aspirations of both sides of the partnership in the years to come.

References

Aristovnik, A., Karampelas, K., Umek, L. and Ravšelj, D. (2023) *Impact of the COVID-19 pandemic on online learning in higher education: A bibliometric analysis. Frontiers in Education*, 8, 3 August. frontiersin.org.

Bartasevicius, V., Roberts, E., Liddar, A., Sharrock, S., Rantanen, K. and Barton-Crosby, J. (NatCen) (2020, July) *Pilots of alternative assessments to AssetPlus: Evaluation report*. London: Department for Education. https://assets.publishing.service.gov.uk/government/uploads/system/uploads/attachment_data/file/932333/Asset_Plus_alternative_assessment.pdf.

Barton, A., Davis, H. and Scott, D. (2019) Quiet silencing: Restricting the criminological imagination in the neoliberal university. In Diver, A. (ed.) *Employability via higher education: Sustainability as scholarship*. Cham: Springer. https://doi.org/10.1007/978-3-030-26342-3_34.

Becker, H. (1967) Whose side are we on? *Social Problems*, 14(Winter), 239–247.

Bond-Taylor (2021) *Evaluation of the Joint Diversionary Panel and Youth Restorative Intervention: Final report*. University of Lincoln, July. https://eprints.lincoln.ac.uk/id/eprint/49676/1/JDP%20Evaluation%20Final%20Report.pdf.

Bond-Taylor (2021) Youth justice live! Transporting professional partnerships into blended learning spaces. *IMPact*, 4(3). https://bpb-eu-w2.wpmucdn.com/blogs.lincoln.ac.uk/dist/e/8583/files/2023/02/Dr-Sue-Bond-Youth-justice-live.-Transporting-professional-partnerships-into-blended-learning-spaces-1.pdf.

Bond-Taylor, S. and Davies, C.T. (2020) Youth justice live! Flexible pedagogies in an online/offline community of practice. In Dennis, C., Abbott, S., Matheson, R. and Tangery, S. (eds) *Flexibility and pedagogy in higher education: Delivering flexibility in learning through online learning communities*. Leiden: Brill/Sense.

Bozalek, V.G., McMillan, W., Marshall, D.E., November, M., Daniels, A. and Sylvester, T. (2014). Analysing the professional development of teaching and learning from a political ethics of care perspective. *Teaching in Higher Education*, 19(5), 447–458.

Bundred, S. (2006). Solutions to silos: Joining up knowledge. *Public Money & Management*, 26(2), 125–130.

Case, S. and Browning, A. (2021) Child First Justice: The research evidence-base. Loughborough University, 3/3/21. https://repository.lboro.ac.uk/articles/report/Child_First_Justice_the_research_evidence-base_Full_report_/14152040.

Case, S., Creaney, S., Deakin, J. and Haines, K. (2015) Youth justice: Past, present and future. *British Journal of Community Justice*, 13(2), 99.

Cranmer, S. (2006). Enhancing graduate employability: Best intentions and mixed outcomes. *Studies in Higher Education*, 31, 169–184.

Creaney, S. and Smith, R. (2014) Youth justice back at the crossroads. *Safer Communities*, 13(2), 83–87.

Dickinson, J. (2022) How have the TEF and the B3 bear landed in universities? *WONKHE*, 16/3/22. https://wonkhe.com/blogs/how-have-the-tef-and-the-b3-bear-landed-in-universities/.

George, M., Lim, H., Lucas, S. and Meadows, R. (2015) Learning by doing: Experiential learning in criminal justice. *Journal of Criminal Justice Education*, 26(4), 471–492.

Gray, P. and Smith, R. (2019) Shifting sands: The reconfiguration of neoliberal youth penality. *Theoretical Criminology*, 25(2), 304–324.

Gray, P., Smithson, H., Larner, S. and Jump, D. (2022) The youth justice system's response to the Covid-19 Pandemic, YOTs' adaptations and challenges to service delivery: A national picture. Research paper 4. Manchester Centre for Youth Studies, April. https://www.mmu.ac.uk/media/mmuacuk/content/documents/mcys/COVID-19_and_Youth_Justice_Paper_4.pdf.

Haines, K. and Case, S. (2015) *Positive youth justice: Children first, offenders second*. Bristol: Policy Press.

Haines, K. and Case, S. (2018) The future of youth justice. *Youth Justice*, 18(2), 131–148.

Hart, A., Davies, C., Aumann, K., Wenger, E., Aranda, K., Heaver, B. and Wolff, D. (2013) Mobilising knowledge in community–university partnerships: What does a community of practice approach contribute? *Contemporary Social Science*, 8(3), 278–291.

Hester, R. and Case, S. (2010) Professional education in youth justice: Mirror or motor? *British Journal of Community Justice*, 8(2).

Jameson, J., Strudwick, K., Bond-Taylor, S. and Jones, M. (2012) Academic principles versus employability pressures: A modern power struggle or a creative opportunity? *Teaching in Higher Education*, 17(1), 25–37.

Keeling, R.P. (2014) An ethic of care in higher education: Well-being and learning. *Journal of College and Character*, 15(3), 141–148.

Lave, J. and Wenger, E. (1991) *Situated learning: Legitimate peripheral participation*. Cambridge: Cambridge University Press.

Lea, M. (2005) 'Communities of practice' in higher education: Useful heuristic or educational model? In Barton, D. and Tusting, K. (eds) *Beyond communities of practice: Language, power and social context*. Cambridge: Cambridge University Press.

Long, J.L. and Utley, M.E. (2018) An afternoon spent behind bars: The impact of touring a correctional facility on student learning. *Journal of Correctional Education*, 69(3), 32–48.

Martinson, R. (1974) What works? Questions and answers about prison reform. *The Public Interest*, 35, 22–54.

Meisel, J.S. (2008) The ethics of observing: Confronting the harm of experiential learning. *Teaching Sociology*, 36(3), 196–210.

Miner-Romanoff, K. (2014) Student perceptions of juvenile offender accounts in criminal justice education. *American Journal of Criminal Justice*, 39, 611–629.

Mountz, A., Bonds. A., Mansfield, B., Joyd, J., Hyndman, J., Walton-Roberts, M., Basu, R., Whitson, R., Hawkins, R., Hamilton, T. and Curran, W. (2015) For slow scholarship: A feminist politics of resistance through collective action in the neoliberal university. *ACME: An International E-Journal for Critical Geographies*, 14(4), 1235–1259. https://acme-journal.org/index.php/acme/article/view/1058.

Neary, M. and Winn, J. (2009) The student as producer: Reinventing the student experience in higher education. In Bell, L., Stevenson, H. and Neary, M. (eds) *The future of higher education: Policy, pedagogy and the student experience*. London: Continuum.

Office for Students (2022) Securing student success: Regulatory framework for higher education in England. OfS, 24/11/22. https://www.officeforstudents.org.uk/publications/securing-student-success-regulatory-framework-for-higher-education-in-england/.

Piché, J. and Walby, K. (2010) Problematizing carceral tours. *British Journal of Criminology*, 50(3), 570–581.

Price, J., Wilkinson, D. and Crossley, C. (2023) Children and young peoples' lyrics and voices capturing their experiences within youth justice services. *Safer Communities*, 22(3), 186–199. https://doi.org/10.1108/SC-08-2022-0029.

Ryan, A. and Tilbury, D. (2013) *Flexible pedagogies: New pedagogical ideas*. York: Higher Education Academy.

Saleh-Hanna, V., Williams, J. and Coyle, M.J. (eds) (2023) *Abolish criminology*. London: Routledge.

Speight, S., Lackovic, N. and Cooker, L. (2013) The contested curriculum: Academic learning and employability in higher education. *Tertiary Education and Management*, 19(2), 112–116.

Strudwick, K. (2017) Debating student as producer: Relationships, contexts and challenges for higher education. *Prism: Casting New Light on Learning, Theory and Practice*, 1(1), 73–96.

Strudwick, K. (2019) Learning through practice: Collaborative policing partnerships in teaching in higher education. *The Police Journal: Theory, Practice and Principles*, 94(1), 58–74.

Wenger, E., McDermott, R.A. and Snyder, W. (2002) *Cultivating communities of practice: A guide to managing knowledge*. Boston MA: Harvard Business School Press.

Yates, J. (2012) What prospects youth justice? Children in trouble in the age of austerity. *Social Policy and Administration*, 46(4), 432–447.

YJB (Youth Justice Board) (2019) *Standards for children in the youth justice system*. https://www.gov.uk/government/publications/national-standards-for-youth-justice-services.

5 The Dyfed Powys Hwb Doeth partnership

Kathy Hampson

Chapter objectives – this chapter will address the following questions:

- What opportunities are afforded by informally devolved youth justice operations within Wales?
- What is the Welsh 'Hwb Doeth' knowledge transfer partnership?
    a national pan-Wales level
    b regional Dyfed Powys level
- How has the Dyfed Powys Hwb Doeth group facilitated positive developments in youth justice for the region?
    a for academia and research
    b for practitioners in the field
- What challenges remain for Dyfed Powys Hwb Doeth?

Introduction

This chapter examines a specifically Welsh youth justice-focused knowledge transfer partnership called Hwb Doeth. It will explore how Wales has differed from England in its approach to developing effective practice and innovation and how the development of the 'Hwb Doeth' knowledge transfer partnership has contributed to both national and regional developments in the field. The focus will then narrow onto one of the regional groups – Dyfed Powys, and how that group has developed to facilitate bilateral communication and knowledge between those delivering youth justice to children and those researching it. Limitations of the operation of the group will also be explored, with potential areas for future development, illustrated through anonymised responses of Dyfed Powys Hwb Doeth members.[1] Firstly, Welsh youth justice development will be considered to contextualise the Hwb Doeth initiative.

The context of Welsh youth justice within a wider jurisdiction

Although Wales and England are one legislative jurisdiction for justice matters, Welsh youth justice has developed along a somewhat different trajectory to that of England, reflecting other policy approaches in devolved areas (like social care). Whilst England was firmly in the grip of risk-focused youth justice which concentrated on addressing assessed risk factors (see Case and Hampson, 2019), Wales was concurrently developing a more

DOI: 10.4324/9781003411192-6

positive approach by seeing children as 'children first and offenders second' (WAG/YJB, 2004: 3), derived from Haines and Drakeford's (1998) work. This led to a much more positive and strengths-based youth justice approach in Wales (at least in policy, as far as it was in the gift of the Welsh Government to give, given the joint jurisdiction); for more discussion on this especially regarding translation into practice, see Janes (2022), based around children's rights, as enshrined in the *Rights of Children and Young Persons (Wales) Measure 2011*, which ensures that all policy in Wales relating to children must 'have due regard' to the United Nations Convention on the Rights of the Child (United Nations, 1989). Welsh policy developed beyond mere regard to rights (which could be seen as a minimum requirement) towards the idea of entitlements (looking more at maximising outcomes)

This divergence, despite legislative union, was facilitated by the fact that Welsh youth justice was overseen by a regional sub-division of the Youth Justice Board (YJB; responsible for delivering youth justice strategy and policy across England and Wales), YJB Cymru (YJBC). This allowed the Welsh emphasis on children's rights and entitlements (especially incorporating '*extending* entitlements', ensuring that *justice-involved* children were not excluded from considerations which other children could take for granted; WAG, 2002) to develop into 'Child First' justice (later adopted by the YJB more generally as the 'strategic approach and central guiding principle' for youth justice across the jurisdiction; YJB, 2021: 10). The YJBC developed much closer and collaborative (rather than purely oversight) relationships with Welsh Youth Offending Teams[2] (YOT), paving the way for a more emancipatory approach to youth justice development and innovation more generally. Across Wales, this specifically developed through the establishment of the 'Hwb Doeth' knowledge transfer partnership.

What is Hwb Doeth?

'Hwb Doeth' translates from Welsh as 'wise hub'. It seeks to bring together practice and academia to 'provide advice, guidance and support to youth justice services to develop, improve and share practice innovation by encouraging, listening positively to and respecting ideas put forward' (Hwb Doeth, 2018: 2). Thus, it fulfils the definition of a knowledge transfer partnership as involving 'the bidirectional transfer of knowledge between academia and business' (Smithson and Jones, 2021: 351). It was developed through the Welsh Centre for Crime and Social Justice, which is a collaboration between all Welsh universities and a variety of criminal justice agencies (e.g. YOTs, probation, police; see https://wccsj.ac.uk/en/ for more information). Hwb Doeth's stated aims include collaboration between youth justice agencies and universities, innovation, and learning/practice development (Hwb Doeth, 2018: 3).

There are two operational levels of Hwb Doeth – national and regional, both of which meet quarterly. The national group includes members from the YJBC and Welsh Government, YOT Managers Cymru and the secure estate, as well as representation from each of the (four) regional Hwb Doeth groups. When the initiative began, the seven Welsh universities were allocated to one of the four regional groups to identify main collaborative partnerships, ensure that all universities were involved and that all regions had academic support. The regional groups, initially based purely on YOT and university representation, were free to include others deemed useful for the development of effective practice, and to develop their own agendas according to what was regionally important. All regional groups now feed back into the national Hwb Doeth organisation, sharing regional meeting minutes, helpfully facilitated by utilising the same national secretariat for all four groups.

The national Hwb Doeth organisation also initiates other support for Welsh YOTs (of which there are 17), for example an annual 'training day' covering policy and practice developments, good practice and research innovations. Content is driven by the needs of YOTs and delivered with the support of the universities (and other contacts). This provides excellent opportunity to securely embed research findings into practice and develop practice along more innovative directions than might perhaps otherwise have been possible. Welsh YOTs have, through such initiatives, kept close relationships with those developing policy (YJBC and Welsh Government) which, coupled with the fact that Wales is a small country, means that those working in this area generally know each other well and collaborate in an environment built on trust and good relationships. The importance of Hwb Doeth within this was expressed by one academic with a national role overseeing both strands (national and regional): '*I believe Hwb Doeth is a precious tool for those who recognise its potential. It's currently the only platform in Wales where YJ [Youth Justice] and academia can come together. I think this connection can be immensely beneficial for both parties and, if fully developed, has the potential to shape students who are interested in a future career in YJ*'. Written practitioner member feedback (see note 1) illustrates the importance of this: '*In relation to the Hwb Doeth Annual Training Day my colleague's feedback was it is good to network and gain up to date information. YJB members were there and talking about future plans and developments*'. Comparing Hwb Doeth to the nearest English equivalent, the Developing Practice Fora, identifies some interesting differences, as the latter are 'closed groups for staff that work in youth justice, and are generally attended by operational and team managers, or specialist workers where relevant' (YJB, n.d.a). They also operate regionally, but only include representatives from practice, thereby compromising their ability to function as knowledge transfer partnerships. So, whilst they are categorised together on the YJB Resource Hub, they appear to be entirely different in practice.

Dyfed Powys Regional Hwb Doeth

As previously explained, alongside the national Hwb Doeth organisation are the regional groups, of which Dyfed Powys is one. The Dyfed Powys region covers the centre of Wales, including the counties of Powys, Ceredigion, Pembrokeshire and Carmarthenshire. It is a very rural area with a sparse population in places, characterised by small villages and towns, featuring agriculture as a dominant economic activity. There is one YOT within each of the four counties, and the whole region is covered by the Dyfed Powys police force. This area encompasses two universities – Aberystwyth and Trinity St David's. Dyfed Powys Hwb Doeth (DPHD) has representation from all four YOTs (at management level), both universities, the office of the Police and Crime Commissioner (OPCC) and a national Hwb Doeth staff member (who attends all regional groups, thus assuring good communication both ways, and consistency of approach, where appropriate; she also provides the secretariat for the meeting). The development of this regional group is an important part of creating a youth justice system which is bespoke to the idiosyncrasies of this area, which has a particular issue with rurality and widely spread sparse populations, and the resultant issues this can cause for children and young people, including the challenge of attending a venue which may not be easy to access (Brooks-Wilson, 2020; see also Glass et al., 2020). As previously stated, the group is supported by the national Hwb Doeth secretariat, and an academic from

Aberystwyth University as its current Chair. Since the Covid-19 pandemic, Hwb Doeth meetings have taken place online, which has been overwhelmingly successful in terms of attendance, given the challenges posed by the wide geographical spread of the region and the busyness of all members; there are no plans to return to in-person meetings, which is perhaps a lasting pandemic benefit.

A strong principle of DPHD is that it exists for the mutual benefit of all members, so the agendas reflect the diverse needs of both practice and academia. Those in practice see it as an opportunity to discuss issues with other YOTs, comparing notes and developing joint processes: *'it is an opportunity to identify what other YOTs are doing'* (practitioner member feedback); those in academia see it as a way to embed good research into practice and base future research on what YOTs need, thereby increasing its impact: *'academics have opportunity to understand research needs as highlighted by practitioners and current issues faced by practitioners'* (academic member feedback).

DPHD example activities

The agendas are set by the membership but have included a wide range of activities. There are some standing items which meet the stated aims and the needs of those attending. For example, there is an 'interventions forum' slot to facilitate the sharing of good intervention practice between the attending YOTs; contributions can be small and interesting or much more large-scale in nature – as long as they are of potential benefit to the other YOTs. There is also a slot each time to share (and discuss) new research or articles of interest, which allows for better embedding of quality research into practice and also enables YOTs to see research to which they may not otherwise have access (given the need to pay for many research journal articles to which the attendant universities already have institutional access).

Current practice developments or changes in policy can be approached regionally, which has enabled a more coherent response. An example of this is a Dyfed Powys police initiative called 'INTACT' (Dyfed Powys Police, 2022), which was intended to address serious and organised crime, but seemed rather to be used for children at a very low level of offending – the YOTs were able to discuss their concerns together on this, and report through the OPCC representative inconsistencies of application. Another subject of detailed debate has been the use of Outcome 22 (deferred prosecution to allow for diversionary intervention; YJLC, n.d.), where issues of communication between police and YOTs were raised. Discussions also highlighted some inconsistencies of application across the region which may not otherwise have been identified.

Cross-YOT communication has also facilitated some shared resource development. An example of this is the common referral form now used by police to refer children to YOTs for prevention work. Previously each area had its own process and form, but now the four YOTs all use the same form, which was developed through the YOTs working together. This has created a better and more consistent process between police and YOTs, the usage of which is being monitored by DPHD. In a similar vein, the interventions forum has facilitated some innovative practice to be discussed. One example has been a strengths-based programme, delivered one-to-one (called 'Dyma fi' or 'This is me'), particularly helpful in the context of Wales where Welsh medium resources are often rare, or after-thought translations. Another project one YOT has proposed for future discussion once it is operational is a mentoring volunteer project they are hoping to introduce to widen the offer to children.

One of the academic Hwb Doeth members benefitted from easy access to youth justice practitioners (from the four member YOTs) for a piece of work looking at how well the model of Child First justice, now espoused by the YJB (YJB, 2021), is being put into practice. The issues raised by respondents led the academic to suggest the provision of a free training event for the member YOTs, which was enthusiastically accepted by them. It was well attended and helped to address some of the gaps in knowledge left by delayed and limited training which had been offered more centrally (see Hampson, 2023), with attendees also appreciating the opportunity to discuss practical application with practitioners from other regional YOTs. This then led to a further training session for magistrates and volunteers from the four member YOTs and court areas, about which attendees communicated not only enjoyment, but a significant development of understanding which would affect the way they worked in future (Hampson, 2023).

The universities also benefited from access to YOTs for student research projects. Two students have attended DPHD meetings to discuss their projects and call for participants (one master's student and one undergraduate). The projects focused on practitioners' views of the need for children to admit guilt for the provision of a service, and the use of language with justice-involved children and the effect of this on relationship-building. The projects received good buy-in from practitioners which allowed the students to gather quality data for two excellent projects, with findings able to be communicated directly back to the DPHD membership to complete the circle. The master's student commented: '*Attending a Hwb Doeth conference allowed me to discuss my research plan with regional YOT representatives who happily agreed to promote my project and assist me with recruiting participants. Thanks to their intervention, I got swift responses to my survey, and I managed to schedule enough one-to-one interviews with willing participants ... I can confidently say that the Hwb Doeth conference and the spirit of partnership it promotes were significant helping factors in my endeavour*'. However, this kind of relationship is also reciprocal, with YOTs being encouraged to consider student researcher potential in areas of interest to them, for example in evaluating a new project or intervention. Universities can offer several levels of research support: undergraduate-led empirical dissertation, master's empirical dissertation, Ph.D. empirical thesis, staff small-scale university-funded research and staff larger-scale externally funded research. This flexibility offers a good range of options to build on the evidence-base of effective practice in the region.

One example of a collaborative research project in the region was the YJB Targeted Prevention Pathfinder project, which involved Ceredigion YOT and academics from Aberystwyth University. This was funded by a grant from the Welsh Government, and awarded jointly to both organisations, to fulfil the brief to 'be a pathfinder project to research, develop, and evaluate prevention approaches' (Norris, 2021: 4) from the prevention work in Ceredigion, and applying this pan-Wales (in accordance with the 'Youth Justice Blueprint for Wales'; Ministry of Justice/Welsh Government, 2019). The outputs from this project have included a new screening tool to facilitate the targeting of prevention services towards children for whom it is more likely to be beneficial (Norris, Griffith and West, 2018), and a guidance document on good practice for gathering children's views on prevention services received (Hampson, 2022). This demonstrates the benefits of involving both YOTs and academia in funding bids and associated research, rather than this being the responsibility of universities alone.

Further benefits of DPHD

> A knowledge transfer partnership can offer a wide range of benefits to all concerned, as it gives businesses access to university facilities, knowledge and data within an R&D-focused context, and so delivers multiple positive impacts: it helps bring new products, services and processes to market; embeds expertise; creates research impact; seeds a culture of innovation; and opens up exceptional career opportunities for graduates.
>
> (UKRI, 2020)

The benefits of DPHD are also multidimensional, varying depending on viewpoint, as those in practice and those in research will have different goals.

YOT members have commented on the benefits of getting together with the other YOTs from the region: '*It is a great opportunity to hear from other YOTs/YJS what they are doing and raising any emerging practices*'; '*sharing good practice examples* [and] *challenges practitioner meet in their field*'; '*beneficial to share practice across the region*'. The fact that there have been specific practice developments rolled out across the whole region (e.g. the police common referral form) illustrates the improvement this group adds to the development of youth justice in Dyfed Powys. The YOTs also perceive benefits of being in the same forum as academics ('*hearing about research*'; '*it is beneficial that they include academics as they can view things through different lenses*'), especially when this has translated into practical training ('*the training provided through HD has empowered colleagues and volunteers alike*'; '*we have received some excellent training (child first)*'; '*Child first training reminded and highlighted how we should be practicing* [sic]'). Perhaps this YOT member's comment sums up the variety of benefits felt: '*Hwb Doeth has been helpful to listen to other examples of good practice and pieces of research and training needs that can be incorporated into day-to-day practice*'.

University members have commented on the benefits of being in close and frequent contact with those in practice, that this has reduced the risk of becoming detached from what is happening in the field ('*Hwb Doeth is a valuable and vital way to keep in touch with the practice, as it allows academics to observe what the issues are for practitioners and keep research relevant to practitioners*'). The relationships which have been built over time through the development of DPHD between the YOTs and the universities provide a basis for navigating the on-going change which has been a feature of youth justice policy/practice for generations, as it has often been used as something of a political hot potato in electoral campaigns (Case and Hampson, 2019). In Wales this is likely to continue with the potential development of a devolved youth justice system on the horizon (Welsh Government, 2023). As one academic member explained: '*potential devolution will impact everybody, and this could be a forum where practitioners could feed their concerns to academics*'. The development of a devolved system is being explored by the Wales Youth Justice Academic Advisory Group, on which several academic DPHD members sit, so this presents an ideal mechanism for the Dyfed Powys region to actively contribute to this process.

Further benefits of the relationships for both universities and YOTs forged through this close partnership have included YOT staff giving practice-informed lectures to students studying youth justice (useful for the YOT staff participating for expanding their experience and CV and for universities in being able to maintain a close relationship between delivered content and youth justice in the field) and students accessing volunteering or employment opportunities within the YOTs. Employability is becoming ever more important to the university offer for students (Cheng et al., 2022), so having practitioners available not only to give students a taste of working in the sector, but also to answer any questions they might have, is an invaluable resource. Within youth justice there are several volunteering roles (YJB, n.d.b); for example, acting as an Appropriate Adult (National Appropriate Adult Network, n.d.), supervising reparation activities (sometimes called 'pay back'; see for example, Barnet Youth Justice Service, 2021), helping on prevention programmes (Norris, 2021), becoming a member on Youth Justice Panels for Referral Orders (Ministry of Justice/YJB, 2018), to which students have good access because of the relationships built up between staff of both universities and YOTs. Some of these roles can also be paid, allowing students to work in relevant roles whilst studying, rather than resorting to less relevant employment, like bar work. In the area of youth justice, relevant work experience is vital to be successful in gaining employment (see National Careers Service, n.d.), as it is a competitive market, so universities able to offer close contact with youth justice agencies (as Welsh universities can through Hwb Doeth) are likely to increase their students' employability once they leave. Aberystwyth University offers two work-based modules (see Aberystwyth University, n.d.), specifically designed to incorporate such work (either paid or voluntary) into the qualification structure – youth justice opportunities play a significant role each year in the range of options available to students on those modules.

From the point of view of the national Hwb Doeth organisation, which supports the regional groups, the Dyfed Powys area group has been a great success, as expressed by one of the national organisers:

> If I were to rank the group's engagement levels from 1 to 4, with 1 being the most engaged and 4 the least, Dyfed Powys would take the top spot ... the key to the success of the Dyfed Powys and Gwent Hwb Doeth groups lies in the active involvement and dedication of both YJ practitioners and academic representatives. They have shown a genuine interest in engaging, sharing valuable information, and investing their time in making the meetings productive.

The main reasoning for this was around leadership (*'they have a strong and enthusiastic academic lead'*) and the inclusion of the OPCC member (*'the presence of the OPCC adds another dimension to the meetings, something the other groups are considering adding to their sessions'*) which represents *'a fast and easier route for escalating concerns about matters to PCC'*. The success of DPHD has also enabled the national member to re-enliven less active regional groups, having identified what makes for a successful approach.

The challenges of DPHD

Although little has been written about knowledge transfer partnerships, what there is has identified challenges in relationships, communication and culture difference between the different organisations involved (Sigal, 2021). It is unsurprising therefore that despite being supported and championed by the WCCSJ and YJBC, the regional Hwb Doeth groups have not been without their challenges.

Sometimes it is extremely difficult to identify a time for a meeting to take place which can accommodate every member's schedule (although the placing of the meeting online has improved this, due to the removal of travel time), as some members identified as a specific challenge: *'Ensuring I have protected time to attend'*; *'attendance has been a struggle*'; '*Not all YOTs always represented*'. When there are only four YOTs within a region, discussions with one missing results in a large gap. It also seems that non-attendance tends to be from the same areas, which invites a question about organisational engagement, as the national Hwb Doeth member has observed: '*it's been noted that only two YJS from that region actively participate and often lead the meetings, whereas the other two seem less engaged*'. Recent changes in leadership and representation from at least one of those areas will hopefully go some way to addressing this issue. However, time pressures also affect post-meeting actions, as one YOT member identified as a challenge: '*meeting colleagues to address some of the action points agreed*'. There are many meetings which result in the roll-over of actions because there has not been enough opportunity for specific-issue working groups to meet in the meantime.

Although various options for research have been offered to YOTs, the dearth of region-specific research was highlighted by some as a weakness. One academic member suggested that a useful future development would be '*focus on development of research at Dyfed-Powys level*'. This was echoed by one of the YOT members, who also proffered a possible reason for this: '*not much research has been happening in* [county], *but this might be due to YJS* [Youth Justice Service, another term for YOT] *not bringing research areas/topics to the meetings*'. Perhaps more needs to be done to encourage the YOTs to make use of the research offer from the universities, or the generation of more regular joint funding bids (between YOTs and universities) should become a staple part of the discussions, rather than exceptional.

One issue with KTPs is getting the right membership. Ensuring the right people are around the table makes the difference between something which remains mere talk and a group which has real impact, which has previously been found when Reintegration and Resettlement Boards were being established in Wales (Hampson and Kinsey, 2016). One aspect identified through that project was that representation had to be at a high enough level for action to be possible from agreed actions; this required reasonably senior management attendance (Hampson and Kinsey, 2016). As well as the right level of attendee, the right agencies need to be in attendance. The original configuration of the Hwb Doeth regional meetings only included universities and YOTs. DPHD has extended this to include the OPCC, identified as a particular strength by the national Hwb Doeth member: '*the OPCC's presence at the table and updates on matters relevant to YJS work demonstrated to be extremely useful (i.e., sharing of recently published reports on matters relevant to YJS (Youth Forum Consultation Report))*', which combines with expedited access to the Dyfed Powys PCC to create a very useful addition. More recently, one of the YOTs has changed its remit to exclude working with children in a preventative way, passing this over to the Youth Service instead, who have now been invited to join the group. This shows the importance of maintaining a flexible approach to both membership and meeting content – responding to changes and developments in order to maintain relevance. However, there are still gaps, as identified by one of the academic members, who said '*police not represented*'. As there is constant overlap in DPHD discussions and police business, this has been a persistent issue, leaving many issues unresolved, which police representation would go some way to solving. Attempts to bring the police to the meeting have met with agreement in principle, but no follow-up, so this is still an issue to be addressed, which competing organisational priorities are clearly going to continue to frustrate.

In a system which is, quite rightly, seeing the increasing importance of involving children in meaningful participation in systems and processes concerning them (Aldridge,

2017; as indeed 'collaboration' is one of the four main tenets of Child First; YJB, 2021), it is also notable that there are no children on DPHD (or indeed on the national Hwb Doeth group). This constitutes a significant gap, and possibly surprising that it has not been discussed as a future development either at the regional or the national level. However, this perhaps reflects the generally late development of true participation within justice spaces specifically, as if justice-involved children waive their right to participation when they break the law (Hampson and Case, forthcoming). Involving children in such fora is complex, necessarily in some ways ceding a measure of power from adults to children, which can be difficult for the adults who have created systems (and in this case, fora between practitioner groups and academia) to accept (Creaney and Burns, 2023). However, it is an issue which both the regional DPHD and the national group should seek to address.

Conclusion

The DPHD knowledge transfer partnership (as a regional expression of a wider pan-Wales practice-academia group) is an important part of the development of a regionally appropriate youth justice system for children living in the Dyfed Powys area. It allows practitioners to get together to develop more consistency and a joined-up approach, where this is feasible (within the differences between the individual counties). It also facilitates academics and those delivering youth justice interventions for children to have a much closer alliance, leading to better embedding of good research, identification and fulfilment of practitioners' training needs, and better understanding for academics concerning what practitioners' experiences are, which should feed into better informed and useful research projects. Research can be bespoke, arising from within the group to meet specific needs (e.g. the evaluation of a specific programme) or the result of joint funding bids to develop more in-depth work within the context of practice and academic collaboration. Such groups can be challenging to maintain as competing demands draw members away, sometimes creating gaps which severely affect the efficacy of meeting the group's aims. Should content be perceived as not useful then engagement is likely to be reduced, so ensuring that all content derives from within the group itself (rather than a general agenda or the ideas of the Chair) is crucial.

The DPHD group certainly has its challenges, but in general the commitment of the members has ensured its continuation through five years of operation so far, with some useful outputs produced which evidence its utility. This was summed up by the national Hwb Doeth member on this regional group, who said:

> the key to the success of the Dyfed Powys and [region] Hwb Doeth groups lies in the active involvement and dedication of both YJ practitioners and academic representatives. They have shown a genuine interest in engaging, sharing valuable information, and investing their time in making the meetings productive.

This commitment should ensure the continuance of this practice-academia partnership for years to come, provided it remains firmly wedded to the needs and requirements of all members and member agencies, to achieve (according to the national Hwb Doeth member) *'the ultimate goal of promoting continuous learning and practice development through collaboration between universities and youth justice services'*.

Notes

1 Dyfed Powys Hwb Doeth members were consulted on four questions regarding the group's benefits, challenges, development and future possibilities; these questions were asked in the context of exploring its utility and development more generally, but also in terms of inclusion of quoted matter in this chapter, for which specific consent was sought and gained.
2 Youth Offending Teams (YOT) are multi-agency teams responsible for the day-to-day delivery of youth justice interventions to children, established by the *Crime and Disorder Act 1998*. They are generally now referred to as Youth Justice Services (although still 'YOT' in legislation), to distance the work from the label of 'offending'.

References

Aberystwyth University (n.d.) B.Sc. Criminology. Available at https://courses.aber.ac.uk/undergraduate/M900-criminology/#modules-september-start–.

Aldridge, J. (2017) Introduction to the issue: 'Promoting Children's Participation in Research, Policy and Practice'. *Social Inclusion*, 5(3): 89–92.

Barnet Youth Justice Service (2021) *Young people speak on reparation activities*. Video. Available online at https://yjresourcehub.uk/working-with-children-and-families/item/946-video-describing-what-reparation-is-by-children-barnet-yos-october-2021.html.

Brooks-Wilson, S. (2020) Rethinking youth justice journeys: Complex needs, impeded capabilities and criminalisation. *Youth Justice*, 20(3): 309–327.

Case, S. and Hampson, K. (2019) Youth justice pathways to change: Drivers, challenges and opportunities. *Youth Justice*, 19(1): 25–41.

Cheng, M., Adekola, O., Albia, J. and Cai, S. (2022) Employability in higher education: A review of key stakeholders' perspectives. *Higher Education Evaluation and Development*, 16(1): 16–31.

Creaney, S. and Burns, S. (2023) Freedom from symbolic violence? Facilitators and barriers to participatory practices in youth justice. *Youth Justice* (online first), https://doi.org/10.1177/14732254231156844.

Dyfed Powys Police (2022) Specialist INTACT PCSOs support more than 235 referrals for those at risk of serious violence and organised crime. Available online at https://www.dyfed-powys.police.uk/news/dyfed-powys/news/2022/january-2022/specialist-intact-pcsos-support-more-than-235-referrals-for-those-at-risk-of-serious-violence-and-organised-crime-neighbourhoodpolicingweek/.

Glass, J., Bynner, C. and Chapman, C. (2020) Children and young people and rural poverty and social exclusion: A review of evidence. Glasgow: Children's Neighbourhoods Scotland. Available online at https://pure.sruc.ac.uk/ws/portalfiles/portal/34056820/CYP_Rural_Review_02112020.pdf.

Haines, K. and Drakeford, M. (1998) *Young people and youth justice*. Basingstoke: Macmillan.

Hampson, K. (2022) Child first prevention pathfinder: Gathering children's views on prevention services. Available online at https://yjresourcehub.uk/images/Wales/Child_First_Prevention_Pathfinder_Gathering_Childrens_Views_Ceredigion_YJS_2022.pdf.

Hampson, K. (2023) Cementing child first in practice. In S. Case and N. Hazel (eds) *Child First: Developing a new youth justice system*. London: Palgrave Macmillan.

Hampson, K. and Case, S. (forthcoming) Participation in youth justice research: Involving children in the telling of their own stories. In G. Martin and E. Pearce (eds) *Research handbook on youth criminology*. Cheltenham: Edward Elgar.

Hampson, K. and Kinsey, T. (2016) Reintegration and resettlement boards: Good practice guide. Available online at https://www.academia.edu/22333022/Reintegration_and_Resettlement_Boards_good_practice_guide_Reintegration_and_Resettlement_Partnership_Boards_RRPB.

Hwb Doeth (2018) Terms of reference. Unpublished document.

Janes, J. (2022) To what extent does the existing Welsh devolution settlement enable youth offending teams to develop bespoke and innovative approaches to youth justice in Wales? Unpublished Ph.D. thesis, Swansea University. Available online at https://cronfa.swan.ac.uk/Record/cronfa63453.

Ministry of Justice/YJB (Youth Justice Board) (2018) Referral order guidance. Available online at https://assets.publishing.service.gov.uk/government/uploads/system/uploads/attachment_data/file/746365/referral-order-guidance-9-october-2018.pdf.

Ministry of Justice/Welsh Government (2019) Youth justice blueprint for Wales. Available online at https://www.gov.wales/sites/default/files/publications/2019-05/youth-justice-blueprint_0.pdf.

National Appropriate Adult Network (n.d.) How to become an AA. Available online at https://www.appropriateadult.org.uk/information/become-an-appropriate-adult.

National Careers Service (n.d.) Youth offending team officer. Available online at https://nationalcareers.service.gov.uk/job-profiles/youth-offending-team-officer.

Norris G. (2021) A Child First Pathfinder evaluation: Ceredigion Youth Justice and Prevention Service: Towards a common preventions approach across Wales. Available online at https://yjresourcehub.uk/images/Wales/Child_First_Prevention_Pathfinder_Evaluation_Ceredigion_YJS_2022.pdf.

Norris, G., Griffith, G. and West, M. (2018) Validation of the Ceredigion Youth Screening Tool (CYSTEM). *International Journal of Offender Therapy and Comparative Criminology*, 62(12): 3727–3745.

Sigal, S. (2021) Knowledge exchange, HEIs and the arts and culture sector: A systematic review of literature in the field. National Centre for Academic and Cultural Exchange. Available online at https://ncace.ac.uk/wp-content/uploads/2022/01/Sigal-Sarah-Knowledge-Exchange-HEIs-and-the-Arts-and-Culture-Sector-2.pdf.

Smithson, H. and Jones, A. (2021) Co-creating youth justice practice with young people: Tackling power dynamics and enabling transformative action. *Children and Society*, 35: 348–362.

UKRI (2020) Innovation recommendation: Leveraging knowledge transfer partnerships (KTPs). Blog posted 15 December. Available online at https://iuk.ktn-uk.org/perspectives/innovation-recommendation-leveraging-knowledge-transfer-partnerships-ktps/.

United Nations (1989) Convention on the Rights of the Child. Available online at https://www.ohchr.org/en/instruments-mechanisms/instruments/convention-rights-child.

WAG (Welsh Assembly Government) (2002) Extending entitlements. Available online at https://www.gov.wales/sites/default/files/publications/2018-02/direction-and-guidance-extending-entitlement-support-for-11-to-25-year-olds-in-wales.pdf

WAG (Welsh Assembly Government)/YJB (Youth Justice Board) (2004) All Wales Youth Offending Strategy. Available online at https://core.ac.uk/download/pdf/4160146.pdf.

Welsh Government (2023) Written statement: Preparing for devolution of justice (25 April). Available online at https://www.gov.wales/written-statement-preparing-devolution-justice.

YJB (Youth Justice Board) (n.d.a) YJB resource hub. Available online at https://yjresourcehub.uk/developing-practice-fora-and-hwb-doeth-mobile.html.

YJB (Youth Justice Board) (n.d.b) Get involved. Available online at https://yjresourcehub.uk/get-involved.html.

YJB (Youth Justice Board) (2021) Strategic plan 2021–2024. Available online at https://assets.publishing.service.gov.uk/government/uploads/system/uploads/attachment_data/file/966200/YJB_Strategic_Plan_2021_-_2024.pdf.

Youth Justice Legal Centre (n.d.) NPCC guidance on Outcome 22: An alternative to an out of court disposal. Available online at https://yjlc.uk/resources/legal-updates/npcc-guidance-outcome-22-alternative-out-court-disposal.

6 Supporting practice in Scotland

Lessons from the Children and Young People's Centre for Justice

Ross Gibson, Nina Vaswani and Fiona Dyer

By the end of this chapter, you should understand:

- the role of CYCJ in the exchange of knowledge within Scotland
- the factors that have helped and hindered the impact of CYCJ
- what changes this approach has made to youth justice policy and practice, and how this was achieved

Introduction

This chapter describes the role played by the Children and Young People's Centre for Justice (CYCJ) in informing and influencing youth justice policy and practice in Scotland. CYCJ is a knowledge exchange centre predominantly funded by the Scottish Government, established to support improvements across the youth justice sector. Thus, CYCJ's very purpose pivots around improving practice in all aspects of the youth justice systems, whilst seeking solutions to the challenging problems that hinder the delivery of care and support to children and young people in conflict with the law. Naturally the production, collation and synthesis of knowledge, in all its forms, as well as ensuring that this knowledge reaches the relevant decision-makers, are key components of these endeavours. This chapter sets out the process by which this knowledge exchange is facilitated by CYCJ.

First, a brief history of the centre is provided, before exploring the structure and operations of the centre in more detail. The chapter then reflects upon CYCJ's unique position aside and across the many services, organisations and institutions that form the Scottish legal and civic system responding to children in conflict with the law. In outlining CYCJ's novel role and function within this context as that of a boundary-spanning organisation, this chapter helps to articulate how this position facilitates effective knowledge exchange and creates an environment in which policy and practice change can occur. In particular, the chapter focuses on the key features of credibility, access and constructive relationships. Two case studies are offered in order to bring to life the contribution that CYCJ has made to policy and practice (alongside partners) and highlight how these three factors each contributed to the outcomes achieved. Finally, consideration is made to the replicability of the centre in other jurisdictions and what conditions may be necessary in order to do so.

Youth justice and evidence in Scotland

Youth Justice practice in Scotland is founded upon the principle of the welfare of the child being of paramount importance, with the Kilbrandon Report of 1963 – which

DOI: 10.4324/9781003411192-7

proved the impetus of the 1968 Social Work (Scotland) Act and the creation of the Children's Hearing System – explicitly making this point (Vaswani et al., 2018). More recently a renewal of Scotland's commitment to a welfare-based approach can be found within the conclusions of Scotland's Independent Care Review in 2020 and through existing policy drivers such as Getting It Right For Every Child (GIRFEC) and the Whole System Approach (WSA). At its core, this calls on those who support children in conflict with the law to employ a holistic approach that focuses not only on the behaviour in question, but the wider ecological, environmental and family situated issues at play.

To achieve this, Scotland – like many other jurisdictions – has placed an increasing emphasis on evidence, and evidence-based policies and practices. Traditionally evidence-based practice has meant the application of research evidence to guide interventions, programmes and approaches, or knowledge *for* practice. A key exemplar of this in Scotland is the longitudinal *Edinburgh Study of Youth Transitions and Crime*, and its identification that sustained and formal justice system contact has a detrimental, rather than beneficial impact on desistance (McAra and McVie, 2007). This study, and its multitude of outputs, has been credited with informing, shaping and influencing the principal youth justice policy in Scotland, the *Whole System Approach*, and its emphasis on maximum diversion from formal justice systems (Murray et al., 2015). The focus on evidence-based practice has necessitated a corresponding emphasis on the transfer or mobilisation of knowledge from academia (or other areas of research) into practice. Whilst terminology, approaches and methods vary across sectors, put simply knowledge transfer is the relocation of knowledge to where it is most useful (Ward, 2017). Yet the rational-linear assumption that transferring knowledge to where it is needed will result in the subsequent *use* of that knowledge has been described as an unsophisticated conceptualisation which fails to acknowledge the often complex, nuanced, indirect and iterative nature of how evidence informs and influences policy and practice (Davies et al., 2008).

How knowledge is transferred tends to fall into three broad approaches: connecting and building relationships with knowledge users; disseminating and synthesising knowledge into useable forms; and more interactive transfer, e.g. action research (Ward, 2017). These approaches also tend to assume the predominance of the unidirectional transfer of a specific type of knowledge, that is research evidence from academia to research users (typically policymakers or practitioners). More recently there has been a recognition that evidence comes in many forms and from various sources, including from lived experience or practice wisdom (Davies et al., 2015). The term knowledge exchange better reflects this multidirectional travel of explicit and tacit knowledge, perspectives, ideas and experiences (Polkinghorne, 2011).

Furthermore, with the increasing shift to co-producing policy, practice and knowledge, the term knowledge exchange better reflects the blurring of the distinction between those who are users and those who are the creators of knowledge. While there are many definitions of co-production, principally it means working in partnership with key stakeholders (service users, the public, practitioners, managers, policymakers, etc.) and sharing expertise, skills and resources in order to create, change or improve policies or services (SCIE, 2022). Specifically in relation to producing knowledge or research evidence, co-production has been embraced as a means to produce more relevant or impactful research (Redman et al., 2021) in that, being created *with* and *for* the end users of research, this knowledge is more readily translated into policy or practice change. The voice of lived experience is central to co-production, because it aims to place lived experience on an equal footing with professional knowledge and academic research.

CYCJ as a boundary-spanning intermediary organisation

CYCJ was established in 2013 with the purpose of supporting and developing youth justice policy and practice in Scotland. With CYCJ primarily funded by the Scottish Government, based in an academic institution (University of Strathclyde) and within the context of a "'Scottish Approach' to policymaking" (Cairney, 2020) this, naturally, meant using evidence to inform these developments. However, by design, CYCJ acknowledged the different forms of knowledge and evidence, placing a great emphasis on knowledge *from* practice, or practice wisdom, by predominantly employing youth justice practitioners, or those in related fields, with recent practice experience. Indeed, CYCJ's work is formulated around three key interconnected workstreams: practice and policy development; research; and participation and engagement. Each workstream is operationally distinct in terms of core skills, structure and line management, but in practice there is near constant overlap and constructive collaboration between the workstreams.

The Practice and Policy Development workstream forms the original core of CYCJ, with ten staff (9.6 WTE) bringing recent practice or policy experience from a range of disciplines including (most recently) social work, residential care and psychology. This workstream engages in a range of nationwide, local or sector targeted activities aimed at ensuring that Scotland's approach to children and young people in conflict with the law is rights-respecting and grounded within evidence. Key components of this work include: supporting policy and legislative developments; project managing the Scottish Government's implementation groups; providing a bespoke practitioner support service; delivering training and events, including a Post-Graduate Certificate; coordinating regular "practitioner forums" where knowledge can be shared and skills developed; representation on various local and national committees, networks and working groups; responding to policy consultations; connecting people through coordinating and networking activities; and publication of resources, including an annually updated practice guide to working with children in conflict with the law. The Practice and Policy Development Team connects with the Participation and Engagement workstream to ensure that the voice of lived experience is translated into tangible action, and also acts as conduit between the Research workstream and practice/policy by helping to identify and prioritise knowledge and evidence gaps, undertaking research themselves, as well as ensuring the continued development of evidence-informed policy and practice resources.

The Research workstream, initially an important but relatively small component of CYCJ, has grown substantially over the years to currently comprise eight staff (6.7 WTE), bringing together researchers from a range of disciplines, each benefitting from diverse expertise. This growth reflects not only the increasing demand for evidence to support policy and practice developments, but also a shift in the main sources of funding, away from Scottish Government core funding provided on a yearly basis to external funding sources such as Research Councils, Local Authorities and the Third Sector. Researchers engage in a variety of research and related activities, including conducting primary research, synthesising existing research and knowledge exchange to ensure dissemination, translation and impact from research. The Research workstream interfaces with the other workstreams in various ways, such as by generating new knowledge, theories or identifying gaps and suggesting future directions; generating evidence from practice through monitoring and evaluation; and innovation through participatory research methodologies and youth-led research.

The Participation and Engagement workstream comprises five staff (5.0 WTE) and seeks to ensure that children and young people who have experience of the justice system have meaningful opportunities to share their views and to actively shape youth justice policy and practice. In doing so, CYCJ adopted the Lundy Model of participation (Lundy, 2007), which proposes that simply allowing children their voice is insufficient for genuine participation, but that adequate supports must be provided to ensure that children have the *space* to share their views, that their *voice* is heard, that their voice reaches the relevant *audience* of those who have the power to make change, and that their views carry weight and can therefore *influence* these power-holders. Moreover, the centre remains mindful that it does not constitute a body to speak for those with experience of care or for justice, but rather to amplify, echo and act in concert with the voices of those who have lived experience of these systems. This is perhaps best put by one care experienced young person who wrote in a CYCJ blog:

> Participation is not about giving young people a voice. They already have that. Participation is about letting children and young people's voices have real weight. It is about recognising that every young person has the right to be actively engaged in the making of decisions that will influence their lives.
>
> (Maloney, 2018: para. 8)

Participation and Engagement work comprises formalised and regular activity, such as Youth Justice Voices, who are a group of care and justice experienced children and young people aiming to influence change; or more time-limited and reactive activities, for example a short-term group of children and young people brought together to help shape the Bairns' Hoose Standards. The Participation and Engagement workstream cuts across all of the work of CYCJ through, for example, directly supporting and facilitating participatory research; piloting research materials; raising issues for the attention of the Practice and Policy team; creating opportunities for children and young people to provide responses to government consultations; or by encouraging partners and stakeholders to make participation of justice experienced children and young people the norm across Scotland. To achieve this CYCJ has partnered with third sector organisations to develop participation projects which privilege and amplify the voice of those with experience of youth justice and of secure care, leading to the formation of Youth Just Us, Inside Out, STARR and other shorter-term projects. Training and practice support has also been offered to statutory bodies who have since replicated the approach taken by CYCJ.

While CYCJ's work spanned policy, practice, research and lived experience from the outset, it was an external evaluation of CYCJ (Stocks-Rankin, 2020) that enabled closer reflection and formalisation of CYCJ's role, position and identity within the youth justice landscape. This evaluation articulated CYCJ's contribution to youth justice as an intermediary, boundary-spanning organisation. Intermediary organisations have been broadly defined as those focused on building organisational or system capacity to bridge the gap between (research) knowledge and policy or practice (Franks and Bory, 2017). Importantly, intermediary organisations can be seen as a function, as a relationship and as a process (Howells, 2006). The primary function may often be seen to be knowledge gathering and facilitating knowledge transfer (Howells, 2006), but also includes the building of relationships and networks (Stocks-Rankin, 2020; Gagnon et al., 2019); problem-solving and technical assistance (Stocks-Rankin, 2020; Howells, 2006); research (Bednarek et al., 2016); and evaluation (Franks and Bory, 2017); policy and practice design or implementation (Franks and Bory, 2017); leadership and other training; and communications and publication (Bednarek et al., 2016). Boundary spanning organisations sit between different systems, organisations and communities (Sturm, 2009) and such a position provides three key benefits to an intermediary organisation: connections, overview and in-depth knowledge (Stocks-Rankin, 2020).

Although CYCJ is not formalised or articulated using the terminology of Knowledge Transfer Partnerships (KTPs), there is near identical overlap between the role and function of CYCJ and that of a KTP, that KTPS are "intermediary organisations, initiatives or networks whose intent is to overcome a range of inter-relationship and contextual challenges ... using a multitude of strategies and tools" (Schmidt et al., 2022).

The implications of being a boundary-spanning organisation

This articulation of CYCJ as an intermediary boundary-spanning organisation had a positive impact on CYCJ's professional and organisational identity. While long-established and respected as a knowledge exchange centre for excellence based in an academic institution, the natural fit and positioning of CYCJ was not immediately apparent. For example, the research process is typically slower than the policy cycle (Nutley et al., 2003) and although the increased use of open access publishing has improved access to research (Shaw and Barker, 2023), until recently few policymakers and practitioners had sufficient access to academic journals. Thus, despite a continued emphasis on rigorous and ethical research, disseminating findings in a timely and distilled manner for a policy and practice audience frequently took priority in CYCJ, over publication in academic journals or writing for the Research Excellence Framework. This approach was not always a neat fit with university research priorities nor career development paths. And despite the Practice Development Model being predicated upon staff's recent practice expertise, the reality was that while staff remained credible and retained significant practice knowledge and skills, they inevitably over time became one step removed from the direct realities and pressures of the frontline. Similarly, while CYCJ team members brought significant experience in policy development and implementation, and worked closely alongside policymakers, CYCJ itself is not an organisation that bears the responsibility for making policy a reality. Lastly, while hearing and amplifying the voice of lived experience has been a core part of CYCJ's value base and conduct since it came into existence, few CYCJ members themselves had significant experience of the justice system as a child.

The setting out of these tensions and ambiguous identities is not intended to paint CYCJ in a poor light, operating as a "Jack of all trades", instead the realisation of our key role as a boundary-spanning organisation underscores that this is not a limitation or flaw. That CYCJ simultaneously belongs, and does not belong, within these spaces is part of its role, part of its *modus operandi*. It is precisely this positioning that gives CYCJ the credibility, the empathy, the knowledge, the skills and, importantly, the capacity from which to create change. Despite these benefits, practice at the boundaries is acknowledged to be complex in that operating in such a space "presents numerous overlapping tensions and trade-offs related to process, participation, power, credibility, relevance and legitimacy, and timing" (Bednarek et al., 2016:3). However, as Stocks-Rankin (2020:22) observes, "Boundary spanners have an overview of the issues, activities and interventions in the system. They also have a detailed understanding of the way those issues might manifest in different places or parts of the system. And finally, the connections that boundary-spanning work provides gives the organisation an ability to challenge and support development".

This positioning provides three key opportunities to facilitate knowledge exchange, influence and impact in the youth justice sector: (a) credibility, (b) access, and (c) constructive relationships. This has benefits for each of our workstreams. In relation to Practice and Policy Development the model of CYCJ involves recent practitioners as key staff in the organisation. Providing practitioners with the capacity and thinking space to reflect and build upon their up-to-date insider knowledge and existing practice connections means that CYCJ can build trust and credibility in the field as well as facilitating honest relationships that can withstand constructive challenge. This is documented in the CYCJ Evaluation:

> I think because they challenge you about what you're doing and you're able to see what they see. And I suppose try and put things right. Or they'll be able to track or identify where there isn't data. And help you to have a good in depth understanding of your business. (Public Sector Manager 5)
>
> (Stocks-Rankin, 2020:45)

This means that CYCJ staff frequently have early access to emerging practice issues and concerns in the field and can act swiftly to understand and address these matters by facilitating knowledge exchange across policy, practice, research and lived experience. For example, while a large focus of CYCJ's work involves interacting with those at the coalface, CYCJ also regularly sits around the table at high-level strategic discussions such as the national Youth Justice Improvement Board, meetings with senior civil servants, and the Age of Criminal Responsibility Steering Group:

> CYCJ is very well connected. They have an awareness function because of their connections in the system. Because there is a lot of trust and credibility, they're able to engage with those that deliver services, you're talking about Polmont, secure care units, the criminal justice system, prosecution and so on. (Civil Society 2)
>
> (Stocks-Rankin, 2020:48)

Access to practice wisdom, both within and external to CYCJ, also enhances the work of the Research Workstream by ensuring that CYCJ's research priorities are driven by current policy or practice needs, or is responding to those with lived experience. This close relationship with practice ensures that CYCJ research has credibility among its primary users, and in turn facilitates the production of meaningful research that is feasible and deliverable (e.g. through providing access to participants, research data, or research funding). As evidenced by Stocks-Rankin (2020:87):

> I think they've got a mutually beneficial relationship with us because they obviously need local authorities to participate in research activities and to inform them about what's developing into really good practice and what's blocking practice. And then they share that learning nationally. (Public Sector Service Manager 4)

This connection with policy and practice also helps to ensure that research has impact, as the motivation behind the research is often to respond to a particular knowledge or practice need (for example, by evaluating the effectiveness of a service, or understanding the experiences of service users). Thus the desire and scope for impact is often established at the outset. As Stocks-Rankin (2020:44) observed:

> CYCJ's leadership was I think in the Scottish context, certainly in the criminal justice end of the Scottish context, ahead of the game on that and getting us all thinking differently about how we imagine the whole process of engagement with academic partners in making research that did something in the world. (Academic 1)

Furthermore, CYCJ's extensive policy and practice networks and communication channels provide a vehicle for dissemination and reach beyond the original commissioning organisation.

CYCJ's credibility across research, practice and policy also benefits the work of the Participation and Engagement workstream by providing meaningful opportunity for those with lived experience to influence change.

> A number of interviewees talked about the importance of CYCJ "walking the walk" (Civil Society 5) and their contribution in helping to create the conditions where lived experience is beginning to be valued on par with other kinds of knowledge.
> (Stocks-Rankin, 2020:89)

The accessible, creative and purposeful approaches to participation employed in CYCJ often produces powerful testimonies and evidence that can challenge perceived wisdom and the status quo. CYCJ's status, relationships and access to those in positions of decision-making power in the youth justice sector certainly provide ample scope for the application of Lundy's conceptualisation of voice, space, audience and influence. Leveraging this privileged position alongside – but not directly affiliated to – decision makers enables CYCJ to create meaningful opportunities to shape, influence and demand change, which in turn enhances CYCJ's ability to reach, support and engage those with lived experience who wish to use their experiences to improve the system for others.

Adopting youth-led, creative, activity-based approaches to this work further extends the appeal that participation and engagement with CYCJ's has. Sport, music, art, gaming, poetry and a multitude of other approaches have been utilised that ensure that the offer of engaging in discussion of the youth justice systems is an appealing one. The creation of safe spaces where young people can speak openly and without fear of judgement have been cited as factors that encourage participation, whilst a recent review of one group led to comments regarding the benefit of personal developmental, skills and abilities. As one young man said, "I have confidence to be myself" following their involvement in the group, whilst another felt that the group had "opened so many doors" by leading to opportunities to speak directly to those in positions of power.

Influencing policy and practice

In 2023 the then Children and Young Person's Commissioner for Scotland, Bruce Adamson, commented that

> CYCJ has had a huge impact on law, policy and practice in Scotland over the last 10 years, with children's rights at the heart of their work; including through a name change to reflect the priority that they give to children. CYCJ has been a key partner

for the office of the Children and Young People's Commissioner Scotland over the last decade, providing expert research and being a strong ally in our role to promote and safeguard the rights of children and young people. This group of amazing human rights defenders has been right at the forefront of the world leading work to reform Scotland's approach to children in conflict with the law. Their expertise, bravery and passion has directly led to changes in the age of criminal responsibility, new approaches to child justice and focus on restorative justice, changes to secure care and other forms of detention, a focus on remand and deaths in custody, and a commitment from Scottish Government to stop the imprisonment of children. But most importantly of all, they have given children a voice. Children who had been constantly failed and often forgotten. CYCJ has put those children's voices at the centre of Scottish decision making, and challenged those in power to do better.

Achieving this is a result of years of endeavour during which CYCJ has collaborated with partners across a spectrum of constituencies to foster trusting relationships that afford the organisation the opportunity to speak candidly and as a critical friend (Costa and Kallick, 1993). It sought to position itself as a centre promoting and supporting evidence-based practice, whilst latterly focussing on the rights of those children and young people who come into conflict with the law in order to achieve change across the youth justice system, and indeed across the wider Scottish polity.

The role of relationships within this process is of particular importance. Having established close relationships with the relevant stakeholders over several years, CYCJ enjoy a position of trust within the sector that affords them the opportunity to speak candidly and honestly to the traditional custodians of the youth justice systems. Grounding their opinion within research and evidence allows for CYCJ to speak with credibility and proficiency.

However, there are inherent risks associated with speaking out in this fashion, no less the potential to damage relationships with partner organisations who may not feel able to express their concern, or who may hold contrasting views. This often requires private conversations, support and providing the evidence – of all kinds – that enables partners to feel equipped and confident to embrace organisational risk. This is not always successful, however, and a balancing act is required at times. Media relationships have also been developed over the years, meaning that CYCJ can occasionally advance the cause for change by informing the public debate and highlighting the benefits of a particular approach.

Whilst primarily funded by the Scottish Government, the autonomy afforded CYCJ and relationships that have developed over time allow them to challenge the government on their policies and advocate for a change of tack. Risks of being "co-opted" as an arm of government have been avoided; no doubt their positioning within the University of Strathclyde – and the academic freedom that comes with it – contributes to their ability to "speak truth to power". The composition of the CYCJ Practice and Policy Development workstream further cements the relationships between the organisation and statutory provision. With each member of the team being assigned to a specific local authority and area of expertise, dialogue and relationships are fostered through regular formal and informal meetings which maintain close links to those delivering support to children and young people in conflict with the law.

This chapter will now highlight two case studies which provide concrete examples of how CYCJ have achieved the impact alluded to by the quote above. These examples consider the positioning of CYCJ as a boundary spanning organisation, and how that unique position facilitates opportunities to exchange knowledge which in turn creates tangible change within youth justice policy and practice in Scotland. The case studies highlight how CYCJ's workstreams intersect, overlap and influence each other and how the conditions of access, credibility and constructive relationships create an environment that is ripe for knowledge exchange. In doing so, the authors acknowledge the tensions and trade-offs (Bednarek et al., 2016) that exist in being a boundary spanning organisation.

Case study one: Co-production of the Secure Care Standards

The co-production of the Secure Care Pathways and Standards, against which all four secure care providers in Scotland are now annually inspected by Scotland's Care Inspectorate, is an example of what has been achieved through the combined knowledge of those with lived experience, practitioners, academics and policymakers. Following on from a dedicated project which examined the delivery of secure care in Scotland (see Gough, 2017; Gough, 2018) CYCJ and partners across the sector encouraged the Scottish Government to explore opportunities to raise and harmonise standards of care within the secure care sector through the creation of standards which set benchmarks expected of care before, during and after a child's journey through secure care. With an ambition to amplify the voice, expertise and experiences of children, young people and adults who have personal experience of living in secure care, CYCJ acted as a mediatory between those with lived experience and a range of traditional stakeholders including Scottish Government, secure care providers and local authorities. The net result was the creation of 44 standards which were later adopted and endorsed by the wider secure care sector and their partners.

Taking advantage of well-developed relationships, and their impartial and objective positioning within the sector, CYCJ facilitated dialogue and open conversation which saw those currently living within secure care – and those with prior experience of it – shaping and critiquing draft proposals, which were in turn presented to the various stakeholders. Doing so involved workshops, conversations and participation in numerous meetings that brought together those with an interest in this area of care, and a ceding of power by some. Achieving this required a move away from the traditional meeting format by creating the space and audience that Lundy (2007) calls for, and ensuring that the views of those with lived experience of secure care were given appropriate weight throughout discussion. As such, the work undertaken to ensure meaningful participation was central to the co-production of the standards, but this was by no means a simple task. It is time-consuming, "deep" work that requires a very particular set of skills and qualities, including development of trusting relationships (Ross et al., 2018; van Bijleveld et al., 2020). Developing and enhancing the Participation and Engagement workstream was therefore an important step to achieve this, recruiting skilled practitioners with the expertise and competence to undertake such delicate and complex work.

Importantly these standards were not only co-produced and inspired by those who had intimate knowledge of secure care, but were written in a style that was centred solely on the child who is now accommodated there, using first person prose and clear language appropriate for children aged 12–18. These standards – which relate to the child's experience of secure care not only during their time there, but before and after – feature statements that were unlikely to have been included had the standards been produced through traditional, bureaucratic means, and address aspects of a child's journey through secure care that may have otherwise been overlooked. Similar approaches have seen CYCJ support children to co-produce standards that govern practice within Scotland's Bairns' Hoose; an approach which responds to episodes of harm towards a child, or harm caused by a child under the age of criminal responsibility (ACR).

Following the publication of the aforementioned secure care standards CYCJ again made use of its positioning alongside the relevant stakeholders to promote its roll-out and uptake, creating spaces within which discussion of the challenges and opportunities posed by the standards could take place. Online and in–person "secure care champs" forums were created where secure care practitioners could meet, speak openly about challenges they face and share ideas of how best to incorporate the standards into practice. Furthermore, CYCJ-dedicated secure care practitioners established multi-agency practitioner forums where participants could share ideas on how to achieve the ambitions set out by the standards. This called on CYCJ to draw on its existing relationships across the secure care sector, whilst expanding its reach into those adjacent organisations whose role was not always as prominent within the delivery of secure care. As such, contact was made not only with the secure care providers – who in Scotland are run by independent charities – and local authority social work departments, but also with colleagues in education, police, third sector organisations and in health services such as Child and Adolescent Mental Health Services. In short, CYCJ sought to engage with Corporate Parents – those statutory bodies with a legal responsibility to consider the needs of care experienced children and young people – and other organisations who had a legal obligation to support children within, and on the edges of secure care.

In the first two years after implementation CYCJ delivered roadshows (interactive briefings and training sessions on the standards and on relevant research in this area) to 21 of Scotland's 32 local authorities, as well as presenting to each of the secure care providers. Scores of colleagues from across the youth justice workforce had attended both the "secure care champs" group and the practitioner forum, whilst CYCJ responded to more than 200 practice queries relating to secure care in the two years prior to October 2023. Through the combined efforts of the various stakeholders and actors, a review of the implementation of the standards found that many children were receiving a good standard of care, whilst highlighting areas for further development (Care Inspectorate, 2023). Those delivering secure care benefitted from CYCJ's expertise, with one provider referring to the "valuable input from CYCJ at a team development day" (Nolan et al., 2023:11) and support provided through CYCJ's dedicated secure care advisor being cited by partners as a key factor in securing progress towards implementation.

As an evaluation of the roll-out of the standards showed, the opportunity to bring the diverse range of organisations and practitioners into one space, and thereafter dedicate time to this discussion, was invaluable in contributing to a better understanding of their respective roles and a more comprehensive adoption of the standards (Nolan et al., 2023). Stocks-Rankin (2020) previously highlighted the impact that CYCJ makes to the youth justice sector by facilitating such discussions, whilst also instigating them where necessary. Importantly, these discussions take place not in the "silos" of organisations, but are encouraged across boundaries, bringing stakeholders from all constituencies together in the belief that a flow of knowledge and opinion will lead to a clearer understanding and improved situation for children in conflict with the law and the communities they belong to.

This piece of work, and other similar initiatives resulted in the co-chairs of Scotland's National Youth Justice Advisory group to comment that:

> the blend of research and practice gives the CYCJ both credibility and relevance and provides valuable support to agencies working across complex and diverse systems where children's rights are often overlooked. As it increasingly integrates the voices of young people into its day-to-day work, we know that CYCJ will continue to challenge and inspire agencies to strive towards the best outcomes for children in conflict with the law.

Case study two: Age of Criminal Responsibility

A further example of CYCJ seeking to improve outcomes for children in conflict with the law can be found in the legislative field. Whilst not progressing anywhere near as much as many wanted, and with calls to increase the age further (Donnelly, 2020), the increase in Age of Criminal Responsibility (ACR) from eight to 12 represents a modest step forward in Scotland's response to children in conflict with the law following decades of campaigning that required persistence (McAra and McVie, 2023). Acting alongside a range of interested partners including children's groups, civic society, local government, academia, social work practice and children's rights organisations, CYCJ contributed to the campaign which ultimately led to an increase in Scotland's acutely low ACR.

This entailed the blending of research and practice wisdom, the amplification of the voice of lived experience and helping decision-makers think through the ways in which policy developments can be introduced. Alongside various partners, CYCJ influenced sufficient cross-party political support to lead to a change of legislation in 2019. This was the outcome of various approaches, including facilitating discussions amongst decision-makers and producing accessible evidence-based literature which sought to centre the debate on knowledge (of all kinds), seeking to avoid moral panic and political point scoring. Contribution to Scottish Parliament committee debates, provision of written consultation responses and seeking to inform Parliamentarians all featured within the actions of CYCJ, mindful that changes in legislation require political appetite and provision of evidence to shape decision making.

This appetite was in part due to the work that CYCJ and a range of partners had undertaken to raise the profile of this issue. Over the preceding years blogs, conferences and other opportunities to amplify the voice of children and young people affected by the low ACR had featured within CYCJ's work and the work of several partner organisations. CYCJ sought to create the spaces and gather audiences that needed to hear the lived experience of the situation, and the evidence that proved the rationale for a change in legislation.

This task was made somewhat easier through the work of Professors Lesley McAra and Susan McVie, whose *Edinburgh Study of Youth Transitions and Crime* provides robust, empirical evidence of the corrosive impact of justice systems upon children and young people, and provided a firm base upon which rational debate could take place. CYCJ therefore sought to communicate the findings of this study into digestible, accessible resources that could be consumed by practitioners, policymakers and political representatives. Likewise, studies regarding the neurological immaturity of children and the impact this has on criminal responsibility (Delmage, 2013) and the impact of Speech, Language and Communication Needs amongst the youth justice cohort (Anderson et al., 2016) were highlighted.

Fusing these approaches together with practical and operational solutions enabled CYCJ not only to support the campaign for a change in the law, but to point to the material reality that would be faced by children, families and practitioners following any change. This included highlighting international comparisons and linking this issue to Scotland's wider ambition of incorporation of, and compliance with, the United Nations Convention on the Rights of the Child (UNCRC) and other international human rights obligations. The expertise of the CYCJ team also meant that practice wisdom amongst its staff could create solutions to the challenges that would be faced by those tasked with the responsibility of delivering care to children and young people. This approach included offering robust and realistic alternatives at an early stage of the debate; producing papers which considered the various options available to practitioners and other organisations should a change be made, and generally seeking to better inform the debate.

Whilst participation and engagement helped in framing the issue and doing so within the lived reality of those experiencing the issue, CYCJ's position crossing the boundaries of research, policy, and practice meant that it was able to blend various strands of knowledge together to create a broader, more vivid picture of the issue. As well as highlighting the ethical and rights-based reasons for the change, they were able to point to evidence which highlighted why an increase in ACR would be effective in meeting the needs of those who caused harm, and of those who had been harmed. CYCJ's distillation of all these forms of knowledge also meant they were well positioned to assist in the roll out of the new ACR, delivering training to practitioners across the youth justice workforce and remaining connected to each constituent part of the systems responding to the change.

Work relating to ACR continues today, with a CYCJ representative chairing one of the working groups set up to review data and research stemming from the change in law. Another representative is involved in examining the operational implications of any further increase to ACR whilst the CYCJ research team have recently completed an exercise collating salient literature from across the globe. Supplementing this, CYCJ supported a young person with lived experience of the justice systems to undertake a large-scale survey of several hundred children and young people in Scotland (Logan, 2021), thus collating and amplifying their collective voice, whilst CYCJ used existing connections to ensure that their views received the audience they deserved. With the aforementioned ACR working groups tasked with providing further insight and evidence to Scottish Ministers over the coming months, there may be a possibility of a further increase to the ACR, but any change would require the political will be present and the relevant services be properly equipped to deliver it.

Simultaneously, CYCJ contributes to the multi-agency training of practitioners who now need to undertake their role within a new framework for responding to episodes of harm by those both under and over the age of 12. In advancing this work, CYCJ collaborated with colleagues within Police Scotland and local authority social work departments to hold practice focussed conferences, at which experience of the legislative change and its impact upon practice could be shared. Practitioners from both police and social work provided presentations on the challenges that had been faced, and how they were overcome. Importantly, attendees received a presentation from a young person who had previously come into conflict with the law, providing an insight and reflection that would otherwise have been missing from the event.

Feedback from attendees highlighted the benefit of this approach, with post-event evaluation stating that the event "provided an opportunity to come together and explore how best to support children in crises" and that "we need more events like this to talk about support and practice". Those in attendance had been provided with case studies reflective of the change in legislation, resulting in one participant saying "it was great to get together with practitioners from so many agencies and local authorities and work through some of the challenges faced by children. The case studies provided some of this opportunity". Involvement of young people with experience of contact with the police was similarly praised, with attendees stating that their input had "made me think more about what he had gone through in police custody." Support from a trusted adult – in this case a CYCJ participation worker – was necessary to create this knowledge exchange opportunity, once more underlining the importance of that role in facilitating the sharing of knowledge and opinion.

This approach – which has been replicated by CYCJ on numerous occasions over the past ten years – demonstrates the broad attitude to knowledge that the organisation adopts, with practice wisdom, lived experience and research all being given appropriate levels of weighting and equally respected. Whilst the focus here has been on secure care and on ACR, this approach has been utilised in many other instances such as Diversion from Prosecution, disproportionate criminalisation of children within residential childcare, and the expansion of Restorative Justice. The Chief Executive of the Scottish Children's Reporter Administration (SCRA) – the organisation tasked with overseeing Scotland's Children's Hearings – recently reflected on the impact that such an approach has had, stating that "CYCJ fuse research, evidence, practice, policy, influence and learning into a really compelling offering across our sector – and we have all benefitted greatly from that."

Conclusion

With a population of only 5.4 million, Scotland benefits from a youth justice sector – and indeed a wider social welfare landscape – in which connections and networks are fairly easy to establish and maintain. This in turn allows for those with credibility to play a central role in the civic discourse and to influence the body politic. Whether or not CYCJ could be replicated in a nation that is far larger where such connections are more difficult to establish, or within a smaller nation where it may be more challenging to secure the correct blend of expertise remains to be seen. The depth and proximity of relationships between CYCJ and the distinct branches of the youth justice workforce and sector has been central to their success, however, and thus any attempt to replicate this model elsewhere ought to bear this in mind.

Compared to its southern neighbours, Scotland's parliament has shown a willingness to move towards a Rights Respecting response to children in conflict with the law (Kilkelly, 2023), with steps to incorporate the UNCRC into law and the raising of the ACR evidence of a more progressive approach. It may be that a favourable attitude to addressing issues such as children's rights and an equitable justice system are prerequisite features of any nation that would seek to replicate the model that CYCJ has undertaken, or to mimic its impact. CYCJ's ability to nudge and encourage decision makers at all levels of national and local government may well have been hampered had a political ideology that is more apathetic towards progressive issues been dominant. Indeed, McAra and McVie (2023) suggest that progress towards an increased ACR would not have been possible without the political desire to do so.

Likewise, access to those making decisions at the largest of organisations, as well as directly to practitioners engaging directly with children, has allowed CYCJ to share knowledge, produce knowledge and to absorb knowledge. This ability to speak to distinct and separate, although interconnected, constituencies within the youth justice sector has enabled it to contribute to changes in Scotland's response to children in conflict with the law. Adopting an approach that creates spaces to communicate with senior policy officers, *and* frontline practitioners *and* people with lived experience of the justice system *and* academics; indeed, with relevant parties from *all* areas of the sector, has been key. Those seeking to replicate CYCJ's influence would therefore need to invest in the relationships and capacity that allows them to cross the boundaries that these stakeholders exist within, and in doing so bring together actors that may otherwise have worked in isolation. Any organisation seeking to replicate this would be required to develop the credibility and relationships that afford such ease of access; it is impossible to span boundaries that are closed off.

References

Anderson, S. A., Hawes, D. J. & Snow, P. C. 2016. Language impairments among youth offenders: A systematic review. *Children and Youth Services Review*, 65, 195–203.
Bednarek, A., Wyborn, C., Meyer, R., Parris, A., Leith, P., McGreavy, B. & Ryan, M. 2016. Practice at the boundaries: Summary of a workshop of practitioners working at the interfaces science, policy and society for environmental outcomes. Washington, DC: Pew Trust. Available from http://www.pewtrusts.org//media/assets/2016/07/practiceattheboundariessummaryofawork shopofpractitioners.pdf (accessedApril 2017).
Cairney, P. 2020. 463 The "Scottish approach" to policymaking. In Keating, M. (ed.) *The Oxford handbook of Scottish politics*. Oxford University Press.
Care Inspectorate (ed.) 2023. *Secure care pathway review*. Dundee: Care Inspectorate.
Costa, A. L. & Kallick, B. 1993. Through the lens of a critical friend. *Educational Leadership*, 51, 49–49.
Davies, H., Nutley, S. & Walter, I. 2008. Why "knowledge transfer" is misconceived for applied social research. *Journal of Health Services Research & Policy*, 13, 188–190.
Davies, H. T., Powell, A. E. & Nutley, S. M. 2015. Mobilising knowledge to improve UK health care: Learning from other countries and other sectors – a multimethod mapping study. *Journal of Health Services Research & Policy*, (18)(3), suppl. https://doi.org/10.1177/1355819613502011.
Delmage, E. 2013. The minimum age of criminal responsibility: A medico-legal perspective. *Youth Justice*, 13, 102–110.
Donnelly, M. 2020. Scottish youth justice and the legacy of Kilbrandon: A provocation paper. London: The British Academy.
Franks, R. P. & Bory, C. T. 2017. Strategies for developing intermediary organizations: Considerations for practice. *Families in Society*, 98, 27–34.
Gagnon, S., Mailhot, C. & Ziam, S. 2019. The role and contribution of an intermediary organisation in the implementation of an interactive knowledge transfer model. *Evidence & Policy*, 15, 7–29.
Gough, A. 2017. *Secure care in Scotland: Young people's voices*. Glasgow: Centre for Youth & Criminal Justice.
Gough, A. 2018. *Secure care in Scotland: Cross border placements*. Glasgow: Centre for Youth & Criminal Justice.
Howells, J. 2006. Intermediation and the role of intermediaries in innovation. *Research policy*, 35, 715–728.
Kilkelly, U. 2023. Child First and children's rights: An opportunity to advance rights-based youth justice. In Case, S. & Hazel, N. (eds) *Child First: Developing a new youth justice system*. Cham: Springer International.
Logan, B. A. 2021. *Age of criminal responsibility: Children and young people's views*. Glasgow: Children and Young People's Centre for Justice.

Lundy, L. 2007. "Voice" is not enough: Conceptualising Article 12 of the United Nations Convention on the Rights of the Child. *British Educational Research Journal*, 33, 927–942.

Maloney, E. 2018. Listening to young people is not enough… Available from: https://www.cycj.org.uk/listening-to-young-people-is-not-enough/.

McAra, L. & McVie, S. 2007. Youth justice? The impact of system contact on patterns of desistance from offending. *European Journal of Criminology*, 4, 315–345.

McAra, L. & McVie, S. 2023. Raising the minimum age of criminal responsibility: Lessons from the Scottish experience. *Current Issues in Criminal Justice*, 1–22.

McCartney, G., Collins, C., Walsh, D. & Batty, D. 2011 *Accounting for Scotland's excess mortality: Towards a synthesis*. Glasgow Centre for Population Health.

Murray, K., McGuinness, P., Burman, M. & Mcvie, S. 2015. *Evaluation of the whole system approach to young people who offend in Scotland*. June. Glasgow: SCCJR.

Nolan, D., Whitelaw, R. & Gibson, R. 2023. *Secure Care Pathway and Standards Scotland: The journey of implementation*. Glasgow: Children and Young People's Centre for Justice.

Nutley, S., Davies, H. & Walter, I. 2003. Evidence-based policy and practice: Cross-sector lessons from the United Kingdom. *Social Policy Journal of New Zealand*, issue 20, 29–48.

Polkinghorne, M. 2011. *Review of the use of the terms "Knowledge Transfer" and "Knowledge Exchange"*. Technical report. Bournemouth University.

Redman, S., Greenhalgh, T., Adedokun, L., Staniszewska, S., Denegri, S. & Committee, O. 2021. BOTC-POKCS. Co-production of knowledge: The future. *BMJ*, 372, n434.

Ross, C., Kerridge, E. & Woodhouse, A. 2018. *The impact of children and young people's participation on policy making*. Edinburgh: Children in Scotland, on behalf of the Scottish Governmant.

Schmidt, B. M., Cooper, S., Young, T. & Jessani, N. S. 2022. Characteristics of knowledge translation platforms and methods for evaluating them: A scoping review protocol. *BMJ Open*, 12, e061185.

SCIE 2022. *Coproduction: What it is and how to do it*. London: SCIE.

Shaw, T. & Barker, A. 2023. Open access in scholarly publishing: Where are we now? In *Research information yearbook 2022/2023*. Cambridge: Europa Science.

Stocks-Rankin, C. R. 2020. *The contribution of CYCJ: Boundary-spanning and system development*. Glasgow: CYCJ.

Sturm, S. 2009. Activating systemic change toward full participation: The pivotal role of boundary spanning institutional intermediaries. *St. Louis University Law Journal*, 54, 1117–1138.

Van Bijleveld, G. G., Bunders-Aelen, J. F. G. & Dedding, C. W. M. 2020. Exploring the essence of enabling child participation within child protection services. *Child & Family Social Work*, 25, 286–293.

Vaswani, N., Dyer, F. & Lightowler, C. 2018. *What is youth justice? Reflections on the 1968 Act*. Edinburgh: Social Work Scotland.

Ward, V. 2017. Why, whose, what and how? A framework for knowledge mobilisers. *Evidence and Policy*, 13, 477–497.

7 Advancing best practice in juvenile justice in Belarus

Vicky Palmer

Chapter objectives

By the end of this chapter, you should be able to:

- Understand the context of juvenile justice in Belarus.
- Appreciate the significance of knowledge-transfer partnerships on an international platform.
- Recognise that Belarus, as with the UK, strives purposefully to reconcile the sensitive balance between welfare and justice policies for juvenile offenders.

Introduction

This chapter explores a knowledge-transfer partnership between British and Belarusian academics and legal professionals, in conjunction with the British Embassy and Belarus State University, concerning practice-focused advancement in Belarusian juvenile justice. It will examine the current context of their juvenile justice system, briefly surveying its underlying political landscape and the constituent parts of its juvenile sentencing practices. It will then provide a discussion on Belarusian children's rights, something which arose as a consequence of project delivery. A detailed analysis of the partnership project is then provided, including its origins, purpose, implementation and accomplishments. It aims to assess the impact that the project has had, including its evaluation and recommendations for change, along with some reflections on its challenges. Finally, the chapter brings us up to date by investigating post-project developments and by reflecting upon a new era for Belarusian juvenile justice. It concludes by reinforcing the importance of knowledge-transfer partnerships locally, nationally and internationally, placing such initiatives firmly on the agenda as a community of practice for the global evolution of youth justice; one which collaborates over shared intelligence and objectives in an open and reciprocal manner.

Belarusian juvenile justice in context

The Republic of Belarus is a presidential state in Eastern Europe which is centrally governed as a single nation by a government that maintains absolute control over its country's domestic and foreign policies (Khodosevich et al., 2019). It gained its independence following the dissolution of the USSR and achieved its state sovereignty in 1990 and has been described as 'the last remaining true dictatorship in the heart of Europe' (White et al., 2010: 5). Elected

DOI: 10.4324/9781003411192-8

in July 1994, Alyaksandr Lukashenko remains the first President of the Republic of Belarus and he upholds a state ideological system which is disseminated to all its citizens via its state educational system as well as through the workplace (IFHR, 2008). As a means of sustaining this ideology, the state has control of most media outlets and there are no independent radio or TV channels (White et al., 2010).

The Belarusian legal system is rooted in Romano-Germanic law, also known as civil law; a practice used by some 60% of the world (Khodosevich et al., 2019). Its focus is upon the freedom of the individual and human cooperation, and it is 'the most ancient and widely extended system in the world' (David and Zhoffre-Spinozi, 1998: 186). Its criminal justice system relies upon an 'inquisitorial' system of justice; one where its judges are actively involved in investigating the facts of the case, questioning witnesses and preparing evidence (Block et al., 2000), whereas the UK utilises an 'adversarial' system; one which relies upon two opposing parties disputing the facts of a case to convince a neutral judge. The UK system is rooted in 12th-century common law and was historically administered by the Kings' Courts, starting with King Henry II. It relies upon two advocates – defence and prosecution lawyers – to represent the defendant and the Crown's position before an impartial judge who then, with the assistance of a jury, determines the truth and passes sentence (*ibid.*).

The penal system in Belarus is managed by the 'Department of Execution of the Punishment' (Foreign and Commonwealth Office, 2023). Individuals can be arrested and detained by either the police, the Border Guards or by the *Komitet Gosudarstvennoy Bezopasnosti* (KGB) – Committee of State Security (*ibid.*). Their minimum age of criminal responsibility (MACR) is set at 16 years; however, it is lower for more serious offences such as murder, rape, and robbery with violence; where it is set at 14 years (CRC, 1993). The rationale for the lower age for what we would consider 'indictable only' offences are that at 14 years, young people should have acquired life experience, rational mental development and a prior comprehension of the dangerousness of their behaviour (Barcov et al., 2018). Whilst the age of 14 clearly falls within the recommended age set by the UNCRC (United Nations Convention on the Rights of the Child), their juvenile justice policies have not been without controversy. Much of this focuses upon the more recent addition of 'illegal traffic in narcotic drugs' to the list of offences punishable at 14 years of age (*ibid.*). Since its inclusion, it has been reported that 'thousands of teenagers and young people were sentenced to long terms of imprisonment (8–15 years)' (ICCI, 2020: 1). The controversy arises from the assertion that many of these children and young people have been coerced into child criminal exploitation, either online or offline, and hence should be treated as victims (UNODC, 2019; Amnesty International, 2020b; ICCI, 2020). Belarus is not alone in this area of contention, since the UK has also been criticised for similar approaches (The Children's Society, 2019, Marshall, 2023). Marshall (2023) informs us that although England and Wales have been moving away from the criminalisation of children involved in such exploitation, there remains a problem in terms of their identification through the National Referral Mechanism which may further ensconce some young people in the youth justice system. However, Belarus operates a zero-tolerance policy towards all drugs offences and such crimes are considered by its President as so heinous, in terms of their effects, that he mandated that any offender should be incarcerated in conditions so intolerable that prisoners would 'pray for death' (Urgent Action, 2019: 2).

Even children who have broken the law who have not reached the MACR can, by decision of the court, be incarcerated in a correctional institution for up to two years, and in this scenario no minimum age is stipulated (Gasyuk, 2006; Moestue, 2008). Once they have met the MACR, Belarusian juvenile community sentencing options, like their adult counterparts, comprise the equivalent of an absolute discharge, conditional discharge, fine, enforced education, community service, liberty restrictions, banning from activities, curfews and conditional sentences such as suspended sentence supervision orders (Gasyuk, 2006). In addition, where a juvenile has committed low-risk offences, the courts have further non-custodial disposals such as a public apology, payment of compensation, placement under the supervision of a labour collective or in a special educational establishment (CRC, 1993).

For those juveniles who have committed more serious offences, sentences of detention may be imposed. There is no equivalent of our children's secure estate in Belarus, meaning that there are no dedicated prisons for children (Just Arrived, 2023). Sentences of detention for juveniles are served initially in adult Pre-Trial Detention Centres whilst they are being investigated or subject to their hearing or trial, and time spent here can sometimes exceed a year (*ibid.*). Following sentence, they are transferred to Youth Detention Centres of which there are only two; one is a facility for teenage boys aged 14–21 called 'Bobruisk Children's Educational Colony No. 2' (ICCI, 2022), and the other is for girls called 'Gomel Correctional Colony No. 4'. The latter facility is for both girls and women who have been imprisoned for either the first time, for political activity or for drug trafficking offences committed under article 328 of the criminal code (ICCI, 2021). Once those incarcerated have turned 21 years of age, they are transferred to one of 16 corrective colonies, where the emphasis for them is on gaining an education and they are able to access the support of psychologists (Just Arrived, 2023). Corrective colonies vary in size, ranging from occupancies of fourteen convicts to several thousand (*ibid.*).

It is difficult to determine a holistic picture of whom exactly is incarcerated in each of these facilities, as statistics are not available on specifics concerning age ranges or male versus female juvenile prisoners. In addition, it is difficult to obtain data regarding the total number of children arrested in any one year, those held in police custody or those on remand (Moestue, 2008). Neither is there any readily available information regarding institutional size, staffing levels and whether education is available. Machalou (2018: 1) articulates this frustration thus, 'who has been researching in the secure facilities? You can't even get in … we do not know what is happening in children's prisons'. Figures that are available can be found from the Institute for Crime and Justice Policy Research website (ICPR, 2023) which informs us that the number of juveniles aged 14–17 sentenced to detention fluctuates year on year. For example, in 1989, there were a total of 948 incarcerated, rising to 1,680 in 1999, then decreasing again to 733 in 2005. By 2018, numbers had increased again to 1,302.

The percentage of the prison population that are juveniles is low and remains relatively stable at around 0.8% (World Prison Brief, 2018). By comparison, in England and Wales, there are presently (August 2023) 456 children under the age of 18 in detention, but there were as many as 3,200 in October 2002 (HM Prison and Probation Service, 2023). More recently, a more complete picture of Juvenile crime in Belarus has emerged. In 2020, their Ministry of Internal Affairs announced that juvenile crime is falling; from 5.5 thousand juvenile offenders 10 years ago to 1.5 thousand in 2020 (BelTA, 2020).

It is difficult to ascertain the conditions in Belarusian penal facilities owing to difficulties of access, however, Andrey Machalou (2018), of the Minsk Regional Bar Association, has made some observations. He reports that their football pitches are not used and that in one Colony, there were boxes of laboratory equipment which had been sent to the institution for educational purposes in 2006 that remained unopened in 2014. He believes that this is because of a lack of funding to pay for its usage. Conditions generally in these facilities are reported as better than those in adult prisons (United States Department of

State, 2017), but they remain in need of improvement, with juveniles having restricted access to education, healthcare and their families, and receiving harsh sanctions for petty wrongdoings (OHCHR, 2019). These trivial infringements are noted in a 2020 report by the International Centre for Civil Initiatives (ICCI 2020: 2) to be 'a bad shave, a badly made bed, an unbuttoned button – to prevent them from being released early for good behaviour'. The implication here is that children's rights are deliberately violated to ensure that they serve the maximum length of time in secure facilities. The same report also alleges that on occasion, forms of torment are applied to young people such as the deprivation of oxygen via gas mask, the throwing of darts at their backs and threats to inject them with syringes of brown liquid (*ibid.*). In the same year, Amnesty International (2020b: 1) reported on the case of a 17-year-old prisoner who was made to clear snow 'with his bare hands'. Further violations are purported to include minors provided with ill-fitting, seasonally inadequate and damp clothing and footwear (Urgent Action, 2019).

Violations of children's rights in detention are not unique to Belarus. In the UK, the use of physical restraints contradicts Article 37 of the UNCRC which states that 'children must not suffer cruel or degrading treatment'. The use of force is a concern throughout the UK secure state, where it has previously been deemed premeditated, improper and unsafe (Carlile Report, 2006). More recently, some practices have been deemed to be especially dangerous and contentious, particularly the use of the 'prone restraint' (House of Commons, 2019: 3). It has also been reported by one child that, 'one of them twisted my arm up, and almost snapped it' (Gooch, 2015: 9). Hence it still remains a controversial issue that infringes human rights legislation.

Although Belarus has no real equivalent of our pre-sentence report, juveniles appearing before the courts will have certain information taken into consideration. This includes their living conditions, physical and mental health, any influence exerted by others, social background and 'other personality peculiarities' (Gasyuk, 2006: 1). When the latter is involved, it should be proven whether the defendant was aware of the full consequences of their actions, hence their teachers, parents and other relevant parties are interviewed with the help of a psychologist (CRC, 1993). Should it be found that the defendant was not fully culpable, they may be granted a conditional pardon or be made subject to compulsory measures of an educational nature (Gasyuk, 2006). In addition, regarding treatment, the Committee on the Rights of the Child (CRC, 1993) observes that the use of weapons or straightjackets for security measures is disallowed for juveniles; they are entitled to better standards of nutrition than are adults and they are entitled to food parcels which they may purchase or have sent in (CRC, 1993). Children are allowed visits from relatives once a month and are permitted two-hour walks. Furthermore, whilst Belarus continues to be the sole executioner in Europe and the previous Soviet Union (Amnesty International, 2020a), under their criminal code, juveniles under the age of 18 are exempt, just as they are from life imprisonment, exile or deportation (CRC, 1993; Belarusian Helsinki Committee, 2023).

The next part of the chapter seeks to explore children's rights in Belarus, since they are intrinsically related to the implementation of juvenile justice practice.

Surveying children's rights in Belarus

The Republic of Belarus ascribes significant importance to the administration of juvenile justice as well as to the protection of their interests and rights (Barcov et al., 2018). In terms of the 1989 UNCRC, all states should endorse the establishment of procedures and laws that specifically deal with children who find themselves in conflict with the law (Moestue, 2008). Moestue (2008: 40) informs us that

> this includes protecting children's privacy in court proceedings, ensuring that children are not detained with adult offenders and training staff to be sensitive to children's rights.

In addition, article 37 of the Convention maintains that the arrest, detention, or imprisonment of a child should only be for the shortest length of time and as a measure of last resort (UNICEF, 2020). However, according to Schmidt and Shchurko (2014), respecting children's rights remains a challenge for post-soviet countries, and they still rely upon residential care for educating children with disabilities, for juvenile offenders and for safeguarding purposes. Where Belarus does differ significantly in the upholding of children's rights may be seen in the repression of its own people in times of political crisis; including children (UNHR, 2020).

In August 2020, Lukashenko was re-elected as President for a sixth term, and this resulted in countless Belarusians protesting the results in both towns and cities (Bedford, 2021). The police on the streets were alleged to have used excessive force and many Belarusians were arrested, detained, prosecuted and imprisoned; many proclaiming that they were subjected to torture (Bedford, 2021; Human Rights Watch, 2021; Machalou, 2021). The use of torture was reportedly not confined to adults, and Amnesty International (2022) have announced that children were threatened in schools by staff for their or their parents' political views, that parents were threatened with the removal of their children into residential care and suspected child protestors were subjected to police violence on arrest and in detention. Amnesty International (2022) investigated several such cases and the testimony from the children and their parents is concerning. The children's very presence in an area staging a protest was sufficient to warrant their arrest and detention. A 16-year-old boy told his father, 'dad they beat us every day' (*ibid*.: 4), another claimed, 'I was hit several times with a baton all over my body; back, leg and hips' (*ibid*.: 3) and the mother of a 14-year-old boy maintained that the police, 'beat him, pulled his hair and pulled his fingers back to force him to unblock his phone' (*ibid*.: 5).

The next section addresses how the Belarusian judiciary are currently looking at developing methods of fully integrating juveniles into their own special and separate category of justice for the purposes of sentencing, taking more careful consideration of their status as minors who lack maturity. It will examine the drivers behind this desire for change and the knowledge-transfer partnership that helped to cement its impetus.

The project: Placing juvenile justice reform on the map in Belarus

Up until 2017, Belarus did not have a developed juvenile justice system sufficient to comply with the UNCRC 1989 (Blackman, 2017). Although there were differences in how the Belarusian justice system operated for juveniles and adults, it had never had a distinct juvenile justice system in terms of the provision of dedicated juvenile courts, specially trained judges and lawyers or a separation in terms of the delivery of specific youth justice services (SIHRG, 2018). Where it does differ is in the provision and use of distinct institutions for incarcerated young people (Just Arrived, 2023). In 2008, UNICEF maintained that it needed to reform its procedures by creating a separate, dedicated system that recognised the fact that young people had not yet reached maturity (Moestue, 2008).

It proposed a system based on constructive, non-punitive responses where the emphasis should be on helping young people to avoid unlawful behaviour, rather than punishing them; all in conjunction with the UNCRC to bring them into line with international standards (*ibid.*). The criticism from signatories of the UNCRC drove the government into action, and it commissioned a training package to be delivered to its judiciary to begin the process of advancing best practice in Belarusian juvenile justice (SIHRG, 2018).

In 2017, owing to my position as Course Leader for Nottingham Trent University's B. A. (Hons) Youth Justice course, I was approached by the founder of Solicitors International Human Rights Group (SIHRG) to collaborate on a programme to provide the theoretical and practical input for a project being spearheaded in Belarus. The project aimed to effect advancement in their administration of juvenile justice in the full spirit of co-operative knowledge and skills exchange. SIHRG is a network of academics and legal practitioners based in England which delivers training and education packages on a broad range of topics relating to human rights. It has been supporting seminars at the Belarus Judicial Institute in Minsk since 2014 (Blackman, 2017). In January 2017, the President of Belarus appointed judges to specialise in juvenile cases, and their Supreme Court invited the Judicial Institute to deliver their training. This provided a unique opportunity to draw upon British expertise to deliver a comprehensive training programme for their judiciary, with particular emphasis on improving the use of discretionary legal powers affecting juveniles and to spread the norms of a rehabilitative approach to juvenile offenders (*ibid.*).

The project would entail five separate visits to Belarus State University in Minsk between September 2017 and February 2018, delivering two full-day programmes of seminars on each occasion. I took the academic lead on programme design and delivery, and on each of the visits was accompanied by the founder of SIHRG and one other co-teacher; two of whom were academics, two were practising solicitors and one a youth offending team officer. Each of these co-teachers helped to deliver the package of lectures that I had devised. This undertaking would be in partnership with the Belarusian Institute for Training and Qualification Upgrading of Judges and Other Legal Professionals, SIHRG and the British Embassy. This work comprised an internationally collaborative, cross-sector, and cross-cultural project via the delivery of ten high-quality seminars on UK and international practices in juvenile justice for Belarusian judges, prosecutors, investigators and lawyers.

The remit was clear, Belarus State University and the British Embassy wanted traditional didactic lectures with inbuilt time for questions and discussion. Following a series of planning meetings with SIHRG, I designed the full seminar programme to be delivered on five occasions to different, discrete groups of legal professionals at Belarus State University. This included Russian sub-titled video interviews with a UK Court of Appeal Judge, a youth justice police officer, the Chief Youth Justice Judge and a rehabilitated juvenile offender.

In the drafting of the PowerPoints onto British Embassy templates, I was mindful of the advice given by Young (2008: 1): 'you want people to remember you standing there telling them something rather than that you used swishy information on your slides', hence the presentations were judicious in their content with the added benefit of reducing the costs of translation. In the crafting of the materials, I took account of the promotion of 'deep' rather than 'surface' learning with the inclusion of provocations for debate, the provision of real-life case studies and anonymised court reports for the sentencing of young offenders from my own previous practice as a probation officer. This 'deep learning' base utilised methods of 'doing' in the form of learning activities (Ramsden, 2003). This was intended to foster a more inclusive means of practice for the participants, stimulated by 'getting the audience to think, make decisions, formulate questions and learn' (Brown and Race, 1995: 14). All the written materials were quality assured and the content agreed by SIHRG to ensure that they provided equity of experience and adhered to Belarusian ethics and values. We were mindful, for example, not to include any case studies relating to drugs offences because of the exacting nature of their drugs laws for all ages, compared to those in England and Wales.

A further feature of the work on this project was mentoring to ensure that each co-teacher was familiar with and understood the sessions that they would be delivering. This proved an easy task for the academics as both were familiar with all of the programme content, having taught alongside me on the Youth Justice course at Nottingham Trent University (NTU) since its inception. As Course Leader, I and my practice-experienced colleagues had been involved in its design, together with the Youth Justice Board (YJB), since 2005. It was originally designed as a foundation degree and was delivered in person across the country to large cohorts of youth justice practitioners. Once delivery was completed, we were then commissioned to design and write a third year B.A. (Hons) top-up programme which was delivered to the same groups of learners on the same basis. The provision of these courses was finally completed in 2008 so we took the decision to maintain the course curricula and embed them at NTU for undergraduate students with no experience of the field, and it remains in place to this day.

The course is currently constructed to align with the YJB's Skills and Knowledge Matrix (Youth Justice Board, 2021) and is inclusive of modules around the evolution of the youth justice system, child and adolescent development, effective practice, the secure estate, restorative justice, safeguarding, and youth sentencing practices. As the course evolved, we developed strong links with employers via the provision of student place-ments, and introduced elements of student enrichment with field trips to Nottingham Magistrates' Courts, the Crown Court, the National Justice Museum and the ICJ at The Hague.

The outside co-facilitators, two solicitors and a youth offending team officer, were not aware of the course; hence time was spent helping to familiarise them with the materials and in the thinking behind the allocation of their sessions that played to their strengths. I was also able to identify where they could make additional contributions from their own areas of expertise. The final programme looked innovative, stimulating and con-temporary, and was underpinned by my doctoral research on the traits of children in the youth justice system. The sessions included the legal framework applicable to youth jus-tice in England and Wales, the context of children's rights, sentencing approaches, the secure estate for children and young people and a historical analysis of the English pro-gression from juvenile punishment to rehabilitation. Case study and court report analysis was built into the programme, where participants were encouraged to offer opinions, debate, and make comparisons with their own justice system regarding methods of juve-nile justice processes and sentencing.

Because neither I nor my colleagues speak Russian, we needed to embrace digital technology supported learning, i.e. erudition that is sustained using information and communication technologies (Weller, 2011). All the teaching was simultaneously trans-lated by two Russian interpreters located in sound-proofed booths at the rear of the lec-ture theatre, each sharing the translating. We spoke into a wired microphone directly into the interpreters' headphones and all participants were provided with headsets so that they could only hear the interpreters speak. These roles were then reversed when the participants asked questions. All the materials had been pre-translated into Russian, and each video interview had been augmented by Russian subtitles.

Following delivery of the first training day, it became clear that there were two areas of our lecture content that were proving contentious to this group of learners. The first was the comparative ages of criminal responsibility; 10 in England and 16 in Belarus (14 for the most serious offences). This issue generated a barrier to learning concerning 'areas of good practice' as it became clear that despite their lack of a separate youth justice system, the Belarusians believed their current system to be better than that in England in this regard. The second area of contention was around the cultural positions on sentencing practice, for example, Belarusians do not recognise 'violence' between children as a criminal offence, but merely as an 'administrative case' to be dealt with by social workers rather than the courts. At the time of programme delivery (2017–2018), 40% of children in custody had been incarcerated for offences of violence against the person in England and Wales (Youth Justice Board, 2019: 39). Participants once again questioned the progressiveness of British juvenile justice policy when we imprison children for such acts.

Though these issues fostered a two-way learning experience which enlarged and broadened our knowledge (Seldin, 1997), they became a considerable hindrance as they invoked excessive discussion and debate, some heated and prolonged, thus shortening the time available for the remaining sessions. Reflecting on the first day's training and learning from these mistakes triggered by culture clashes (Schön, 1983), we revisited the areas of contention within the case studies and increased the ages of the children whilst changing the emphasis and types of offences committed to more neutral territory – acquisitive offences. This modified approach, combined with an added explicit acknowledgement that many identified areas of good practice were to be found in Belarus, encouraged more harmonious and receptive engagement. Belarusians were further heartened to learn that we have actively been lobbying for change in England and Wales (see for example Brown and Charles, 2019). This meant that with a more collegiate programme, the project's overarching learning outcomes could all be met. These included, 'to improve participants' understanding of the vital role of juvenile justice reform', 'to develop rehabilitative sentencing and diversion of juveniles from the criminal justice system', 'to promote an international human rights base for modern juvenile justice systems', 'to ensure that children are dealt with in a manner appropriate to their well-being' and 'to promote an understanding of juvenile psychology' (Blackman, 2017). Participants were eventually able to construct meaning through learning activities that held more value to them, and in the spirit of constructive alignment, learning that they had inadvertently created for themselves (Biggs, 2007).

The materials still required further tweaking as we began to appreciate that the differing professions of the ten cohorts provoked more interruptive and prolonged debate depending upon their angle of practice. By example, the cohort of judges found it difficult to understand the UK 'adversarial' system of justice. Since Belarus relies upon an 'inquisitorial' system of justice, this cohort frowned upon the lack of fine-detailed, thorough investigation that they themselves would employ and picked holes in one of the case studies that demonstrated this perceived UK failing. These extended debates meant that sessions overran their time allocation, and it soon became clear that no matter how much we modified the content of the training, we would never be able to fully pre-empt areas of conflict, so we made no further changes to the content; preferring to encourage debate at the potential expense of missed session content.

The next section identifies some challenges faced by this knowledge-transfer partnership.

Reflections on the knowledge-transfer partnership: Some challenges

At the time of programme delivery, I was unaware of any of the allegations of abuses of children's rights in Belarus noted earlier. There were, however, some indications during the final seminar delivery where several NGOs participated. During one of the breaks, a number of women entered the break-out area and handed out flyers. These women were members of 'Mothers 3:2:8', a lobby group campaigning for support for the release of their sons who had been incarcerated for prolonged periods of time for drug-related offending. Amnesty International (2020a) alleges that thousands of children and young people are being convicted of non-violent, drug-related offences and are serving sentences of between 8 and 15 years. They had been detained under Article 328 of the Belarusian Criminal Code for illicit trafficking of narcotic and psychotropic substances. Each of the women's flyers stated their son's name, their charge and their sentence. The testimony they gave seemed astonishing, with hefty sentences for both possession and for naive and unsophisticated involvement in drug trafficking. However, it would appear that the women's narrative was accurate in that it has been widely acknowledged that this is a frequent occurrence (see Amnesty International, 2020a; ICCI, 2020; OHCR, 2019; UNODC, 2019; and Urgent Action, 2019). The most common explanation provided for teenagers' involvement in drug trafficking takes the following form, 'I saw an advert on the internet about working with a well-paid wage. I contacted the employer, I received assurances that the job was fully legal, became a "courier" and was detained and sentenced to half a life' (ICCI, 2020: 1). Although this was clearly a case of child criminal exploitation, and in most cases these children had been identified as being involved in an organised crime group, no other members of the group were ever identified or prosecuted (Amnesty International, 2020a).

The mothers' campaign has led to some positive changes in relation to Belarusian drug policies in that the lower threshold of punishment has been reduced by two years and some categories of offenders have been granted amnesty (ICCI, 2020). Also, in 2019, the Office of the High Commissioner advocated that Belarus begin to treat drug use and dependency as a health issue as opposed to a criminal matter (OHCHR, 2019; UNODC, 2019). Furthermore, Belarus has been looking into how the UK deals with the trafficking of children for coerced criminality. At an international conference which took place in Minsk in 2018 called 'Prevention of Crimes Related to Illegal Drug and Psychoactive Substance Trafficking by Children', the presenters examined judicial cases concerning cannabis cultivation and noted how the UK courts take an innovative approach where it is recognised that children committing drug-related crimes are actually victims of human trafficking (UNODC, 2019). Belarus is now looking towards making this issue a specific defence for forced criminality (*ibid.*). This is yet another clear instance of where a transfer of knowledge between the United Nations Office on Drugs and Crime, and intelligence from the UK judiciary, is advancing an agenda of positive international juvenile justice. The agenda for change was certainly impacted by our project, as the next section will highlight.

Project impact: Fostering the landscape for change

Regarding project evaluation and feedback, participants were required to complete an evaluation form, the results of which were summarised in a letter dated 4 July 2018 from

Her Majesty's Ambassador, Fiona Gibb in an official letter to SIHRG, as 'excellent feedback from the participants. [They] especially appreciated the diverse range of experts that you engaged in the seminars as well as the visual and interactive education materials building on case studies and interviews'. Concerning impact, the seminars were delivered to a total of 338 legal professionals of various ranking, serving to increase their understanding of international principles regarding child rights, and presented aspects of UK best practice in the rehabilitation of youth offenders. They also assisted in the creation of a receptive climate across relevant strata of Belarusian society to the development of dedicated youth justice services necessary to deliver a reformed approach based on the principles of rehabilitation and restorative justice. In addition, there is the likelihood that the impact of the seminar series has an indirect multiplying effect on the belief that juvenile justice reform is on the agenda in Belarus and has provided a catalyst for receptiveness to change.

This responsiveness is evidenced in the subsequent collaborative production of a textbook, the first of its kind in Belarus, entitled *A Guide to Juvenile Justice: The Republic of Belarus and International Law* (Barcov et al., 2018). The Guide seeks to provide a detailed resource for judges in Belarus concerned with juvenile justice. It was produced following the culmination of a collaboration between British academics and Belarus State University with the financial support of the British Embassy. It specifically advocates 'the need to create courts for juvenile cases ... via the formation of one juvenile court per region' and 'the creation of a comprehensive system of specialised juvenile justice bodies'. Moreover, to implement these recommendations, 'it is necessary to make the required amendments in the "Code of the Republic of Belarus on the Judicial System and Status of Judges", the "Criminal Procedure Code" and other normative legal Acts concerning the organisation and implementation of juvenile justice' (Barcov et al., 2018: 93). Although the textbook acknowledges the plethora of challenges presented by such a progressive response, the series of seminars has clearly had a significant impact on another country's policy, practice and legislation in relation to youth justice, as illustrated through the accounts of key stakeholders presented in this chapter.

On reflection, every aspect of contention noted in this case study that highlighted the differences between Belarusian judicial practice and that of England and Wales had a positive impact. It advanced our own knowledge of comparative youth justice, meaning that this new comprehension is now conveyed to colleagues and students of youth justice and criminology at NTU concerning the 'international perspective'. The findings have been presented at two staff conferences located in the School of Social Sciences, and they are also incorporated into two of our course modules which cover comparative youth justice. So, what next for Belarus? The next section will examine some of the post-project developments that have occurred.

Post-project developments: A new era for Belarusian juvenile justice

Immediately following completion of the project, an initiative that was driven by the UNCRC (1989) Articles 40 (3) and 40 (4) directives, several of the academics responsible for its organisation recommended the establishment of several specialised services. These included probation, counselling, supervision, and day treatment centres that could be managed by NGOs for the re-socialisation and rehabilitation of minors (Barcov et al., 2018). Some of these recommendations have already been acted on, with the establishment of counselling centres which provide children with psychological and legal assistance (United Nations Belarus, 2020).

Belarus continues to further its juvenile justice reform programme. and the baton for promoting and implementing change has since been handed over to the Intergovernmental Organisation (IGO) UNICEF, which has its own dedicated offices in Minsk. UNICEF maintains the undisputed stance that 'children are children. Children make mistakes sometimes' (UNICEF, 2022: 2). They recognise that their involvement in the justice system is stigmatising and can lead to their loss of freedom, childhood and their future (*ibid.*). They welcome any initiatives that steer the Belarusian judiciary away from 'punishment and intimidation of the guilty' (*ibid.*: 2). They wholeheartedly endorse the plans that were put in place after the project to evolve state juvenile justice policy which provides for the re-integration of young offenders back into society.

Worldwide, it is suggested that one of the causes of juvenile delinquency is children's lack of legal literacy (UNICEF, 2021). If young people were provided with legal education, they could be empowered to refrain from criminal acts and may be more guarded and equipped to desist from falling victim to deceit and into drug trafficking as couriers (*ibid.*). Under the guidance of UNICEF, Belarus has launched the innovative 'Children's Legal Library Educational Project' to educate children on laws that impact their rights and interests. This has been supplemented by a 'Children's Legal Website' where, under the guise of 'gaming', children can access legal information in an accessible and entertaining manner. In addition, children now have access to a free 'Telegram Chat Bot' and a 'Lawyer Mobile App' to help them to understand their rights and as a method of accessing legal assistance (*ibid.*).

Plans are also in place to develop state juvenile justice policy via the use of mediation and restorative justice (BelTA, 2018; 2019). Valery Mitskevich, Deputy Head of the Belarus President Administration, believes that 'restorative juvenile justice … is an important instrument which prevents the criminalisation of a child's personality' (BelTA, 2018: 1). He stresses that the provision of alternatives to criminal punishment will procure socially useful models of behaviour which will help adolescents to understand the consequences of their wrong deed, which in turn will help prevent criminal conduct in the future (*ibid.*). By 2019, Belarus had already trained and certified 700 mediators to undertake restorative work with teenagers, parents and victims (*ibid.*). Mediation enables all parties to work voluntarily with a neutral third party to agree upon a solution that is mutually beneficial, and this may involve a decision on compensation (UNICEF, 2022). This means that children in conflict with the law can bypass liability within the court system and instead, turn to a mediator, whilst still being made aware of the consequences of their actions. Noskevich (2018: 1) further explains that 'abandoning criminal law measures in the context of restorative justice is one of the ways to realise the interests of both a child and the society at large'. In this instance, Noskevich (2018) is potentially alluding to the way in which the use of restorative justice enables victims to feel more secure, with less fear of re-victimisation and diminished feelings of revenge towards the perpetrator; thereby enabling both victim and offender to move on in their lives (Shapland, 2016). This has now been accepted into the juvenile justice criminal process as a result of a partnership cooperation between UNICEF, the Mediations and Law Centre, and the Ministry of Justice (UNICEF, 2020).

It should perhaps be acknowledged that restorative justice is a contested concept as a form of 'justice' as it potentially erodes an individual's human rights, could result in the effect of net-widening, may trivialise crime and could result in discriminatory outcomes (Morris, 2002). However, Belarus believes that this new way of thinking about meting out justice for young offenders offers a more conciliatory process of offender rehabilitation (Noskevich, 2018). So much so that the restorative justice initiative is being strengthened via educational programmes. For instance, UNICEF continually invites secondary educational and high school students to submit essays about the value of restorative justice for minors. Their topics include the significance of restorative justice, how to make the law accessible to children, and the stigmatisation of a criminal record (United Nations Belarus, 2020). This has long been mirrored in NTU's Youth Justice curriculum where an entire module is taught to students entitled, 'Restorative Justice, Victims and Victimology'.

These are just some of the ways that Belarus is continually striving to widen the scope of not only promoting methods of desistence to children and young people, such as by identifying an openness to change, and overcoming any barriers and obstacles to transformation (Bottoms and Shapland, 2011), but also by seeking viable and sustainable alternatives to their official prosecution processes.

Conclusion

It is clear that the importance of knowledge-transfer partnerships cannot be underestimated and the employment of them can not only lead to significant improvements in social justice, but also to the generation of new knowledge. As Creaney (2017: 1) advocates, by joining forces, 'universities can bring academic theory to those working in youth justice services and allow practitioners access to expert advice and training'. This chapter has highlighted just one example of a community of practice. Such a community is one that acts as a living curriculum; the coming together of a group of people who share a mutual concern and wish to share best practice in order to create new knowledge (Farnsworth et al., 2016). Here, a university, together with partners, ran a series of seminars for the Belarusian judiciary who are practising in the field of juvenile justice. This resulted in the co-production of knowledge which not only provided a platform for the further advancement of best practice in their statutory work with minors, but afforded students at NTU a tangible glimpse into how youth justice operates in an Eastern European country which has been under-researched.

The resultant exchange of knowledge from this project facilitated a detailed understanding of the context of juvenile justice in Belarus, including its intrinsic 'inquisitorial' system, its minimum age of criminal responsibility, and sentencing options, including the use of their own secure estate.

Following project completion, Belarus continues to forge ahead with clemency measures by widening the scope of alternatives to custody and even circumstances under which juveniles may avoid official prosecution (Noskevich, 2018). It is aware that children's criminalisation should be limited, with the use of a range of diversionary schemes corresponding to international standards, and that prevention is also key to reform (Moestue, 2008). It also recognises the need for an improvement in the legislation that allows for better reintegration of juvenile offenders, and this is currently being debated in its appropriate ministries and departments (BelTA, 2019).

It would be useful for Belarus to adopt a 'Child First, Offender Second' partnership approach to driving their systemic change, where those young people involved in their juvenile justice system may participate in service design and delivery (Haines and Case, 2015; Smithson and Jones, 2021). This would ensure that 'children are part of the solution, not part of the problem' (Haines and Case, 2015: 45). Creating knowledge in the social sciences and transforming juvenile justice can then be incorporated as a reflexive activity, one which champions a unique synergy of networking between the stakeholders, including the judiciary, academia, practitioners and young people themselves. These reciprocal relationships can then co-construct their learning as a new form of community of practice that is more culturally aligned and context-sensitive (Case and Haines, 2014). In this way, Belarusians could further enhance their drive to improve effective practice for children in their juvenile justice system.

References

Amnesty International (2020a) *Belarus: Juvenile Justice and Fair Trials.* Minsk: Amnesty International.

Amnesty International (2020b) Belarus: Serious Human Rights Concerns Persist – Submission for the UN Universal Periodic Review, 36th Session [Online]. Available at: http://www.amnesty.org/en/documents/eur49/1781/2020/en/. [Accessed 15. 10. 21].

Amnesty International (2022) *Crackdown on Children.* London: Amnesty International.

Barcov, A., Blackman, L., Godunov, V. and Zaytseva, L. (2018) *A Guide to Juvenile Justice: The Republic of Belarus and International Law.* Minsk: Four Quarters Publishing House.

Bedford, S. (2021) The 2020 Presidential Election in Belarus: Erosion of Authoritarian Stability and Re-politicization of Society. *Nationalities Papers.* 49 (5) 808–819.

Belarusian Helsinki Committee (2023) Death Penalty in Belarus: Facts and Numbers [Online]. Available at: https://belhelcom.org/en/topic-material/death-penalty-belarus-facts-and-numbers [Accessed 22. 09. 23].

BelTA (2018) Belarus Ready to Make New Steps towards Restorative Juvenile Justice [Online]. Available at: https://eng.belta.by/society/view/opinion-belarus-ready-to-make-new-steps-towards-restorative-juvenile-justice [Accessed 17. 05. 23].

BelTA (2019) UNICEF Looks Forward to Early Adoption of Juvenile Justice Concept in Belarus [Online]. Available at: https://en.belta.by/society/view/unicef-looks-forward-to-early-adoption-of-juvenile-justice-concept-in-belarus-123081-2019/ [Accessed 26. 04. 23].

BelTA (2020) Protection of Juvenile Prisoners in Belarus: Who and How Supports Them [Online]. Available at: https://www.belta.by/society/view/v-belarusi-za-desjat-let-podrostkovaja-prestupnost-snizilas-v-chetyre-raza-mvd-416428-2020/ [Accessed 02. 10. 23].

Biggs, J. (2007) *Teaching for Quality Learning at University.* 3rd edn. Maidenhead: Open University Press.

Blackman, L. (2017) *Conflict Stability and Security Fund Project Proposal.* London: SIHRG.

Block, M., Parker, J., Vyborna, O. and Dusek, L. (2000) An Experimental Comparison of Adversarial versus Inquisitorial Procedural Regimes. *American Law and Economics Review.* 2, 170–194.

Bottoms, A. and Shapland, J. (2011) Steps towards Desistance in Male Young Adult Recidivists. In: Farell, S., Sparks, R., Maruna, S. and Hough, M. (eds) *Escape Routes: Contemporary Perspectives in Life After Punishment.* London: Routledge, 43–80.

Brown, A. and Charles, A. (2019) The Minimum Age of Criminal Responsibility: The Need for a Holistic Approach. *Youth Justice.* 21 (2) 153–171.

Brown, S. and Race, P. (1995) *Assess Your Own Teaching Quality.* London: Kogan Page.

Carlile Report (2006) *Independent Inquiry into Physical Restraint.* London: Howard League.

Case, S. and Haines, K. (2014) Reflective Friend Research: The Relational Aspects of Social Scientific Research. In: Lumsden, K. (ed.) *Reflexivity in Criminological Research.* London: Palgrave Macmillan.

CRC (Committee on the Rights of the Child) (1993) Juvenile Justice Information Portfolio: State Party Reports [Online]. Available at: UNDOC.CRC/C/3/Add.14 [Accessed 21. 09. 20].

Creaney, S. (2017) *Creating Youth Justice Communities of Practice.* London: Children and Young People Now.

David, R. and Zhoffre-Spinozi, C. (1998) *Main Legal Systems of the Present*. Moscow: International Relations.

Farnsworth, V., Kleanthous, I. and Wenger-Traynor, E. (2016) Communities of Practice as a Social Theory of Learning: A Conversation with Etienne Wenger. *British Journal of Educational Studies*. 64 (2) 1–22.

Foreign and Commonwealth Office (2023) Arrested or Detained in Belarus [Online]. Available at: https://www.gov.uk/government/publications/belarus-prisoner-pack/arrested-or-detained-in-belarus–2 [Accessed 22. 09. 23].

Gasyuk, G. (2006) *Children in Conflict with the Law in Belarus*. Minsk: Ministry of Statistics and Analysis.

Gooch, K. (2015) Who Needs Restraining? Re-examining the Use of Restraint in an English Young Offender Institution. *Journal of Social Welfare and Family Law*. 37 (1) 3–20.

Haines, K. and Case, S. (2015) *Positive Youth Justice: Children First, Offender Second*. London: Policy Press.

HM Prison and Probation Service (2023) *Youth Custody Report: August 2023*. London: HM Prison and Probation Service and Youth Custody Service.

House of Commons (2019) *Youth Detention: Solitary Confinement and Restraint: 19th Report of Session 2017–2019*. London: House of Commons.

Human Rights Watch (2021) *Belarus: Events of 2020* [Online]. Available at: https://www.hrw.org/world-report/2021/country-chapters/belarus [Accessed 29. 04. 23].

ICCI (International Centre for Civil Initiatives) (2020) Children – 328: Goals and Objectives of the Campaign [Online]. Available at: http://news.house/40773 [Accessed 29. 08. 22].

ICCI (2021) How Women's Rights Are Violated in Penal Colony No. 4 in Gomel [Online]. Available at: http://news.house/41494 [Accessed 09. 05. 23].

ICCI (2022) Slave Labour and Disciplinary Penalties: What Is Happening in the Walls of the Only Educational Colony in Belarus [Online]. Available at: https://news.house/43526 [Accessed 22. 09. 23].

ICPR (Institute for Crime and Justice Policy Research) (2023) World Prison Brief [Online]. Available at: https://www.prisonstudies.org [Accessed 24. 04. 23].

IFHR (International Federation for Human Rights) (2008) *International Fact-Finding Mission: Conditions of Detention in the Republic of Belarus*. Viasna: IFHR.

Just Arrived (2023) Prisons in Belarus [Online]. Available at: https://justarrived.by/en/blog/prisons-in-belarus [Accessed 02. 10. 23].

Khodosevich, T., Shalygina, N. and Sarbay, D. (2019) Update: Legal Research in Belarus [Online]. Available at: https://www.nyulawglobal.org/globalex/Belarus/1.html [Accessed 10. 02. 23].

Machalou, A. (2018) *Belarus Solutions to Challenges in the Juvenile Justice System: Views on Juvenile Justice from Children and Other Stakeholders*. Presentation to the Monastrysky Hotel Civil Society. 15.01.18.

Machalou, A. (2021) The Belarusian Authorities Have Unleashed a Scorched Earth Policy [Online]. Available at: http://omct.org/en/resources/news/the-belarusian-authorities-have-unleashed-a-scorched-earth-policy [Accessed 09. 05. 23].

Marshall, H. (2023) Victims First? Examining the Place of Child Criminal Exploitation Within Child First Youth Justice. *Children and Society*. 37 (4) 1156–1170.

Moestue, H. (2008) *Lost in the Justice System: Children in Conflict with the Law in Eastern Europe and Central Asia*. London: UNICEF.

Morris, A. (2002) Critiquing the Critics: A Brief Response to Critics of Restorative Justice. *British Journal of Criminology*. 42 (3) 596–615.

Noskevich, I. (2018) *Abandoning Criminal Law Measures in the Context of Restorative Justice*. Minsk: The Investigative Committee of the Republic of Belarus.

OHCHR (Office of the High Commissioner for Human Rights) (2019) Belarus: UN Expert Deplores Child Jail Sentences for Drug Related Offences [Online]. Available at: https://www.ohchr.org/en.NewsEvents/Pages/DisplayNews.aspx? [Accessed 08. 12. 19].

OHCHR (Office of the High Commissioner for Human Rights) (2020) Belarus: Establishing Independent Judicial System Should Top the Agenda for Future Reforms Says UN Expert. New York: UNHCR.

Ramsden, P. (2003) *Learning to Teach in Higher Education*. 2nd edn. London: Routledge.

Schmidt, V. and Shchurko, T. (2014) Children's Rights in Post-Soviet Countries: The Case of Russia and Belarus. *International Social Work*. 57 (5) 447–458.

Schön, D. (1983) *The Reflective Practitioner: How Professionals Think in Action*. Aldershot: Ashgate.

Seldin, P. (1997) Using Student Feedback to Improve Teaching. *Professional and Organisational Development Network in Higher Education*. 16, 335–346.

Shapland, J. (2016) Forgiveness and Restorative Justice: Is It Necessary? Is It Helpful? *Oxford Journal of Law and Religion*. 5 (1) 94–112.

SIHRG (Solicitors International Human Rights Group) (2018) *Belarus Project Report: Advancing Best Practice in Juvenile Justice in Belarus*. London: SIHRG.

Smithson, H. and Jones, A. (2021) Co-creating Youth Justice Practice with Young People: Tackling Power Dynamics and Enabling Transformative Action. *Children and Society*. 35 (3) 348–362.

The Children's Society (2019) *Counting Lives: Responding to Children Who Are Criminally Exploited*. London: The Children's Society.

UNCRC (1989) *The United Nations Convention on the Rights of the Child*. London: UNICEF.

UNHR (United Nations Human Rights) (2020) Belarus: Establishing Independent Judicial System Should Top the Agenda for Future Reforms Says UN Expert. New York: UNHR.

UNICEF (2020) Statement on the Situation of Children in Belarus [Online]. Available at: https://www.unicef.org/press-releases/unicef-statement-situation-children-belarus [Accessed 26. 04. 23].

UNICEF (2021) Legal Education: Knowledge of the Laws Allows the Child Not Only to Refrain from Illegal Acts, but Also Not to Become a Victim of Violence and Deceit [Online]. Available at: https://www.unicef.org/belrus/en/legal-education [Accessed 22. 02. 23].

UNICEF (2022) Restorative Justice: Building and Reforming the Juvenile Justice System in Belarus [Online]. Available at: https://unicef.org/belarus/en/justice-children-and-adolescents [Accessed 22. 02. 23].

United Nations Belarus (2020) UNICEF in Belarus Supported Campaign to Celebrate UN's 75th Anniversary [Online]. Available at: https://belarus.un.org/en/49054-unicef-belarus-supported-campaign-celebrate-un's-75th-anniversary [Accessed 17. 05. 23].

United States Department of State (2017) 2016 Country Reports on Human Rights Practices: Belarus [Online]. Available at: https://www.refworld.org/docid/58ec8a6f11 [Accessed 03. 02. 23].

UNODC (United Nations Office on Drugs and Crime) (2019) UNODC Supports Judges and Subject Matter Experts in Belarus to Discuss Juvenile Justice and Crime Prevention [Online]. Available at: https://www.unodc.en/human-trafficking/glo-act/ [Accessed 21. 04. 23].

Urgent Action (2019) Protect Rights of Juvenile Prisoners First [Online]. Available at: UA:36/19Index:Eur49/0100/2019Belarus [Accessed 21. 03. 23].

Weller, M. (2011) *The Digital Scholar: How Technology Is Transforming Scholarly Practice*. London: Bloomsbury Academic.

White, S., McAllister, I. and Feklyunina, V. (2010) Belarus, Ukraine and Russia: East or West? *British Journal of Politics and International Relations*. 12 (3) 344–367.

World Prison Brief (2018) Belarus [Online]. Available at: https://www.prisonstudies.org/country/belarus [Accessed 01. 05. 23].

Young, C. (2008) Working with PowerPoint. *The Times Higher Education Supplement* [Online] 14. 07. 08. Available at: www.timeshighereducation.co.uk [Accessed 08. 08. 08].

Youth Justice Board (2019) Youth Justice Statistics 2017/18 [Online]. Available at: https://assets.publishing.service.gov.uk/government/uploads/system/uploads/attachment_data/file/774866/youth_justice_statistics_bulletin_2017_2018.pdf#: [Accessed 04. 10. 23].

Youth Justice Board (2021) *Youth Justice Skills and Knowledge Matrix*. London: YJB.

Conclusion

Knowledge and skills partnerships

Sean Creaney and Jayne Price

> Research in youth justice is vast and varied, meaning that those seeking to identify 'good practice' or 'evidence' must navigate multiple studies, large and small, from every jurisdiction and academic discipline. The scholarship has been produced using diverse methodologies and approaches, and although there is an increasing focus on policy impact and practitioner perspectives, its breadth and depth can make this vast literature difficult to access by those interested in an evidence-based approach.
>
> (Kilkelly, 2023:4)

The chapters contained within this edited collection, authored by experts in the field, provide in-depth insight into different types of knowledge and skills partnerships in youth justice, illustrating the importance of collaborative working between academics and professionals. As was alluded to in the opening section of the Introduction to the text, there are different types of knowledge relevant and applicable to the youth justice context that can be developed or acquired through engagement in academic study/scholarship and mastered through professional practice. This includes engagement with empirical research, theoretical insights, young people's narratives, and professional knowledge/expertise (Baker et al., 2011; see also Kilkelly, 2023). The focus of this edited collection is on forms of knowledge exchange (transfer) between professionals and academics in the youth justice context. This is an area of interest to the Youth Justice Board for England and Wales (YJB), as the following quote illustrates:

> Five years ago, the [Youth Justice Board] YJB published a working guide for setting up partnerships between youth justice services and the academic community. The aim was to allow youth justice workers to have access to expert advice and training, while giving academics valuable access to data and providing placement opportunities for their students. So, the seeds were sown, and with such clear mutual benefits it was not surprising that partnerships began springing up across the country, and the rest, as they say, is history.
>
> (Keith Fraser, Chair of the Youth Justice Board (YJB, 2022))

Knowledge and skills partnerships between youth justice services and practice-facing academics have been established to evolve youth justice on the ground (YJB, 2018, as cited in Haines and Case, 2018:143). The guidance for academic/Youth Offending Team partnerships published by the Youth Justice Board (YJB) set out arrangements for establishing and formalising knowledge and skills partnerships (Smith-Yau, 2017). One key principle highlighted within the guide concerns power-sharing arrangements (non-

DOI: 10.4324/9781003411192-9

hierarchical relationship-building between professionals and academics). This principle was applied into practice as part of the project across Greater Manchester, for example, which focused on 'the bidirectional transfer of knowledge between academia and business' (Smithson and Jones, 2021:351), building the evidence-base through co-creating principles of effective practice (Smithson et al., 2022; Smithson et al., 2020).

This edited collection builds on this body of work, especially around the formation and operation of multifaceted partnerships, providing expert analysis of knowledge/evidence production and utilisation in youth justice, drawing on national and international empirical research and practice examples. The collection offers a unique insight into the extent to which knowledge and skills partnerships between academia and the youth justice sector can be a vital mechanism to build and interrogate the knowledge base. It has examined how such partnerships are realised in practice, including how students are enabled to undertake innovative research/practice placements and participate in varied educational development projects. These partnerships can provide the space for academics to advise professionals on current and new areas of policy initiatives and practices, enabling valuable opportunities to undertake research. This book presents an expert analysis of knowledge/evidence production and utilisation in youth justice, drawing on empirical research and practice examples, presenting a series of case studies, to showcase the application of theory/evidence to practice. This conclusion chapter identifies key themes and summarises the arguments set out in this collection. It also ends by identifying and reiterating some of the key principles necessary for the development and sustainability of knowledge and skills partnerships across the youth justice sector. Such principles or prerequisite features include relationships, reciprocity and constructive dialogue through collaborative endeavours. This conclusion chapter begins by highlighting key benefits of knowledge exchange/transfer and then proceeds to reflect upon some of the challenges.

Benefits and challenges of creating a synergy between academia and practice

The chapters within this book have highlighted the benefits and challenges of knowledge and skills partnerships. They have showcased knowledge exchange initiatives and approaches to building evidence-based practice that can lead to positive child outcomes. **Dr Jayne Price and Dr Sean Creaney (Chapter 1)** explored how the knowledge and skills partnership between Edge Hill University, Cheshire Youth Justice Services and Chester University facilitated opportunities for criminological theory/research evidence to be applied in practice. The research group they have developed is a useful mechanism to help identify and promote progressive and principled practices. Through collaboration, dialogue and interaction, empirical research and theoretical insights have become more accessible to practitioners. This collaboration also led to a relationship-based practice framework being developed and implemented. This knowledge and skills partnership also founded the 'Building Professional Skills for Youth Justice' (BPSYJ) programme. As **Dr Sean Creaney and Dr Jayne Price (Chapter 2)** note, this programme is a useful mechanism to maximise criminology placements for students, further enhancing opportunities to develop skills and knowledge and apply theory into practice. Similarly, the practice–academia group formulated within the Welsh youth justice context has facilitated student research projects; worthwhile opportunities to evaluate a new pilot or intervention (**Chapter 5**). As part of the BPSYJ programme, students have had valuable opportunities to utilise theoretical/subject-specific knowledge combined with critical thinking skills

(**Chapter 2**). There are challenges to solidifying a commitment to knowledge exchange. Time constraints and workload pressures can hinder the ability of professionals to engage with research findings and bodies of evidence. It can also be difficult to operationalise the principle of knowledge mobilisation when seeking to upskill students with sector specific knowledge, create access to valuable networks/contacts and provide practice experiences. Resource pressures can limit the ability of organisations to host student placements, and universities may find it difficult to navigate logistical challenges when designing learning experience opportunities (field trips) for large cohorts of students. **Dr Robin Moore, Andrea Brazier and Helen Mercer** note other challenges, which include 'keeping an eye on all the latest developments across the entire research community, so identifying the new, up-and-coming academics, while also being alert to relevant findings from other sectors'.

Dr Robin Moore, Andrea Brazier and Helen Mercer (**Chapter 3**) have provided an insightful and engaging account of ways to maximise the knowledge, experience and skills of various stakeholders and interested parties who are invested in the generation, use or application of evidence. The chapter includes a series of practice examples and detailed accounts of how the HM Inspectorate of Probation has worked in collaboration with commissioned partners. In this chapter, Moore et al. also reflect upon some of the challenges, including ways to navigate competing/differing academic perspectives. They also refer to the importance of nurturing research/evaluation cultures within services to progress evidence-informed approaches in youth justice. The chapter also makes reference to the HMIP 'academic insight' series, which contains articles and reports of evidence-based practices, designed to be accessible for practitioners (HM Inspectorate of Probation, 2024). As Dr Robin Moore, Andrea Brazier and Helen Mercer note, 'An evidence-informed approach is one which is guided by the best available research findings alongside professional knowledge and practice wisdom, and the lived experiences of children and their families'.

Dr Sue Bond-Taylor (**Chapter 4**) has provided a detailed account of *Youth Justice Live!*, an educational development project involving students, practitioners and academics, premised on ideas of a Community of Practice. This chapter provides insight into how knowledge and skills partnerships can enhance employability skills of students by preparing them for the workplace. *Youth Justice Live!* maximises creativity and innovation through embracing a collaborative curriculum whereby students are able to engage with practitioners in-person. As noted within the chapter, practitioners have opportunities to 'connect their practice with theory, to remain up to date about the developing research evidence base, and perhaps to be challenged in new ways by the conversations and questions from both staff and students'. Self-reflection is key, as Bond-Taylor highlights:

> opportunities to reflect on our own values, beliefs, and practices … is of immense value in developing critical thinking and reflective practice to improve our work. This includes reflecting honestly upon some of the challenging realities of working in youth justice services, rather than only sharing the success stories as a means to promote the employment opportunities within the sector.

In Dyfed Powys and 'Hwb Doeth', the practice-academia group has created the space for stakeholders to reflect on and discuss current issues and share insights into the application of findings from research studies into practice (**Chapter 5**). **Dr Kathy Hampson** has highlighted how there is space created for members of the academic/practice group to 'share (and discuss) new research or articles of interest', cultivating opportunities for practice to be guided by theoretical/conceptual and empirical considerations (**Chapter 5**). Hampson argues that this knowledge exchange partnership is reciprocal, 'with Youth Offending Teams being encouraged to consider student researcher potential in areas of interest to them, for example in evaluating a new project or intervention. Universities can offer several levels of research support: undergraduate-led empirical dissertation, master's empirical dissertation, Ph.D. empirical thesis, staff small-scale university-funded research and staff larger-scale externally funded research. This flexibility offers a good range of options to build on the evidence-base of effective practice in the region'. (**Chapter 5**). Moreover, as Hampson notes,

> Further benefits of the relationships for both universities and Youth Offending Teams forged through this close partnership have included YOT staff giving practice-informed lectures to students studying youth justice (useful for the YOT staff participating for expanding their experience and CV and for universities in being able to maintain a close relationship between delivered content and youth justice in the field) and students accessing volunteering or employment opportunities within the Youth Offending Team.
>
> (**Chapter 5:91**)

The Children and Young People's Centre for Justice (CYCJ) in Scotland facilitates effective knowledge exchange through adopting and implementing novel approaches (**Chapter 6**). **Ross Gibson, Dr Nina Vaswani and Fiona Dyer** have provided insight into how research evidence can be built, shared and subsequently used to influence policy makers and invoke practice change. The approaches presented by the authors 'demonstrates the broad attitude to knowledge that the organisation adopts, with practice wisdom, lived experience and research all being given appropriate levels of weighting and equally respected' (**Chapter 6**).

In **Chapter 7, Dr Vicky Palmer** has presented insight into an internationally collaborative knowledge transfer partnership between academics and criminal justice professionals in England and Belarus. The author has provided an in-depth account of its origins, purpose, implementation, and accomplishments, including reflections on the challenges of designing and delivering a project of this nature. A series of high-quality seminars was delivered to juvenile justice stakeholders via a range of teaching methods and learning activities, including real-life case studies and anonymised court reports. Palmer concludes this chapter by reinforcing the importance of knowledge transfer partnerships locally, nationally, and internationally. This project has 'not only provided a platform for the further advancement of best practice in their statutory work with minors, but afforded students at Nottingham Trent University a tangible glimpse into how youth justice operates in an Eastern European country' (**Chapter 7**). As Palmer concludes, 'The resultant exchange of knowledge from this project facilitated a detailed understanding of the context of juvenile justice in Belarus including its intrinsic 'inquisitorial' system, its minimum age of criminal responsibility and sentencing options, including the use of their own secure estate' (**Chapter 7**).

As alluded to, there are challenges in creating a synergy between academia and practice, not least resource constraints and workload pressures. Nevertheless, as evidenced throughout this text, a critical factor of successful partnership working is relationship building. The Youth Justice Board's guidance (Smith-Yau, 2017) cites the importance of mutual aims being established. Having a partnership allows for these relationships to develop over time as partners work towards shared aims and mutual benefits.

Concluding thoughts

The chapters within this collection illustrate examples of stakeholders working effectively together. This has included a commitment to build and maintain working relationships (in an open and reciprocal manner), which allows for discussion around mutually beneficial areas of interest. Whilst there can be challenges due to varying professional backgrounds and experiences, collaboration is a useful principle to cultivate, inviting those at the coalface of youth justice delivery, academics, students, and others, to join in a reflective dialogue. Similarly, as Kilkelly, (2023:11) notes, it is important to embrace 'an approach to evidence-based policymaking as a collaborative endeavour, one that is shared between academia and decision-makers in youth justice practice and policy, with a focus on the young people at the heart of this process'. We hope that this collection helps to invoke and nurture a culture that values criminological research; perhaps even a vehicle to facilitate research-informed practice across the youth justice sector, or used to inspire/motivate others to develop or engage in knowledge-exchange activities to enhance practice.

References

Atfield, G., Hunt, W. and Luchinskaya, D. (2021) Employability programmes and work placements in UK higher education. Department for Education, November. https://assets.publishing.service.gov.uk/media/619bc17b8fa8f50381640305/employability_programmes_and_work_placements_in_UK_HE.pdf.

Baker, K., Kelly, G. and Wilkinson, B. (2011) *Assessment in youth justice.* Bristol: Policy Press.

Bramford, K. and Eason, A.L. (2021) Criminology placements: work-based learning and organisational 'buy in'. *Higher Education, Skills and Work-Based Learning*, 11(2), 317–329. https://doi.org/10.1108/HESWBL-10-2019-0133.

Case, S. and Hampson, K. (2019) Youth justice pathways to change: Drivers, challenges and opportunities. *Youth Justice*, 19(1), 25–41.

Case, S., Drew, J., Hampson, K., Jones, J. and Kennedy, D. (2020) Professional perspective of youth justice policy implementation: Contextual coalface challenges. *Howard Journal of Crime and Justice*, 59, 214–232.

Clarke, M. (2018) Rethinking graduate employability: The role of capital, individual attributes and context. *Studies in Higher Education*, 43(11), 1923–1937.

Creaney, S. and Burns, S. (2023) Freedom from symbolic violence? Facilitators and barriers to participatory practices in youth justice. *Youth Justice* (online first), https://doi.org/10.1177/14732254231156844.

Day, A-M. (2022) 'It's a hard balance to find': The perspectives of youth justice practitioners in England on the place of 'risk' in an emerging 'child-first' world. *Youth Justice*, 23(1), 58–75.

Goldson, B. (2019) Reading the present and mapping the future(s) of juvenile justice in Europe. In Goldson, B. (ed.) *Juvenile justice in Europe: past, present and future* (pp. 214–257). Routledge.

Haines, K. and Case, S. (2018) The future of youth justice. *Youth Justice*, 18(2), 131–148. https://doi.org/10.1177/1473225418791416.

Hine, J. (2008) Applied criminology: Research, policy and practice. In Stout, B., Williams, B. and Yates, J., *Applied criminology*. Sage.

HM Inspectorate of Probation (2024) Academic insights. Available from: https://www.justiceinspectorates.gov.uk/hmiprobation/research/academic-insights/.

Kilkelly, U. (2023) Evidence-based core messages for youth justice. HMIP. Available from: https://www.justiceinspectorates.gov.uk/hmiprobation/wp-content/uploads/sites/5/2023/10/Academic-Insights-Evidence-based-core-messages-for-youth-justice-by-Professor-Ursula-Kilkelly-Final.pdf.

Loader, I. and Sparks, R. (2010) *Public criminology*. Routledge.

Local Government Association (2022) Work local: Benefits of improving employment and skills outcomes. May. https://www.local.gov.uk/publications/work-local-benefits-improving-employment-and-skills-outcomes.

Marcella, R., Lockerbie, H. and Bloice, L. (2016). Beyond REF 2014: The impact of impact assessment on the future of information research. *Journal of Information Science*, 42(3), 369–385. https://doi.org/10.1177/0165551516636291.

McCormack, S. and Baron, P. (2023). The impact of employability on humanities, arts and social sciences degrees in Australia. *Arts and Humanities in Higher Education*, 22(2), 164–182.

Office for Students (2022, 10 May) Graduate outcomes survey. https://www.officeforstudents.org.uk/for-students/student-outcomes-and-employability/graduate-outcomes-survey/.

QAA (2022) Subject benchmark statement for criminology. https://www.qaa.ac.uk/quality-code/subject-benchmark-statements/criminology.

Shury, J., Vivian, D., Truner, C. and Downing, C. (2017) *Planning for success: Graduates' career planning and its effect on graduate outcomes*. Research report. Department for Education, March. https://assets.publishing.service.gov.uk/media/5a7583c3e5274a1242c9ee85/Graduates__career_planning_and_its_effect_on_their_outcomes.pdf.

Smith, R. and Gray, P. (2019) The changing shape of youth justice: Models of practice. *Criminology and Criminal Justice*, 19(5), 554–571.

Smith-Yau, W. (2017) *Academic/YOT partnership working guide*. Youth Justice Board.

Smithson, H., Gray, P. and Jones, A. (2020). 'They really should start listening to you': The benefits and challenges of co-producing a participatory framework of youth justice practice. *Youth Justice*, 21(3). https://doi.org/10.1177/1473225420941598.

Smithson, H., Lang, T. and Gray, P. (2022) From rhetoric to reality: Participation in practice within youth justice systems. In Frankel, S. (ed.) *Establishing child centred practice in a changing world, part A*. (pp. 111–122). Emerald Studies in Child Centred Practice. Emerald Publishing.

Smithson, H. and Jones, A. (2021) Co-creating youth justice practice with young people: Tackling power dynamics and enabling transformative action. *Children and Society: The International Journal of Childhood and Children's Services*, 35(3), 348–362. ISSN 0951–0605.

Strudwick, K. (2017) Debating student as producer: Relationships, contexts and challenges for higher education. *PRISM: Casting New Light on Learning, Theory and Practice*, 1(1), 73–96.

UCAS.com (2024) Widening access and participation. https://www.ucas.com/advisers/help-and-training/guides-resources-and-training/tools-and-resources-help-you/widening-access-and-participation.

Watermeyer, R. and Hedgecoe, A. (2016) Selling 'impact': Peer reviewer projections of what is needed and what counts in REF impact case studies. A retrospective analysis. *Journal of Education Policy*, 31(5), 651–665.

Wilkinson, D., Price, J. and Crossley, C. (2022) Developing creative methodologies: using lyric writing to capture young peoples' experiences of the youth offending services during the COVID-19 pandemic. *Journal of Criminological Policy and Practice*, 8(2), 105–119.

YJB (Youth Justice Board) (2021) Strategic plan 2021–24. https://assets.publishing.service.gov.uk/media/603f6d268fa8f577c44d65a8/YJB_Strategic_Plan_2021_-_2024.pdf.

YJB (Youth Justice Board) (2022, 17 June) Keith Fraser speaks at the Child First Youth Justice conference. https://www.gov.uk/government/speeches/keith-fraser-speaks-at-the-child-first-youth-justice-conference.

Index

For Product Safety Concerns and Information please contact our EU
representative GPSR@taylorandfrancis.com
Taylor & Francis Verlag GmbH, Kaufingerstraße 24, 80331 München, Germany